Pearl
[illegible]

Ruth Ottmers

# TOUCH *the* TOP *of the* WORLD

# TOUCH *the* TOP *of the* WORLD

A BLIND MAN'S JOURNEY TO CLIMB FARTHER THAN THE EYE CAN SEE

ERIK WEIHENMAYER

DUTTON

DUTTON
Published by the Penguin Group
Penguin Putnam Inc., 375 Hudson Street, New York, New York 10014, U.S.A.
Penguin Books Ltd, 27 Wrights Lane, London W8 5TZ, England
Penguin Books Australia Ltd, Ringwood, Victoria, Australia
Penguin Books Canada Ltd, 10 Alcorn Avenue, Toronto, Ontario, Canada M4V 3B2
Penguin Books (N.Z.) Ltd, 182–190 Wairau Road, Auckland 10, New Zealand

Penguin Books Ltd, Registered Offices: Harmondsworth, Middlesex, England

First published by Dutton, a member of Penguin Putnam Inc.

First Printing, February, 2001
1 3 5 7 9 10 8 6 4 2



LIBRARY OF CONGRESS CATALOGING-IN-PUBLICATION DATA
Weihenmayer, Erik.
Touch the top of the world / Erik Weihenmayer.
p. cm.
ISBN 0-525-94578-4
Special Markets ISBN 0-525-94936-4
1. Weihenmayer, Erik. 2. Mountaineers—United States—Biography.
3. Blind athletes—United States—Biography. I. Title.
GV199.92.W39 A3 2001
796.52'2'092—dc21
[B]
00-047618

Printed in the United States of America
Set in Garamond Light
Designed by Leonard Telesca

*For Emma*

# Contents

*Acknowledgments* ix
INTRODUCTION: McKinley's Kahiltna Glacier 1

1. Quasimodo 9
2. A World In-Between 33
3. Helplessness 48
4. Faint Recognition 62
5. Blind Warriors 79
6. Wizard, the Chick Magnet 99
7. Flailing to Independence 109
8. Perceptions 125
9. Thirty Sets of Eyes 135
10. Blind Faith 142
11. Preparation 155
12. Zero Zero 169
13. "Big" Changes 200
14. Uhuru 210
15. Moving Through Darkness 221
16. The Nose 243
17. The Slag Heap 258
18. I Did Not Die 274
19. The Song of the Sirens 280

*Epilogue* 301
*Everest* 305

# Acknowledgments

The course of one's life is like the ascent of a mountain. Although a climber may have the privilege of standing on top, it takes a team to get him there. I thank my friends and family, who have been my support team, creating opportunities in front of me, building a foundation of hope and confidence beneath me, and enabling me to reach my own summit.

Thank you to my mother, who loved me fiercely and fought for my future like a mother lioness, and to my father, who taught me the power of action and inspired me with the courage to forge ahead despite formidable obstacles.

Thank you to my grandparents, Martin and Talatha Baker. So much of who I am has come from you.

Thanks to my brothers, Mark and Eddi, and my sister, Suzanne, who have always treated me like any other little brother and are my greatest fans.

Thanks to my teachers and counselors, like Ms. Reddy and Mr. Westervelt, who believed in me long before I was ready to believe in myself.

Finally, thank you to my wife, Ellie, whose spirit and commitment has filled me with the certainty that there is no higher goal than to love fully.

*I am only one, but still I am one.*
*I can not do everything, but still I can do something.*
*I will not refuse to do the something I can do.*

—Helen Keller

## INTRODUCTION

# McKinley's Kahiltna Glacier

For thousands of years, a massive tongue of the Kahiltna Glacier, forty miles long and a mile thick, has been inching its way down the western flanks of Mount McKinley, splintering, cracking, collapsing, and shearing off as if it were alive. Below fourteen thousand feet, giant gaping chasms bisect each other in chaotic patterns, but snowfall blows across the openings and freezes, so that deep crevasses are hidden from sight by a snow cover of only a few inches in places.

On a past training climb, I had made the mistake of bragging to my teammates that I could sense when we were over a hidden crevasse by the soft tremulous feel of the snow and the slightly hollow thunk made by my boot steps. So, they had decided to test my claim by pushing me forward and making me lead across the notoriously suspect snowfield below our fourteen-thousand-foot camp.

"This'll teach you to brag, Super Blind Guy," Jeff, a close friend and one of my teammates, called out as he and the others crept along behind, keeping taut the 150-foot climbing rope connecting us. The tension in the rope assured me they would be ready to hurl their bodies face-first into the snow, their chests driving in the pick of their axes, hopefully arresting me, if I were to plunge through. The dry bitter wind roared across the surface of the glacier, rattling through my GORE-TEX. The wind scoured the top layer of snow into a frozen crust, and I could hear the biting metal squeak of my crampons as they clawed into the ice.

I stepped cautiously, listening as I slowly brought down the full weight of each step, forcing myself to breathe in rhythm. What were the chances of me stumbling upon a hidden crevasse, I thought, in this place, at this moment? I probed a trekking pole in front of me. Initially, it held, but suddenly it popped through the Styrofoam snow into emptiness, with me swooning forward, the pole sliding through to the handle. Then I heard it, the terrifying noise that climbers dread, the slit of a knife across the glacier and increasing to a loud zipper. I had heard this noise before, the sound of ice fracturing, breaking apart and zigzagging across the frozen ground, but I had never been so near. The snow around me collapsed with a *whoomp*. The muscles in my legs turned to putty and the rope stretched tighter as the team braced. I felt the lurch of my body and the snow beneath me dropping away, and I knew at once I had broken through. I could feel the air all around me, filling the space under my feet, along my legs, and against my face. Jeff yelled something, but his voice quickly faded in the rushing snow and gear that came with me. A moment later, I was confused because I was still standing. "It was a false shelf! You only dropped a few feet," Chris, our leader, yelled urgently.

"Huh?"

"What are you doing standing there, waiting for it to collapse again?"

I forced my legs to move, mumbling, "False shelves! I never said I could feel false shelves." The lower shelf I moved across was softer than the first, sagging and creaking below me. I tried not to think of the bottomless cavern beneath the thin bridge. I climbed a jagged little ice hump, swinging my ax above it, biting in and pulling myself over what I assumed was the fracture line, and breathed out deeply, chuckling grimly because I knew everyone else now had to cross.

Later at our fourteen-thousand-foot camp, Sam, my primary training partner, said he could finally see the brilliant white ramparts of the West Buttress leading to the top of Mount McKinley, a mile and a half above us. It had taken us a week to get here, but besides the crevasse danger, it had only been a grueling slog up moderate snow slopes. Tomorrow, the real climbing would begin. Sam took my finger and brought it up the route we would climb, stopping at prominent landmarks like the sixty-degree headwall, Washbern's Thumb, and Pig Hill. He pointed out the second tallest peak, Mount Foraker. Then, I tried to point toward McKinley's summit. I pointed my finger a little higher than Foraker. "No. Higher!" Sam laughed. I raised my finger. "Still higher." I continued to point higher and higher. Finally, I pointed so high, I imagined I was pointing at the sun. "There!" Sam said, his voice softer and deeper now, "There's the summit of McKinley!" That is when I felt the stubborn fear washing over me, beginning in the pit of my belly and slowly seeping into my fingertips, making them tingle.

All my life, fear had nearly paralyzed me. Rock climbing outside of Phoenix had definitely provided a healthy dose of fear, my one hand palming a precarious finger lock while my other hand scanned across the rock face, desperately searching for the next hold. For me, the fear of climbing blind does not come when I am hanging securely from a fat hold or after latching on to the next. The greatest fear is in the reaching, at that moment when I have committed my body and soul to finding the next hold, when I am hoping, predicting, praying I will find what I am seeking. But it isn't all fear. Despite the pain and frustration of going blind, the death of loved ones, the loss of my eyes to glaucoma, none of it had been enough to stamp out the hope. A delicate strand of hope balanced by fear, each keeping the other in its place. It was on the top of one of those rock faces when Sam suggested we try something a little bigger, "Maybe Mount McKinley." I had immediately said yes, and the decision had been like another reach into the darkness, the greatest reach of my life.

That afternoon in the blazing heat, we built snow walls around our campsite. I knew about McKinley's legendary cold, but no one had told me about the heat, reflecting like a mirror off the snow and burning my eyeballs through the leather flaps of my glacier glasses. Then the wind, chilled by the glacier, whipped past me, taking much of my body's warmth with it. "Windburn on top of sunburn. Get used to it," Chris laughed, observing Sam and me constructing snow fortresses out of the glacier. Sam cut blocks of blue ice from the floor while I placed them in a rectangle around the site to block the wind. Soon the walls were as tall as me. Then I cut steps into our fort while Sam packed the small gaps in the walls with snow. Finally the site was ready for the tent. I held one side and threw the other into the wind, which caught it and unfurled it. I laid it on the ground and oriented it by feeling the loops and pockets on the corners through my layers of gloves.

Months before on a training climb on Mount Rainier, a teammate assigned me to set up a tent on the Muir snowfield, on which wind and cold seemed to be the only constants. I was beginning to shiver as I knelt in the snow with the tent laid out in front of me. Through my thick gloves I couldn't feel the delicate sleeves of the fabric. I fumbled with it, clumsily trying to jam the pole through. Then I took my glove off so I could actually touch it. My hands were my eyes, but three frustrating layers of material over them made me feel blind. Only for a second, I thought. Just enough time to get the pole started in the sleeve. But sharp splinters of sleet pricked my bare skin and it went instantly numb. I stuffed my lifeless hand back inside the glove and beat it against my knee. When it came back to life, the pain was so intense I almost vomited from nausea. Not wanting to give up, I whipped off the other glove, but this hand too went numb before it even touched the tent fabric. Sam and Jeff approached. They had finished with the other tents and without saying a word started working on mine. The pain in my hands was nothing compared with my frustration and embarrassment, like a balloon expanding in my chest. I knelt in the snow, listening to the tent lifting up under the pressure of the poles, and I made a promise to myself. The things I could not do, I would let go; but the things I could do, I would learn to do well.

Afterwards in Phoenix, when the temperature was hovering above a hundred degrees, I took the tent to a field near the school where I taught and, with my thick gloves on, worked on setting it up and breaking it down and setting it up again. I heard cars slowing down on the nearby road, to gape, I imagined, at the lunatic in the blazing heat, in a tank top and mountaineering gloves, kneeling over a tent. But I refused to be the weak link of the team. I wanted them to put their lives in my hands, as I would put mine in theirs. I would carry my share. I would contribute as any other team member. I would not be carried up the mountain and spiked on top like a football. If I were to reach the summit, I would reach it with dignity.

That evening on McKinley, we sat on ice benches around the tents we'd set up and our gas stove. I could feel the sun quickly dropping away beneath the peaks, plunging the temperature fifty degrees in minutes. Near eight P.M., climbers all over the mountain awaited Base Camp Annie's weather report over the two-way radio. Instead of the report, however, our radio crackled the news of two Taiwanese climbers who were trapped at nineteen thousand feet. That morning, they had left for the summit with high expectations but had pushed too hard and too fast in a whiteout and were forced to bivy on the Football Field, a hundred-yard shelf of snow just beneath the summit ridge. Now, many hours later, they lay huddled together, freezing to death in the frigid night air. One of them croaked their position to a rescue party. "Sit tight," a ranger responded. "The winds are too high for the Black Hawk." We all sat transfixed, drawn to the desperate events unfolding. An hour later, the same voice, although weaker, crackled over the radio. It was almost a whisper. "My friend, he has stopped breathing."

Sam and I headed dejectedly for our tent. Sitting inside, Sam asked, "What separates us from them? I mean from the guys who die?" Neither of us spoke for a long time.

A year before, we had been no different. Sam and I, in preparation for McKinley, had tried to climb Humphrey's Peak in Arizona, a moderate climb that takes the average hiker only a few hours to summit. But minutes from the parking lot, Sam had hesitated. "What if you get hurt up there?" he said. "How would I get you down?" I had only added to his doubts by leaving a glove in the car. Sam had gone ballistic, seizing the opportunity to reassess our prospects. "If this had been McKinley," he said angrily, "that might have meant your hand." So we had turned back, and I fumed with anger. "You don't understand," he tried again. "When we get up there, I'm the one who has to get us down." And I understood that Sam was not so much questioning me, but his own ability to lead a blind person safely through the mountains.

A week later, when our tempers had cooled, Sam suggested that we try again, this time on Long's Peak, a rough fourteener in the Colorado Rockies. Gauging from our failure on Humphrey's, I didn't think we had any chance of succeeding on a much higher and more difficult peak, one often considered the most grueling in Colorado. And on top of everything, we would be trying it in January. I agreed anyway. On the first day we climbed slowly as I followed the sound of Sam's footsteps over icy boulder fields and up steep snow ridges. We were stopped five hundred feet from the summit by high winds. Retreating back to our high camp, we spent a traumatic night feeling the winds buffeting the tent walls, threatening to rip the tent from its stakes and tumble us down the mountain. The next morning the tent was buried in three feet of fresh snow. We descended slowly, stopping every few seconds to brace against the incredible force of the wind, now over a hundred miles per hour, which constantly picked me up and slammed me back against the rocks and snow. Eventually, I could no longer follow the sound of Sam's footsteps over the howling gale. I couldn't even make out his shouts, only a few feet away. With numb hands, Sam struggled to tie a piece of webbing from my pack to his own and, for the next seven hours, I followed him down by the tension of the webbing. Paying close attention to my footing on the steep slope, I was often blown off balance, but Sam was always there so that we could brace our bodies together against the force of the wind. When we finally reached the parking lot late that afternoon, we were dehydrated and exhausted. We had failed to make the summit. My eyelids had frozen together and Sam had lost a snowshoe in the deep powder, but we both knew, emphatically, that if we could make it through that, we could make it through anything.

Now, sitting next to Sam on McKinley's Kahiltna Glacier, I finally broke the silence. "We've prepared for a year. I've never worked harder for anything. We've earned our right to be here. We're ready," I said, and hoped I was right.

I turned away and began organizing my pack for the next day's carry. In the top compartment I put my extra layers of gloves, thick socks, my face mask, and goggles. My ice ax, pickets, and shovel, I cinched down with the outside straps. Yes, Sam was right, losing a glove or an ice ax could mean losing a hand or a life. Then, as I slid into my down sleeping bag, a thought emerged from the crisp still night. I'd been preparing for this climb my whole life.

# 1
# Quasimodo

Football oozed through my father's veins, from his dramatic linebacker plays on schoolboy teams to his days as a star for the Princeton Tigers. In his late twenties he volunteered as a youth coach and was proud to have his family share his love and passion for the game of football. I was only a few months old when I attended my first game in Hightstown, New Jersey, where I was born. On that crisp autumn day in 1968, Dad coached on the sidelines as my oldest brother, Mark, age nine, led the Hightstown Rams to yet another victory. Both Mom and Dad cheered as Mark ran a kickoff back for a touchdown, caught several passes, and made his efforts complete with several crushing tackles. The postgame celebration on the field was a family affair, with moms and dads circulating among the players. In the midst of celebration, my dad tossed me a tiny bit into the air and caught me. "This guy will score touchdowns too someday," he said as my mom immediately took me back into her arms.

Back home after the game, my dad played with me in his lap, first making funny faces, trying to make me laugh, then getting me to focus on a small football that he moved from side to side. Suddenly, he noticed my eyes shaking as they tried to follow the ball. He stared at them, moved the ball again, stared again, this time a moment longer, and then examined them closely. Finally, he asked my mom if she had seen my eyes shake and if this was normal for a baby. My mom cradled me and carefully studied my eyes. Knowing my mom, she inwardly panicked but outwardly forced herself to stay calm. She told my dad matter-of-factly that she would keep a close watch on it, and later, alone in their room, she called the pediatrician.

That call began a two-year nightmare of doctor visits around the country as specialists tried to diagnose my strange disease. I was subjected to some frightening tests with apparatus frequently placed right onto my open eyeballs, sometimes for hours at a time, as intense beams of light focused on my retinas. When I lay on my back on a metal hospital table, with the harsh smell of antiseptic burning in my nose and throat, the temperature was always cold, no matter how hot it was outside. Hospitals seemed like places ripped out of time, floating beyond the familiar warmth of my life, and the parades of specialists, drifting in and out of my perception, were merely disembodied voices: "Open your eyes wider, please." "Keep your eyes still, please." "Focus on my fingers, please." "This may sting for a moment."

Sometimes, the voices would even talk to each other. "Have you ever seen this pattern of hemorrhaging in the macula, doctor?"

"Unbelievable! What a fascinating case study."

Each specialist had a different diagnosis. A few recommended courses of action that could only be described as bizarre. One specialist pronounced confidently that I suffered from weak retinas. "The solution is a bit obtrusive," he admitted, "but it's the only remedy I know. Erik's retinas need to be stimulated into reattaching themselves to the eyeball. The ideal environment for growth is a liquid environment."

"Liquid environment?" my frantic mother gasped.

"It's completely safe. He'll be attached to a breathing tube and he'll only be submerged for a few months."

"We'll sleep on it," my dad promised, as he took my mother's arm and moved toward the door. "He'll be able to come up for meals, of course," my father half joked.

Another doctor believed a virus was attacking my retinas and wanted to start me on an intensive series of freezing treatments. "I'll inject liquid nitrogen into the diseased portion of the retinas." Then he plucked a leaf from a potted plant in his office and crumpled it in his palm. "You see this leaf?" he asked, thrusting it toward my parents. "That's what liquid nitrogen will do to that virus. Unfortunately, he'll probably lose quite a bit of vision, but, nevertheless, it has to be done. I'll schedule the surgery for tomorrow."

"Maybe we'll hold off," my mom said, glancing nervously at the crumpled leaf.

After dozens of specialists, there was still no medical consensus, not even agreement on whether my condition resulted from a virus or a genetic problem. While my dad concentrated on his job and the rest of the family, my mother scurried from doctor to doctor, hospital to hospital, pacing outside examining rooms, draining herself emotionally and physically in the process.

Finally, when I was three, the path led to the famed Boston eye clinic, Retina Associates, regarded as the best in the world. After more tests and many more doctors, Dr. Brockhurst delivered the bad news. "Erik has retinoscheses, an extremely rare eye disease, which we've never seen before in a child so young. His retinas are already detached in the center of his pupils, so he can't see straight ahead, but he does have limited peripheral vision, which will allow him to get around for a number of years. The pressure, which is causing the damage, though, will continue to increase gradually over time—there is no way we know to stop it. Eventually it will cause total splitting of both retinas."

Almost too quiet to hear, my mother asked, "How long will he be able to see?"

"It's hard to say, it's not very predictable," responded the doctor.

More forcefully, my dad asked again, "What's your best guess?"

"I'm sorry," Dr. Brockhurst said haltingly, "but Erik will be blind by his early teens."

On the way home to New Jersey, my parents were quiet. Just before leaving Boston, we stopped at a cathedral. My mother had heard of a priest who had performed miracles there. The giant church was dark and mysterious as we entered. No clergyman was present. She waited with me for an hour to see someone, trying to be patient, but her anxiety increased minute by minute. When no one appeared, she finally knelt, with me at her side, and prayed aloud for God to restore my sight. I had rarely been to church, and so my mother's hot tears splashing on my forehead combined with the strange dark cathedral were terrifying. I could hear the fear and dread in my mother's voice as she asked God for a miracle. I had never known what full sight meant. I saw what I saw, what I had always seen, but many people close to me, particularly my mom, seemed to be so frightened. Kneeling in the church and listening to my mother's wails, her arms wrapped tightly around me, I prayed along with her. I prayed that I would see like my brothers and be able to catch a football and charge down the basketball court on a fast break. I prayed to put these awful trips to Boston to an end. I prayed for sight so my parents wouldn't bring me to dark places and sound so desperate and scared. All I wanted was to be away from this place, home in my backyard playing in the piles of crisp fall leaves, riding my Big Wheel up and down the sidewalk, and exploring the fallen oak tree, its exposed roots making it my own secret fort.

Before I started my first days in kindergarten, Dr. Friedman, a low vision specialist, gave me special thick magnifying glasses that enabled me to read letters almost as small as those my dad could see. My mother had taught me the alphabet, and I used the bubble glasses to help me find the letters on the page. Even with the bulgy glasses, though, I had to bend over and press my face against the page before the letters came into focus.

As kindergarten approached, my parents looked at various schools for me. The public schools were crowded, and the student-teacher ratio didn't allow any of the special attention I would need: assignments in large print, special seating near the blackboard, after-school help with reading. My mother looked at a private school but, even there, found reluctance. On my first visit, I arrived neatly dressed—alligator shirt, pressed khaki slacks, clean sneakers. I held my mother's hand as she walked me inside the school. She straightened my shirt collar and squeezed my hand with pride. After a review of my medical situation, the discussion turned to my ability to see print. Proudly, my mother reached into her pocketbook and gave me my special glasses with quarter-inch-thick lenses and my cloth-page beginner's reading book. I put my glasses on, carefully opened the book, put my right eye all the way down to the page, and began reading slowly: t-a-b-l-e, c-h-a-i-r. I expected smiles, but was confused by the panel's silence. While my reading ability was pretty advanced for a four-year-old, watching a little boy press his nose against the page was a little alarming to the educators. It was obvious I would never be able to read fast enough to keep up with my class. The school had never had a legally blind student before and was fearful of whether it could provide all that I would need. Ultimately, they concluded that it would be best for me to attend a school for the blind, and they offered to help my mother make arrangements.

"He will not go to one of those schools," she said forcefully.

"I believe the teachers there would be more cognizant of his needs," explained the headmistress.

"I have a second cousin, maybe a third cousin," my mom began. "She was born prematurely and the incubator made her blind. You know what they taught her at that school for the blind?"

"No," the administrators replied politely.

"They taught her to tune pianos. Now there's nothing wrong with tuning pianos. It's perfectly respectable. The funny part is that Penny's tone deaf. She's blind, so they teach her to tune pianos, but they ignored that she was tone deaf." My mother burst into laughter, but it sounded strained. The administrators smiled politely, wondering where she was going with this. "You know what she does now?" my mom asked.

"No." The administrators shook their heads.

My mother paused and then delivered each word separately and deliberately: "She does nothing. She can't make a bed or cook a meal. She can't even peel an orange by herself. And what's going to happen to the poor thing when her mama and daddy die? Where's she gonna go? What's she gonna do? Who's gonna peel her oranges then? My baby can move around the house and neighborhood on his own. He can take out the garbage and vacuum the floor. He can look at comic books. Puts his head right against the page, but he can see them. He can swim in the pool, dribble a basketball. He plays football with his brothers. They let him be quarterback and yell out, 'Erik, over here. This way,' and he throws it right to them. He's not going to tune pianos and he's not going to sit around the house waiting for the dinner bell. He's going to go to a normal school, with normal children, and even if I have to go to school with him, he's going to learn."

I don't know how my mother found the strength to oppose the world. Maybe it's simply a mother's primal instinct to nurture and defend her child. She was as unprepared as the administrators sitting across from us. Somehow though, she believed in me. I was just a little boy with my ink-smudged nose pressed against the page. I had done nothing yet to prove myself, so how she saw strength, opportunity, and promise, while other people saw problems, obstacles, and limits, I'll never know for sure, but her belief in me stemmed from the evidence of her own life.

Ellen Suzanne Baker had grown up in Jay, Florida, a hard-drinking, one-stoplight town near the border of Alabama, picking cotton at two pennies a pound with her younger brother, Kenny, and shelling peas and butter beans from the family garden with her mother, Talatha. Some of the more well-to-do families in town wouldn't allow their children into the cotton fields, but Martin and Talatha Baker had grown up in the Depression, when the battle cry crackling over the radio was "Wear it out and use it up. Make it do or do without," and they weren't training their children, as Martin put it, "to meet the public"; they were teaching them to respect hard work and the bounty that came with it. Until Ellen was an early teen, almost all the food that passed through her lips, the clothes she wore, the dishes she ate from, the vases in which she arranged flowers, were either grown in the red rich soil behind her house, stitched in Talatha's sewing room, or baked in her kiln.

By the time my mom was sixteen years old, while others her age were dropping out of school, having babies, and starting work in the fields, signs of promise shimmered, like waves of heat rising up from the soybean fields, that Ellen Baker was going places. A top honors student and head majorette, Ellen led the school band and town parades while performing twirling baton throws with tricky behind-the-back catches. To honor her talent and beauty, the Soybean Grower's Association of Santa Rosa County voted my mom Miss Soybean Queen. The governor of Florida gave Ellen a special crown and invited her to help cut the ribbon that would open the Florida State Fair. Talatha made her gown, lavender and purple with a sea of ruffles circling from waist to floor. The governor's honor had come with a luxurious prize: a free trip for two to tropical Cuba. So Ellen and her mother, who like most in Jay, had never been out of the Southeast, found themselves laughing and crying with joy as they boarded a jet plane bound for Havana.

They painted the town, sitting in the Tropicana, where Desi Arnaz got his start, watching companies of Latin entertainers dance the tango, cha-cha, and the samba. Once, Ellen slipped away and her mother found her standing at the threshold of a busy casino, staring wide-eyed at twinkling lights, flashing screens, and tall, handsome blackjack dealers wearing stiff tuxedos and rings that sparkled with brilliance as they shuffled and dealt cards in fast-motion. Later Ellen and her mother walked through a park packed with university students lounging around on blankets when one called out, "*Bonita! Bonita! Muy bonita!*" Then many others followed, "*Bonita, bonita,* beautiful." They were entranced by my mother's long blonde hair and fair complexion. One bold young man even stepped in front of Ellen and performed a few lively moves of the cha-cha. Without missing a step, my mother fell right in and they danced in the open park, with no music to guide them and with the other boys laughing and cheering. As my grandmother likes to say, "It was right out of a scene from *West Side Story*," but true to that story's violent undercurrents, my mother's young life was also in store for a tragic surprise.

After graduation, my mother married her high school sweetheart, Jake McNary, a big strapping farm boy with a gentle voice and a kind smile, and soon, they had produced two beautiful children, Suzanne and Mark. Sadly, not even a year through the marriage, Jake was coming home later and later, and sometimes, not at all. When he did come home, his gentle demeanor turned belligerent, a few beers and he could "whip the world." The last straw was on a slurred drunken night when Jake came home and slapped my mother across the room. She was afraid for herself but terrified for her children that his increasing anger would turn on them. My grandfather had finally told her, "Everyone's life's just a batch of changes, some good, some bad, and yorn ain't no different. You wan' leave him, your mama and I'll back you, but if you do, you best look straight ahead and never look back." My mother had assumed marriage was forever. She must have been so disappointed in herself. Unlike so many other locals her age, she had finished high school, had been Miss Soybean Queen, had traveled to an exotic world, and she had married someone she thought was the man of her dreams; but she listened to the words of her strong-willed father, gathered up a few belongings for her and her children, looked straight ahead, and never looked back.

Living in the room she had grown up in, she supported her children by working the factory floor at Chemstrand Manufacturing, a big plant producing nylon carpet fibers. She had worked there almost four years when a friend invited her to a party at the Marine Corps officer's club in nearby Pensacola, where she met my father, a recent Princeton University graduate and student at the flight academy. They fell in love and within a year, they were married under the crossed swords of fellow Marine Corps pilots in a traditional military ceremony. A few years after that, she gave birth to my brother, Eddi. I was soon to follow.

At the end of our meeting with the private school administrators my mother took my hand, and we left. A week later my mother got a letter informing her that they had decided to accept me on a trial basis, provided my mom assist me in the classroom. So my mother was often with me, reading my assignments, practicing with me, and rewriting class work into larger print. Eventually my mother backed away so that I could become more independent. Once, in the first grade, I came home from school bragging that I had gotten all the words right on a spelling quiz. I proudly showed my mother the paper. At first she was ecstatic and then, looking over the paper, she grew silent. The quiz had pictures of animals and we were supposed to spell the names underneath. My quiz had a series of illegible marks scribbled across the page in yellow crayon. A smiley face sat atop the page giving the work its approval. I could hear my mother mumbling, "How . . . smiley face . . . load of . . . !" The next day my mother showed up in class and approached the teacher, quiz in hand. "With fifteen children in a class, I'm sure it's difficult to give special attention to every child, but when a child hands in a paper full of yellow scribbles, surely it doesn't deserve a smiley face. He's blind. He's not stupid, and he can do better work than this. Damn smiley face. Draw a pitchfork and horns next time. Anything but a smiley face."

"I have never taught a student like Erik," the teacher replied defensively. "I was just attempting to boost his self-esteem."

"He doesn't need self-esteem," my mother said. "He needs to know how to spell." That night, my mother sat me down and pulled out the very same quiz. With a black pen, she made me spell out the names of the pictures all over again. I rewrote the words right over my faint yellow marks that even I couldn't comprehend anymore. Each new stroke of the solid black pen gave me a sense of security and comfort, and seemed to bring a layer of order to the mayhem beneath.

My mother always tried to bring order to my world. When she bought groceries, it was my responsibility to put away the food I liked to eat—animal crackers, peanut butter, oranges—so I could easily find them when she wasn't around. The same principle applied to laundry. She'd place the clothes bin in front of me and I'd go through it, folding the underwear, sorting the socks, and putting it all neatly in the drawer. Once, I was in a rush to go out and play, and only stuffed the bundle in haphazardly, but she caught me, pulled the clothes out, and angrily threw them in a heap on the floor. I had to fold and sort all over again and learned my lesson. Even at age six I thought she was a neat-freak, but there was no bending her fierce will. School shoes were to be put away in the closet; jackets were to be hung up. In return, she did the same. She always remembered to close the dishwasher after putting dishes away, so that I wouldn't come screaming around the corner, as I often did, and smash my shins on it. Cabinets were never left half opened, and buckets and mops were never left in the middle of the room.

My father rivaled my mother in persistence, especially when the goal was physical. He came from a strong German family in Pennsylvania. While my mother was eating black-eyed peas and collard greens, my father dined on red cabbage and potato pancakes. Every Saturday, he'd suit up for the big game and every Sunday, he'd don his coat and tie for early morning church. His father owned a concrete factory, and it was as though Ed Weihenmayer was forged of that very same concrete. During his Princeton days, he had worked his body beyond exhaustion, playing football in the fall, wrestling in the winter, throwing the hammer in the spring, and graduating at the top of the engineering department. After college, he had enlisted in the Marines, serving his country as an attack pilot flying A-4 Skyhawks on 108 missions over Vietnam. Years after his service, he still woke up every morning at the crack of dawn and, before starting off on his two-hour commute to his Manhattan job, saluted the Marine flag that flew above our porch and the American flag that flew right above it. Whenever Kennedy's famous speech played on TV: "Ask not what your country can do for you, but what you can do for your country," my father always got teary eyed and, during the president's State of the Union Address, he'd take the phones off the hook and watch with admiration. On weekends, he'd wake his four children—Mark, Suzanne, Eddi, and me—with a familiar but corny, "Rise and shine like the morning sun. Breathe in that fresh morning air." When he was feeling especially energetic, he'd wake us up by putting his fists up to his mouth and playing reveile on a pretend bugle. Mostly, his early morning speeches and bugling were met by groans while Mark and Suzanne buried their heads under their pillows. Some fathers read aloud to their sons from fairy tales or nursery rhymes, but my dad would sit me on his knee and read me his favorite poem, "Don't Quit."

*When things go wrong as they sometimes will,*
*When the road you're trudging seems all uphill,*
*When the funds are low and the debts are high,*
*And you want to smile, but have to sigh,*
*When care is pressing you down a bit—*
*Rest if you must, but don't you quit.*

*Life is queer with its twists and turns,*
*As every one of us sometimes learns;*
*And many a fellow turns about*
*When he might have won, had he stuck it out.*
*Don't give up though the pace seems slow—*
*You may succeed with another blow.*

*Often the goal is nearer than*
*It seems to a faint and faltering man;*
*Often the struggler has given up*
*When he might have captured the victor's cup;*
*And he learned too late when the night came down,*
*How close he was to the golden crown.*

*Success is failure turned inside out—*
*The silver tint of the clouds of doubt,*
*And you never can tell how close you are,*
*It may be near when it seems afar;*
*So stick to the fight when you're hardest hit—*
*It's when things seem worst that you mustn't quit.*

So, it was in the spirit of my dad's favorite poem that, when I was six years old, I begged him to take the training wheels off my bike and teach me to ride. My father and I woke up early on a Saturday morning and wobbled up and down the road, me craning over the handlebars and my father running along behind holding the back of the seat. "Are you still holding?" I'd scream.

"Still holding," he'd reply, "but my hands were just off for five full seconds and you didn't even know."

"I was riding alone," I screamed. "I was really riding alone?"

"They were just off again while you were talking," he screamed back, his voice raising a few octaves in excitement. "You're on your own," he yelled. "You're doing it by yourself." And he ran along beside the bike holding his hands up in front of me.

"Really? Really?" The realization that I was on my own was too much and I swerved crazily, tried to recover, and swerved to the other side of the road. My father sprinted behind me, trying to grab hold of the seat again, but he was too late and I toppled over, bouncing off the pavement with a yelp. I popped up though, hardly feeling my knees and elbows oozing with blood. "I was really riding alone? I was doing it alone?" In less than an hour I was riding alone, a little shakily, my father trying to grab the seat whenever a car passed. Sometimes, though, I was too far ahead and he'd scream out, "Car on your left." I got so nervous, I swerved to the right, bouncing over the curb and down a steep embankment into a ditch. He stumbled right after me, picking me and the bike up out of the poison ivy, weeds and briars. "Do you want to try again? You're really getting it down."

Around noon, my dad burst through the front door, his hand on my shoulder. "Ellen, Ellen!" he screamed. "We can throw out the training wheels. Our boy is riding solo!" But my mother didn't seem to hear his exciting news. She stood silently, her eyes running systematically from my scraped ankles, past my battered shins, to my skinned knees, and finally to my mangled elbows. Her face slowly metamorphosed into a mother lioness. She clenched her jaw and flashed an angry glance at my father before she rushed to me, throwing her arms around me and hurrying me down the hallway to the medicine closet. My father stood by the door, his hands hanging limply at his sides and his smiling lips drooping. My father was like a broom, sweeping me out into the world, while my mother was the dustpan, constantly gathering up the shattered pieces and putting me back together again.

My mother was a fierce protector of her children and especially of me, and especially, I think, because of my blindness. There was a fierceness under the surface, always ready to appear at the slightest provocation. When two neighborhood bullies stood in our yard, playing monkey in the middle with my baseball cap, my mother chased them down the road and whacked one across the butt with her foot. When I was uninvited to trick-or-treat with a group of boys a day before Halloween because the parents felt I would be too much responsibility, my mother stayed up till 2:00 A.M. sewing a Hunchback of Notre Dame costume with Quasimodo embroidered across the front and a huge pillow fastened on the back for a hump. Then she paraded me up and down the neighborhood, to the doors of those very same neighbors. My mother only focused on the costume's originality, on the fact that it would have won first prize in any Halloween contest. The effect on me, however, was that it made me feel exactly like the real Quasimodo.

In the summer of 1976, my parents drove me back to Boston for an appointment with Dr. Friedman, my low-vision specialist. He was excited for me to try out a new type of monocular. My thick bubble glasses helped for reading, but until now, nothing enabled me to see objects at a distance. In his office, I held the high-powered monocular up to my right eye, my only good eye, and the letters in his eye chart, twenty feet away, leaped into clear focus. Before, I couldn't even see the fat capital *E* at the top of the chart, but now I could read the letters, right down to the fourth line. As my parents talked to the specialist, I stood in front of the big window in his third floor office and used the monocular to stare down on people going about their business. I saw a man with brown curly hair wearing a pale worried expression as he hurried down the sidewalk, holding a bundle of papers under his arm. Where was he going so quickly? I wondered. A group of men carried large boxes from the back of a truck to the lobby of a building. I could see their faces straining. A man leaned on a railing, looking out over Boston Harbor. Suddenly I was right there beside him, looking out over the dark choppy water. Before using the monocular, only a few feet away, faces were smooth, flat, blurry masks. The busy landscape of city streets and the endless mystery of the harbor, dotted with oceangoing ships, were beyond my comprehension. Now I leaped into the thick of the world, all vivid with color and texture and I felt for once that I was a part of it all.

After our doctor's visit, my parents took me to see *Star Wars*, playing on a giant screen in Copley Square. Normally I'd sit in the front row, my tiny bits of working retina only allowing me to see a small piece of the large screen. My craning head would jerk back and forth, trying, but usually failing, to follow the action. Now, though, we all sat in a middle row. With the focused monocular, I could now see about half of the screen, and it was plenty. Right in front of me were furry gorillas with giant piercing eyes and wrinkle-faced beasts whose stubby elephant trunks flopped from side to side. I literally ducked to avoid ominous spaceships with large square sides spiraling into focus, shooting luminous beams of light through the dark space.

It was after the movie, celebrating my new miracle seeing-device over banana splits, that I realized my mother's protective hardness was only a thin husk, erected not only to protect me but also to protect herself. Sitting at a booth in the diner, my father attempted to explain all the large words the doctor had used to describe my disease. The words had made my disease seem important: congenital, genetic, recessive gene disorder, mutation. "There are little strips of information that make up each person," my father expounded. "Your disease may come from a defective gene encoded in your mother's side of the family."

I turned to my mom. "Thanks a lot," I joked. She was drinking a glass of Pepsi and began coughing so hard she slammed down the glass, spilling it on the table. Then, the coughing turned into crying and she had to leave the table. "I didn't mean to," I said to my father who was standing up and watching her go. "I was just joking." My seven-year-old brain had never thought to blame her, and I had never thought that she would blame herself for a microscopic defect that may have been carried through the family tree for a thousand years, generation to generation, never surfacing—until now. When she came back from the bathroom, I hugged her and told her that my being blind wasn't her fault, but through the rest of the meal, she only sat there, without speaking, taking short choppy breaths and blowing her nose in tissues she kept in her purse.

A powerful concoction of love mixed with guilt drove my mother's fervor to ensure my participation in all normal childhood activities. In Cub Scouts, to unequivocally guarantee that I would not be left out of any activity, she got herself elected our den mother. After dinner, we'd lie together on her big bed, which smelled of her perfumes, creams, and powders. She'd read aloud from my Cub Scout manual about how to tie knots, build campfires, and how to construct periscopes out of milk cartons. I was mesmerized by her voice, so high and even, almost musical. When I was only one step away from receiving my nature badge, she began to read out of the chapter entitled "Bucky Badger's Road to Nature." For the last step, I was supposed to catch a butterfly and draw a picture of it, "while carefully noticing its color, texture, and design." I was disappointed because the whole process seemed immensely difficult. All a butterfly was to me was a little flicker of color. But she assured me, "Don't worry. It'll be easy." She dressed me up in an annoying matching outfit, a safari print with roaring lions, leaping zebras, and elephants spraying water from their trunks. She dressed in a pair of designer jeans and a bulky, bright red sweater that made her thin face seem even more delicate. I made her promise that when we caught a butterfly, we wouldn't kill it, but only look at it and then let it go, and she agreed wholeheartedly and said it would be fun.

She held my hand as we crossed a busy road to a field covered in prickly pine needles. First, she gave me the butterfly net and let me try to catch one, but the butterflies would sweep into my field of vision and quickly disappear. I even tried to spot them with my monocular, by pointing it toward the sky, but unfortunately, butterflies were too small and stealthy for its power. Then my mother held my hand and, with her other hand, took the butterfly net and began to run and jump and lunge, with me dragging along behind. But together, we still couldn't catch one. Then, she released my hand and continued on her own while I watched. Soon, she forgot I was there. Her bright red sweater danced and dove and then seemed to be writhing near the ground. She cursed and the sweater rose again, flashing across the field, darting, reversing, zigzagging. Then she began swinging the net at butterflies that even I could see weren't there. Between breaths, she snapped, "How do they expect a little boy to catch a butterfly?" Finally, she gave up, throwing down the net and plopping down on the hard mud beside me. "We'll try again another time," she promised.

We drew the picture anyway. I held the black marker near the tip, while her fingers held it at the top. She leaned over my head, which was pressed to the page, and helped guide my strokes. The picture turned out nice, almost as though we had actually caught one. Sitting close to me, she pushed aside her hair, and I could see her eyes up close, so large and green and open like a child's. She said that she didn't know catching a butterfly would be so hard, but that we'd do better next time. I didn't really mind not catching one. I liked the picture we had drawn, but the thought of her sad eyes made my heart swell up so tight with love that I had to concentrate on each breath, pulling the air deliberately into my lungs and then pushing it out again.

As I got older, my mother's love felt overpowering, almost suffocating, while my father allowed me to experience a touch of freedom, even if it meant flopping on my face now and then. When I was eight years old, my dad's company, Pfizer, a pharmaceutical firm, offered him a promotion, heading its human resources function in Asia. The job would require the family to move to Hong Kong. It was a huge leap, but my mother convinced him it would be exciting. We moved into an apartment on Wongneichong Gap Road. My mother enthusiastically filled our new home with dark wooden Chinese apothecary chests holding dozens of tiny drawers, tall bronze Buddhas, pearl-white lamps crammed with lines of swirling, swooping Chinese characters, and hand-carved wooden screens bearing pictures of ancient battle scenes. On weekends, we'd sail a Chinese junk, with a tall wooden mast and an elaborately painted green serpent on the sail. Each weekend, we'd dock the junk and explore a new sparsely populated island. Mark, Eddi, my dad, and I would leave my mom sunbathing on the junk and hike for hours over the mountains, thick with bamboo. As we hiked along in a line, my father would call out in marching cadence, "Up the hill, over the hill, down the hill, through the hill, sound off!"

Eddi—One, two!

Dad—Sound off!

Me—Three, four!

Everyone—We love the Marine Corps!

Mark would hang back a ways, too cool to take part, mumbling things like, "Sound off. One, two. Stepped in dogshit, P-U!" Ignoring him, my dad would continue in a louder voice.

Dad—Who's the best?

Eddi and I—We're the best!

Dad—Who are we?

Eddi and I—We're the Corps!

Dad—Sound off!

Eddi—One, two!

Dad—Sound off!

Me—Three, four!

Everyone—We love the Marine Corps!

Sometimes my dad would let us hike far ahead, and we'd explore deserted beaches with names like Sharks Bay and Deep Water Bay, and climb through caves and old Japanese bunkers, left over from when the Japanese occupied these islands during World War II. Once, when my mother was away on a two-week tour of China, my dad, my brothers, and I explored a patch of land governed by Hong Kong but connected to mainland China. We crawled under a barbed-wire fence and hiked along a narrow beach. All along were signs written in such large red English letters, even I could read them, TURN BACK IMMEDIATELY, YOU HAVE ENTERED THE PEOPLE'S REPUBLIC OF CHINA. I kept waiting for my dad to tell us we had to turn back, but he was even more excited than us. "We can't let your mother have all the fun. What do you say we go explore a little of China too." Leaving the beach, we came into a village comprised of rickety wooden shacks and sandy, beachfront roads. Immediately, throngs of stray yapping dogs and intensely curious children surrounded us. The adults kept their distance and only stared suspiciously. Ready for more adventures, my father negotiated with a sampan driver who agreed to take us to an island across the bay where a market was set up. As we boarded his tiny boat, sirens blared toward us, a jeep screamed up beside us, and Chinese police wearing short pants and holding AK-47s leaped out and surrounded us. I can't imagine we struck a threatening first impression, my dad in his big floppy sun hat and my brothers and I wearing flimsy Boy Scout packs. My father was scolded by the Chinese authorities, fined a hefty HK$200 (U.S.$40), and we were dumped out of an armored truck back across the border. Safely home, my father huddled us together and said, "Personally boys, that was the best forty-dollar adventure we'll ever have, but when your mother gets back and tells us all about her trip to China, let's not show her up with our own adventure. Let's just pretend we were never in China at all," but I suspected that beyond his noble intention of letting my mother have the spotlight, lay the more basic intention of saving his own hide.

My brothers and I didn't have to go all the way to China to taste adventure. The chaotic city streets of Hong Kong were enough. The open markets, crowded with dark, narrow stalls, sold everything imaginable, from long thick eels drying in the sun to barrels of pickled cobras to large white clucking cockatoos. For me, with limited vision and less than ten years old, most of the excitement was off-limits. Double-decker busses spanned the fifteen-mile island, but I was never allowed to travel alone on them. When my mother was still away on her China tour, I persuaded my dad to let me come home alone from a friend's house. His permission might have been spawned as a goodwill gesture of secrecy over our China excursion. My friend walked with me to the bus stop and, when a bus moving in the right direction toward my house stopped, I jumped on. I couldn't see the bus's number, but I knew only two busses went this way, and those were good enough odds for me. I would have eaten a barrel of pickled snakes, had both eyes pecked out by a cockatoo, lived on a double-decker bus for a year, before I would ask a friend for help. On the bus, I excitedly climbed the circular stairway to the top level and sat down in the back, but began to get a little nervous because I couldn't see well enough out the window to track our progress. I could see the dim outlines of white buildings, an occasional tree, and the gray asphalt walls built up the sides of the mountains to prevent erosion, but I couldn't distinguish whether they were the specific buildings, trees, and walls that would lead me to our apartment. I could feel the turns of the bus, and I was sure we hadn't turned right and up the long hill toward Wongneichong Gap Road, but left and down into Happy Valley. As the bus rumbled farther and farther away from my familiar home, I felt like an astronaut shot into space, watching the earth shrink into a tiny blue marble. When the bus finally stopped, I leaped down the stairs, fought my way through a thick crowd of Chinese shoppers, and rushed out the door.

That day, I definitely got to know the island of Hong Kong. Walking along, I watched a group of old, bony Chinese men playing a game with dice. They waved their arms in exaggerated motions and chattered explosively back and forth in Cantonese. One man sipped from a mason jar filled with some kind of brown, slimy liquid. Then he made a noise deep in his throat, like a cat scratching its nails on sandpaper, and spat a long, streaming gob of spit in my direction that landed on the pavement at my feet. The other men laughed and, I guessed, that was my cue to move along. In the distance, I heard a steady beat of drums that piqued my interest. Wandering toward the pulsing noise, I looked out on a row of brightly colored outriggers, narrow and long, with heads of dragons carved into the front and jagged tails near the back. In the front of each, a man sat with a drum between his legs. Facing the back of the boat, they beat out strokes for their crews. From there, I ran through an alley and stumbled upon a flight of stairs, which I climbed. They stopped at a small platform, with a tiny wooden house built into the side of the mountain. To my left, the stairs continued, and even though I knew I was probably trespassing on someone's property, I burned with curiosity. For a half an hour, I zigged and zagged up a countless series of stairways, working their way steeply up the mountain. Each stairway was divided by another small platform and tiny house. Finally, out of breath at the top, I found myself in a tiny red and green pagoda with huge carved dragons guarding it on both sides. Leafy vines grew up the damp walls, and I could hear tiny squawking birds nesting near the ceiling. In the front of the temple lay delicate plates and tea cups, offerings to Buddha. Standing in the silent pagoda, its walls muffling the far-below noises of the city, I knew I had entered a place that was beautiful and sacred, a place that only the rare explorer, with patience and persistence, would ever see. Years later, I would find that this feeling was the same as I would experience on the tops of mountains.

That evening, after three more wrong bus stops, I found my way home and dashed into our apartment only a few minutes after my father arrived home from picking my mom up at the airport. "Where were you?" my mother asked.

"Oh, he was playing outside. I don't know how we missed him," my dad said, well entangled in the conspiracy. When my mother went into her room to unpack, my father drew close enough to me so I could see his angry glare. "We'll talk later," he whispered sternly. "I'm glad you made it home in one piece. A few minutes later, and your mother would have torn me into pieces."

Sadly, only four years after arriving in Hong Kong, my dad was transferred back to the New York City office, and my mom picked out a house in Weston, Connecticut, an hour from the city. Our new house lay on top of a hill, with a long, steep, circular driveway, and while Hong Kong had been a grand adventure, I preferred Connecticut to Hong Kong because I enjoyed even more freedom, every weekend riding my bike fast along the country roads, pumping my pedals up the rolling hills and flying down the other side. I never grew tired of investigating the vast, pungent swamps that formed in the summer, the rugged river cut through steep high rocks, and the empty lots, with their huge, soft mounds of dirt piled up by bulldozers, in which I could roll and tumble without getting hurt. My favorite activity became bike jumping. I'd sit on my bike at the top of my driveway wearing an Evel Knievel T-shirt and black leather gloves. After a few deep breaths, I'd launch myself down the drive, around the corner, and over a wooden ramp positioned at the bottom. I'd soar off the ramp and land on another ramp, eight feet past the first. Then I'd circle the cul-de-sac with one hand on the handle bar and the other raised victoriously in the air, waving to the imaginary crowd.

One day, pedaling back up the driveway for another jump, my bike and the ground seemed to swerve side to side and I just managed to put my foot down before I toppled over. For no apparent reason, my vision was swimming and growing fuzzy. I shook my head, closed my eyes, opened them again, and looked around blankly. I told myself that I was only imagining my diminished sight, that it was only the temporary blinding flash of the sun in my eyes, that I hadn't eaten enough breakfast, or that I hadn't gotten enough sleep; anything but the truth. I decided to prove to myself that nothing was wrong by jumping again. This time I pedaled a little more cautiously, but the brown wooden ramp, only vaguely distinguishable from the asphalt below, was approaching too fast. I hit the ramp crookedly and rolled off the side, barely managing to stay upright. Each subsequent run became slower and slower; I either popped off the side or missed the ramp altogether.

At the top of the driveway, my father was spray painting an old chest. Although I didn't notice him, he couldn't help but notice me. He grimaced each time I missed, wanting so badly to run down and command me to stop before I got hurt, but he held his ground. He knew he couldn't come running each time I confronted a challenge. Finally, he saw me give up in disgust and angrily push my bike into the garage. Saying nothing to my dad as I stormed inside, I slammed the door. My father looked at the dull wooden ramp and at the can of spray paint in his hand. Then he walked into the garage and studied the rack of different colored spray paints until his eyes stopped on bright orange.

The next day over breakfast, my father encouraged me to try the ramp again. I hesitantly pedaled down the driveway as he watched anxiously from the top. When I rounded the corner, I immediately noticed something vastly different. I could clearly see the outline of the ramp; it shone bright orange in the sun. I could smell the aerosol odor of spray paint as I hit the first ramp dead on, flew across the gap, and touched down on the landing ramp. Soon my confidence was back, and I convinced my two brothers, Eddi and Mark, to lie down on their stomachs between the ramps, so I could jump over them. They reluctantly agreed, but both flattened their bodies tensely against the pavement, their flesh quivering and their arms squeezed tightly over their heads. I soared over them in true Evel Knievel style and rode around the cul-de-sac waving my hand in victory. My brothers jumped up, swooning dramatically, holding the back of their heads while pretending they had been hit. Momentarily I was excited, but inside was a looming feeling that my life was closing in on me, that brightly painted ramps, trusting brothers, and the rock-hard stubbornness of my own brain, would not be enough to protect me from an inevitable reckoning with blindness.

The next year my brother Eddi, three years older than me, got his learner's permit for driving. I was envious. I imagined myself behind the wheel, driving with confidence, just like my dad with one arm hanging out the window, the other lightly on the wheel, and the seat pushed as far back as it would go so that my body was a little inclined. Whenever I'd ride with my dad on country roads, I'd beg him to let me try out my driving skills. I'd sit between his knees in the cab of our old Ford pickup and place my hands on the steering wheel while my dad worked the accelerator and brake. Sometimes when the lighting was good, I drove OK, but it wasn't quite what I had imagined. I had to keep my head craned forward almost pressed against the glass to see and both hands squeezed the wheel instead of one, my elbows pointed upward like vulture wings. My dad kept the truck moving slowly, so I had lots of time to react.

One sunny fall day my oldest brother, Mark, flew into La Guardia airport for a Thanksgiving holiday home from college. The whole family met him in the pickup, threw his bags into the back, and squeezed into the king cab for the ride home. As we left the highway for local roads, I began begging my dad to let me show Mark how well I could drive. So, a few miles from home Dad pulled the pickup over, and I scooted myself into position, and we rolled forward very slowly, but the zigzagging shadows cast by the trees overhead and the bright sun reflecting off the hood almost obliterated my vision. I steered into the right curb and then, recovering, into the left curb, the whole time my father, Mark, Eddi, and Mom screaming out, "Left! Right! Now left! More left! Right! Right!" The truck lurched from right tires to left tires, left tires to right tires. The frame of the truck creaked and ground against the axles. My mother rolled down the passenger window, and her face must have been a little green, because Eddi said, "You feeling okay, Mom?" She didn't respond, but when he next said, "This is better than Mr. Toad's Wild Ride at Action Park," she elbowed him in the ribs. I tightened the muscles in my face, trying to stop myself from crying. The tears only made my vision blurrier. Finally my dad took over, and my mother took a few deep breaths. "You should've seen me last week," is all I managed to say to Mark.

Later I lay on my bed, my face in my pillow, when Mark came in and stood over me. "Great job today," Mark said.

"Yeah right!" I replied, surprised.

"I'm serious. I know what you were doing."

"You do?" I asked.

"Yeah, it was obvious. You were avoiding the potholes. I think you avoided every one of 'em." Then he bent his arms in front of him, holding an imaginary steering wheel, and began swerving crazily around the room, with his feet moving in exaggeratedly tiny, fast-motion steps. He motored toward the bookshelf, then the nightstand, and then the chair, each time with only an inch to spare and without losing stride, performing a perfect 180-degree turn.

"Oh ma God!" he cried out in a high-pitched granny's voice. "Look out! Help! Help! There ain't no stopping me now! I'm out of control! Look out for the potholes! I'm comin' through!"

# 2

# A World In-Between

By seventh grade my sight grew worse and refused to stabilize. Each morning I woke up to a new level of diminished vision and the lessened expectations that went with it. My world seemed to be getting smaller, like the old science-fiction movies in which the heroes are trapped between two walls closing in on them. Sometimes I thought it would have been better if it had happened all at once, the violent bang of a door slamming, versus the maddeningly slow squeak as a breeze puffs it shut.

I had been walking to the school bus stop for a year. It was as familiar to me as my bedroom. I knew how the pavement contrasted with the grass and shrubs. I knew the smooth dark sections, newly paved; the lighter bleached places; and the places where the potholes were. I knew all the curves and the slopes uphill and downhill. But my view of the world was changing so fast. It was strange having such a familiar place suddenly become scary and foreign; dim, dark shapes twisted and quivered at the edge of my vision. Nothing I saw was real and, as my vision flickered, I imagined monsters with scaly bodies and bulging eyes waiting just out of view, blending in with the knee-high shrubs on the side of the road. I'd turn my head quickly, trying to see them square on, but they'd creep deftly back to the periphery, transforming into flickers once again. So I'd give up and walk quickly, concentrating on the pavement, hoping that if I kept my sight on the road and blocked the monsters out of my mind, they'd stay frozen in the grass and shrubs. Before, sight had protected me like a warrior's amulet, but now I was easy prey and they were all moving in on me. Each day as I walked to the bus I braced myself, tightening my muscles for their attack.

During school it became harder for me not to notice the increasing differences between myself and other normal kids. After recess my eyes needed at least twenty minutes to adjust to the inside light of the classroom. I felt foolish waiting at the doorway, answering countless questions about why I was standing there. I got good at making up bizarre excuses. Sometimes I'd tell classmates that I was in big trouble and had to meet the principal. Other times I'd say that I was waiting for a pizza delivery.

When I sat in class, using my monocular in the front row, I noticed the letters on the blackboard becoming more and more distant, and the print in textbooks melting away like an ice cube squeezed in my hand. I was forced to use large print books that were more than twice the size of my old books and spanned many volumes. I carried them around in a backpack along with my thick reading glasses, monocular, and magnifying glass.

By now, I had only sketchy peripheral sight; I had to look at the ceiling in order to see straight ahead. I was embarrassed when Mitch, a bully in my class, looked at the ceiling, then back at me, and said, "What are you lookin' at, googly eyes?" In the morning, small hazy shapes hovered in my field of vision and sometimes even expanded to consume my entire field. It was like peering through a translucent glass shower door. When pieces of vision broke away, the brain filled in the gaps with tiny objects. The effect was like a weird fun house with objects twisting and shaking in all directions. Sometimes, the blackboard seemed to shake so violently in front of me that I became dizzy and had to close my eyes. Usually by afternoon my vision grew clearer but, eventually, it would not improve as the day progressed.

Although my vision was disappearing quickly, I was not consumed by the loss itself, but instead was fixated on all the things my friends could do so easily. I desperately focused on trying to keep up with my sighted friends, many of whom played organized sports. Sports like basketball had so many precise rules: when to dribble, when to pass, three seconds in the lane, shooting at a tiny round net. The rules were so confining, I couldn't excel, and instead found myself drifting to a group of kids that had no interest in organized sports. Their games had no rules, or we'd make them up as we went along. Some of the games were riskier and more adventurous than the ones I had given up, but being included was more important than the fear of getting hurt.

Each morning, before the school bell rang, we were corralled into the cafeteria while teachers patrolled the halls, making sure no students escaped. I'd crouch down beside the cafeteria door leading into the hallway, with a scraggly pack of boys. Ted would give the signal, and all together we'd lope down the hallway in the opposite direction of the on-duty teacher. Nine times out of ten a teacher would give chase and we'd zigzag through the halls, the teacher right behind us. On one chase, I misjudged the turns and ran smack into a concrete wall. The teacher paused for a moment, watching my crumpled form on the ground, then hurried off after the other boys. I was blown away in disbelief. He hadn't picked me up roughly and hauled me to the office to fill out a pink slip like the others. He hadn't even indicated that he'd be back for me. I was an insignificant lump on the ground, not even worthy of a lousy detention or an interim report to my parents. His response spawned in me a goal: to elevate myself to the rank of serious offender.

Sometimes my friends and I would gather in a large empty janitor's room. Mitch, the self-appointed leader of the gang, would always have a few ideas to pass the time. "When I say the word, we'll throw our milk containers through the library door. Aim for Yoda." Yoda was our plump, round librarian. Or he'd say, "We'll take these muffins and stuff them inside the guitars in the music room." One day he turned to me. "Blindenheimer, everyone in this room has been in a fight. You're the only one who hasn't. How come? Today's the day you get into a fight . . . or you fight me." I actually stepped back, thinking for a moment that I could make it through the door and back under the scrutinizing eye of the hallway monitor, but then I realized how impossible that would be. "How 'bout at lunch?" I suggested, my heart pumping adrenaline into every corner of my body. Maybe I could find a sixth grader, I thought.

"How 'bout now," he replied challengingly. I peered around the room. Ted was at least a foot taller than me, and the other kids had talked about him having a beard and mustache. To his right was Mike. I had rumbled with him once on the field during recess. His forearms bulged. Even Mitch didn't mess with him. I eliminated each of the other kids in the room. Finally, my eyes focused on Chuck. He was taller than me and much bigger, but the others called him "baby fat." Sometimes in the hallway, Chuck would crouch down and pop up into my field of vision. He'd lean his face close up to mine, so he was sure I could see him. Then he'd widen his eyes and roll them around in his head and crane his neck up toward the ceiling. I didn't like him much and, besides, he was the only kid in the room I had a chance of taking. My eyes were pointed up at the ceiling, disguising whom I had focused on. "I choose . . . Chuck," I shouted, lowering my head and rushing at him. Chuck had a large head, large face, and bright red hair, which made his face easy to spot. My fist connected, and I felt Chuck's face, under my fist, squish back wetly. His head bounced hollowly off the wall. It made me a little sick, thinking about that squishing sensation and the hollow thunk of his head, so I was actually a little glad when Chuck hit me back and I felt my own lip squish back against my teeth. After that, we locked arms and circled around each other. "Look at the two faggots, too scared even to hit each other," I heard Mitch sneer. I was relieved when I heard the bell ring, and we had to disperse. All that day I told friends about the fight. Ted overheard me once. "That wasn't no fight," he scoffed. "That was just two sissies slapping each other." Still, I couldn't get the sensation of my fist against his face out of my brain, both sickening and a little exhilarating.

Ever since I came close to colliding a friend's dirt bike into a moving car that happened to be driven by my mother, my parents began restricting certain activities. But no matter how many times they said no to this and no to that, more untapped dangers awaited, just around the corner. There were caves to slither through, unfinished houses to explore, boulders to jump off, and cliffs to climb. At the Devil's Glen, a fast-flowing river running between high granite rocks, we swam and jumped off the walls. I stood with my friends forty feet over the water on a protrusion of rock. Each dared the other to be the first to jump. None would venture first. I looked down; I could see the sunlit rocky ledge close to me drifting into empty blackness. I knew that there was a fifteen-by-fifteen-foot opening where it was safe to jump. Beyond that, rocks lurked only several feet beneath the surface. I took a stick and began to point toward the water. "Right there?" I'd ask nervously.

"No!" my friend Chris replied even more nervously. A few times I even pointed to areas I knew very well were full of rocks, just to hear what Chris would say. "No," he said urgently. I pointed the stick a foot to the right. "More forward," Chris told me. By pointing and repointing, I figured out the direction of the safe area. Then, with a deep breath and clenched teeth, I leaped off the ledge, forty feet of endless falling into the unknown, and then finally splashing into the water. I landed at the edge of the opening and touched my foot against an underwater rock. A little shaken, I laughed to my friends that I had found a rock they couldn't even see.

Mitch sometimes came to the Glen, but he'd always make excuses for not jumping off the rocks. "Come on Mitch, jump in," Chris would say.

"Can't you see I'm busy smoking a cigarette?" he'd reply. "Maybe later." Over the weeks I began to notice how scared Mitch was of heights. He'd stand at the edge and I'd hear his breaths exhale a tiny bit faster and almost imperceptible groaning sounds escape from his mouth. Then, he'd walk back to a boulder and sit down. "You're scared. Just admit it," Chris would say.

"Yeah, scared of bloodying up your fat head," Mitch would retort. Once, I stood on the edge ready to jump and Mitch scrambled down beside me. "Gonna jump today?" I asked.

"Maybe, maybe not," he said. "I'll tell you one thing, though. If your blind ass can do it, I know I can!"

"Oh, yeah?" I said.

"Yeah," he said. But I knew he was bluffing.

I looked down at the abyss and thought of all the times Mitch had popped me for stupid reasons; the time he had punched me in the face because he said I had sprayed spit on his pizza, the time he had knocked the wind out of me for tripping him by mistake with my cane. "Today's your day," I said.

I grabbed his arm and leaped off the ledge in the direction of the open water, listening as Mitch let out a terrifying cry. When I splashed into the water far below, with Mitch still in swan dive position just above me, I already felt guilty and hoped he wasn't really hurt. I broke away underwater and attempted an escape, but when I crawled up onto the bank, I knew Mitch was just fine, because his fast-bruising fists were there to greet me.

Near my house, a short hike through the woods, was a large network of black, murky swamps. At the edge was a broken-down dock on which I would fish for hours in the summer months. Somebody's old aluminum flat-bottom boat was tied to the end, and often I'd slip away in it for a little adventure. I'd glide through the black, impenetrable water. The head of the boat would cut through a layer of algae and decomposing leaves, creating a trail of open water behind. I could look back and see the layer of scum come together again, cutting off my path home. I tested myself by paddling farther and farther into the narrow channels, eventually learning to maneuver through the confusing maze. I used the familiar patches of sunlight blanketing the water and the gnarled patterns of oak trunks to guide me. Sometimes I got so lost that I was on the verge of panic, but always managed to find my way out. I enjoyed feeling responsible for my own destiny, even if it was scary. Occasionally I glided into a huge sticky spiderweb hanging above the water, and sometimes into a fallen rotten tree, with its mossy tentacles creeping across my face. Once, I almost glided into a large copperhead hanging from a limb in front of me. The reddish-brown color of the snake came into focus only a couple of inches from my face. I threw my body against the metal deck, my heart nearly exploding out of my chest.

Fishing on the end of the dock, I'd purposely scare myself by imagining my body splashing through the thick layer of scum and into the murky warm water filled with striking snakes, eels, and other creatures much worse. I had been listening to a book on tape entitled *The World's Most Dangerous Animals,* and had just finished the chapter entitled, "Sea Crocs, the Savage Man-eater." I peered down at the water, having a hard time convincing myself that the dark slimy tree stumps protruding from the surface weren't the scaly heads of sea crocs.

Sometimes, my friends would fish at the dock too. When I shared the end of the dock with Mitch, I was always a little jumpy, afraid to turn my back.

"I bet there are a lot of eels and snakes under there," Mitch said, looking at the water and then at me.

One day Mitch snagged his lure on an underwater root, and the line snapped. Without a word, he began tearing through my tackle box, looking for another lure. I hated the thought of Mitch's dirty fingers, stained with tobacco, rummaging through my tackle box. "Get out of there," I said.

I heard his breath as he looked up at me. "You mean to tell me you're not gonna share with your good buddy, Mitch?" he said.

"Get your grubby fingers out of my tackle box and then I'll decide," I replied, but I don't think this was the response Mitch had been looking for, because I heard his bare feet thudding toward me and felt his sweaty body plowing into me, pushing me back toward the edge. I fell back, landing on the edge of the dock. My right shoulder hung over the edge, with Mitch's slick flesh on top of me. I could feel his arms digging under my side, trying to pry my body up and over, but it went rigid with fear. I thought of the loud splash my body would make, the first slimy touch of a sea croc as it swam by for a trial run, and finally the razor teeth sinking into my leg. The thought of the teeth was enough. It gave me the energy for one last thrust. I arched my body up and felt Mitch sliding over me. His body jerked and writhed as he snatched for something to grab. Lying on my back on the dock, I heard the splash. He thrashed around, emitting a shrill whimper. I didn't wait to learn whether a sea croc had seized hold of his meaty leg, so I scurried furiously down the dock to safety.

A few days later I shuffled down the dock to go fishing. I had a cooler in one hand and a fishing pole in the other. Although I rubbed my eyes repeatedly, I could not clear the shapes that floated in my vision. Halfway down the dock my field of vision shook and I actually saw the wooden planks of the dock moving in two directions. I chose the dock to the left and as my foot dangled in emptiness, I knew I had made the wrong decision. My arms flailed for something, anything to grab, but there was only air. As I tumbled headlong into unknown space, frantic thoughts flashed through my mind. I envisioned myself splitting my head on a rock, stabbing myself on a jagged stump, or worse, much worse, plunging into the murky blackness and into the snapping swirl of hungry, man-eating predators. Thick water swallowed me up, and I choked for breath. My mouth emitted short high whimpers of fear as I thrashed around, feeling for the post of the dock. If there were sea crocs in the vicinity, they surely would have been on me with the noise I was creating. My arm banged against the wooden post, and I snatched it and shimmied my way up and back onto the dock. Then, I sat there shaking and surveying my scrapes and bruises that I was beginning to feel. Hundreds of splinters were buried in my hands and forearms, and I pulled them out with my teeth. As I untangled myself from my fishing line that had somehow wrapped around my body, I felt so stupid. Mitch, the toughest bully in school, hadn't been able to throw me in, but I had managed to carry it out perfectly on my own. "I could have killed myself," I repeated, until the realization sank in. I didn't feel like fishing anymore, and I was too scared to walk back down the dock, so I crawled on my knees, embarrassed and scared.

As my world darkened, it seemed as though my mother's did too. Ever since we had moved back from Hong Kong, her hard shell began to show more and more cracks. Her moods ebbed and flowed by some mysterious, unpredictable cycle. For days she bubbled over with outpourings of affection, laughed and told stories, and woke up early to make me pancakes and drive me to school. In these times, she was filled with pent-up energy, constantly vacuuming, mopping, and dusting. On her cleaning spurts, she organized Eddi and me into our own little cleaning brigade and ordered us to scrub the bathrooms and weed the garden. On her inspection, she would only accept spotless work. Then on other days she would go into her room, close the door, and sleep all day long, sometimes only getting out of bed to get a bowl of soup. She just lay quietly in her dark room, curled up in a ball. When I came in to talk to her, she scared me by talking about her own death. "If anything were ever to happen to me," she said, "I want you children to have all the things I have collected. If your father marries again, I don't want some young floozy to get any of it."

"Mom," I interrupted, "stop talking like that. You've got a whole future ahead of you." But she must have forgotten her father's advice to "look straight ahead," because it was as though her eyes saw through a rearview mirror to the color and adventure she had left behind in Hong Kong. "And I don't want to be buried, I want to be cremated and have my ashes scattered over the South China Sea."

In the physical world outside my home, my dad had always excelled: he had won the student/athlete award in high school, had been the honor man out of six hundred other Marines in officer's candidate school, and had recently become the head of human resources for a large Wall Street firm. Every challenge he set his mind to, he was the best and the brightest, so why wasn't he the best at bringing my mother happiness? Maybe the responsibility rested on me. Sometimes I would climb from our second-floor balcony and sit on the steep roof for hours. I wanted to rescue her, to sweep her up in my arms and carry her back through time to her brilliant past. Beyond that impossibility, I didn't know what to do. I tried to keep my room very clean, to make my bed every morning and to fold and put my laundry away, but in her solitude she didn't notice.

Maybe, I thought, it was this place that made her so sad, with my father off in the world achieving, leaving her alone in our big house on the hill, filled with the prized furniture and artifacts she had brought back from her travels to India, Pakistan, Korea, and Thailand. Our house was an Asian museum. My sixth grade class had even taken a field trip to my house. At the entranceway my classmates had replaced sneakers with silk Chinese slippers and gone on a tour. They gawked at the four-foot burnished Buddha on the fireplace hearth and at the bronze sculptures of tigers and elephants, the colorfully painted antique chests, the Indian *pishwas* and Tibetan prayer wheels. They jumped back when they saw greeting them at the top of the stairs the life-sized wooden replicas of a sea turtle, Komodo dragon, and a cobra fighting a mongoose. My mother was only forty-two years old, but perhaps, surrounded by these vivid reminders of her past, these glimpses into what she once was and what she might have been, my mother's life began to feel like a tomb.

At Christmas, during one of her worst spells, she hadn't emerged from her room all day, while the rest of the family opened presents in the living room. I was the first to hear her pattering steps as she came down the stairs and around the corner toward the living room. I jumped up and ran toward her. "Are you going to open presents with us?" I asked excitedly. She didn't answer, but instead passed right by me and kicked her prized Chinese pot into the living room. It shattered with a loud explosion. Then she crumpled onto the floor, moaning and crying. My dad and brothers ran over and picked her up as she still fought and screamed, wrestled her into the back of our car, and took her to the emergency room. For the rest of the day I sat on the couch.

Half the presents under the tree remained unopened, but they were the last thing on my mind. I was haunted by the vision of my mother's shuffling body moving past me, and although I might have only imagined it, I thought I glimpsed her eyes, distant and ghostlike, staring past me, perhaps into that imaginary mirror. When she returned that evening under the sedation of medication, I was afraid that when I gathered up the courage to enter her room as she lay on the bed, she would look at me blankly and not know who I was.

When I was younger, I had held my monocular up to my right eye and stood ten feet away from a picture of my dad that hung in our living room. He stood proudly in his Princeton uniform with his number, sixty-two, emblazoned across his jersey and his leather football tucked under his arm. He stood with his chest out and his strong square jaw jutting out. He wore a short flattop, and his deep-set eyes commanded such strength. Then I focused the monocular on a picture of my mom. She was standing in front of the Taj Mahal on a trip to India. She wore a sari, a traditional Indian silk wrap, emerald green with dark gold gods and goddesses leaping and dancing across the material. She was tall and slender and although her face was thin, almost fragile, it radiated confidence, just like my father's. I had stared at the two pictures for a long time, wondering if I would become more like him or more like her. It was so much easier to admire qualities of logic, strength, and power, than the chaos of emotion. I could follow his path by planning and working hard to accomplish big goals, but another, deeper part of me wanted to hang on to my mother's creativity, her softness, her flair, but that also meant taking on her brooding side, her vulnerability, her fragile spirit, laid open to the damage of time. My parents' personalities were polar opposites, and I wondered if I could take a little from each, my father's pragmatism and optimism to keep me safe, and my mother's restlessness to keep me dreaming.

On hot summer days before my freshman year, as my mother slept, I would sit at my window listening to the neighborhood kids below in the cul-de-sac, organizing pickup games of basketball. I could hear the hollow sound of the ball dribbling against the pavement and the convulsive wobble of the backboard. One-on-one basketball was one organized sport that I had clung to, even as my sight diminished. Like the ramp, my dad had painted the backboard at the end of my driveway a bright orange. With only one person on which to focus, versus five, I was a pretty good player. I took a serious pride in being the neighborhood one-on-one champion, even though the boys in my neighborhood were only in fifth and sixth grade, while I was in eighth. In the late spring, I practiced intensely, but throughout the summer, sensing the loss of my sight, I had been avoiding the court. Finally, sitting at my window, the heavy, stale boredom of the house overtook my anxiety, and I went down to shoot around. The outline of the backboard was no longer clear, only a faint illusory form almost indistinguishable from the green and brown forest behind it. Soon Scott, a younger boy who had never come close to beating me, challenged me to a game. My pride would not let me back out. Scott's hazy form seemed to flit around me at will. Sometimes he was around me before I even knew it. I'd spot a little wiggle of movement and then hear the ball against the backboard and through the net. The one time that Scott didn't steal the ball out of my hands, I charged toward the basket, but I wasn't exactly sure I was moving in the right direction. I kept expecting Scott to dash up behind me and snatch the ball away, in fact I hoped he would, because when I looked up, frantically whipping my head around, the backboard was nowhere. Then I simply wanted the ball out of my hands. I guessed at a direction and threw the ball up wildly. It landed in the grass, probably miles from the backboard. Scott actually laughed in astonishment. When we were finished playing, I had lost, ten to zero. I was too shocked even to be angry. Scott threw his fist in the air repeating, "I can't believe it. I've never beaten you!" I threw the ball to Scott and walked away in a daze. The victorious chants faded behind me. "Where you going? Hey, where you going?" Scott's voice trailed off.

I had to escape. A new house was being constructed down the road and I had gone there a few times to think and be alone. I walked down the driveway and through the open door frame. The house was an empty shell. The workmen had left for the day and I stood inside completely alone. I walked through the empty rooms, feeling the cool plaster walls and the new glass windows recently installed. I could see the windows, thanks to the contrast between the light streaming through the glass and the dark wood window frame. I stepped back from one window, counting the paces before it drifted away, indistinct from the wall. Eight paces, only eight damn paces. A week ago I had seen it from eighteen. There could be no more lying to myself. The truth was brutally clear. Up until now, I had done everything in my power to shroud my brain in ignorance, to keep a layer between my life and the inevitable. I had clung to a fleeting belief that the doctors' diagnosis of blindness by the age of thirteen had been wrong, that through force of will alone I would beat them, that I was only imagining the loss today, and tomorrow I would wake up to see the vivid green of the trees and the basketball hoop beyond. But standing in front of the window, only eight paces away, I knew I never would. I picked up a handful of heavy metal nails from a wooden box and hurled a bunch toward the hazy light. Pieces of glass exploded outward, spraying the ground. The air whistled out of my lungs and returned in shallow bursts. I aimed at another glint of light and heard it shatter too. Then I walked around the entire house, aiming and shattering, not wanting one window to be spared. I would gut the house; tear it from the inside out. I was shattering the last window when I heard a siren from a car coming up the driveway. I rushed out a gutted window and stumbled into the woods, barely feeling the trees that I was crashing into and the sharp branches scratching my face. I pushed forward, not knowing where my feet would land, hoping they touched soil. My momentum drove me forward. Another step and my feet soared through the air. I landed only a few feet down in a ditch and lay there trying to hold back my heart that was beating out of my chest. I lay motionless for an hour, listening for the sound of footsteps.

That night, I had a dream in which I was running frantically through the woods behind the empty house. My friends were far in front of me, and although I ran furiously, I was falling farther and farther behind. I could hear leaves and brush crashing behind me and smell rank hot breath on the back of my neck. It was overtaking me, and I was overwhelmed by the fear from knowing that there was nothing I could do. The woods were all shadows and flickers of light, twisting and intermingling, dancing and lunging, and I was running through it and it through me. I bounced off a tree trunk that twisted into the scaly head of a sea crock, opening its jaws to swallow me. I hurled myself back against a tree that held thick, gnarled, thrusting claws, and then I tripped over a slithering snake, thousands of them, wriggling and twisting and striking. Ground, rock, and sky swirled together in a crazy kaleidoscope of color and the whole scene shook monstrously before me. Then, I felt emptiness below me, and I was falling through a void of black sky. Above, I could hear the creature laughing, laughing and laughing, and it was the laugh of Chuck and Scott and Mitch, and it cackled, "Fall, Blindenheimer, fall. There is nothing to catch you." And that was all I could do, fall and fall, strangely slow and suffocating, like sinking into muck, but when I reached out, it was only black empty sky with the faint glimpse of the earth disappearing above me. That is when I woke up, clutching my bed frame, listening to the desperate rasp of my own breathing and trying to shake the sinking motion of the dream.

The fear of blindness had loomed over me for so long, and I had never resigned myself to it. It felt like what I imagined dying would feel like. But no matter what I felt, no matter what I feared most, this death was coming, and whether I denied it was happening, or wished it away, whether I accepted it begrudgingly or embraced it fully, it was coming. It didn't matter what I did or how much I kicked and screamed and fought. I had no say whether it would sweep or trickle over me, or whether it would hurt. It would come at its own pace, in the way it chose, and there was absolutely nothing I could do to change it.

Ironically, as I relinquished my grip on sight, I sank into bitter relief. I had not a clue how I would survive as a blind person, how I would cook a meal, walk around, read a book, but trying to live as a sighted person was becoming more painful than blindness could ever be, and the uncertainty of what each tomorrow would bring was almost more terrifying. I knew nothing about blindness. I had no action plan. All I knew was that I was sick and tired of getting lost on the playground and not being able to find the entrance to the school. I was tired of squinting my eyes and falling off docks, tired of trying to run down a trail in the woods or trying to shoot a basket. I couldn't do any of it well. My head bashed against trees, my skin was always scraped and bleeding. I lived between blindness and sight. While I couldn't see well enough to play visual games, to read a regular-print book, to see an equation on the blackboard, I also couldn't accept myself as being blind. But one thing I knew: compared to this in-between world, total blindness couldn't be any worse, or any more terrifying.

# 3
# Helplessness

I sat in the passenger seat of my mom's car, parked in front of my high school. It was my first day and I was totally blind. A few weeks before, while visiting my grandparents, my eye disease had reached its final stage. I could no longer walk by myself. When shopping at the grocery store, my grandmother saw me stumble into a display rack, and she noticed that I didn't seem to be able to follow her. She asked me if she could hold my arm to guide me. I laughed off her suggestion. Then she said, "I know you don't need any helping, but let me lean on your elbow, to take a little weight off my old weak knees." I agreed, although I wondered who exactly was helping whom. It was strange that my grandmother didn't say anything or show any surprise. In fact, she seemed to be prepped for this moment. So, why wasn't I?

Parked in front of the high school, my mother wanted to walk me inside but I abruptly said no, not wanting to look stupid in front of my friends. Then I noticed by her silence that I had hurt her feelings. I squeezed her hand. "I just want to do this by myself," I said quietly. As I walked up the stairs to the school entrance, I thrust my cane out in front of me, poking each stair before I stepped up on it. The guy who had sold me the cane had given me a quick lesson: right forearm resting on right hip, right wrist flicking the cane in front of each step. If blind people do it that way, I thought, then I will do it differently. Although I didn't know it, Mrs. Mundy, a teacher for the blind sent by the state, watched my stumbling entrance. "Good morning," I heard, and I immediately noticed the overly sweet scent of her perfume. I hoped she wasn't talking to me. "Good morning," she repeated formally; her large fleshy palm and fingers reached out and swallowed my puny hand. "I'll be assisting you several periods a day—every day." Her voice was husky and serious, with no trace of playfulness. "Your cane technique is sloppy and disgraceful," she didn't waste time saying. Then she marched me up and down the hallway demonstrating how to tap my cane in front of one foot and then the other. Who was this total stranger humiliating me in front of the whole school? It was the first day of school, and all I wanted to do was to hang out with friends. Instead, I was providing the entertainment. Until this point, my anger flowed out at the world like water from a sprinkler, spraying in too many directions to be dangerous, but in my brief meeting with Mrs. Mundy, I had found a target, a perfect candidate on whom to focus the force of my rage. I hated my cane almost as much as I was learning to hate Mrs. Mundy. In my mind they both represented the vast gulf that existed between me and everyone else. No matter how hard I tried, I'd never be able to bridge that insurmountable expanse.

Earlier that summer my mother had also pushed me to use a cane, but I swore to myself that I never would. I purposely bent them by placing one end on a bench, the other on the pavement, and the middle beneath the weight of my foot. My mother, just as stubborn as me, continuously bought new ones. One day she had refused to let me leave the house unless I brought the cane. I had refused, and she had refused to let me leave. I felt searing anger flowing up like a volcano. "You're a bitch!" I yelled.

"If I'm a bitch," she replied calmly, "then you're a son of a bitch. And you're still not leaving." Finally I had relented and left with the cane dragging behind me. I met my friend Chris in town and we stood on an overpass, listening to the roar of cars as they sped below us. When I heard a sound break in traffic, I launched the cane like a javelin. It landed helplessly on the road, and to my amusement Chris described it writhing and recoiling, like a snake, beneath the onrushing tires. He counted aloud how many cars it took to snap the fragile metal frame. After repeat visits, I'm sure people wondered about all the snapped canes lying dormant on the side of the road. Another time, feeling the metal sewer grating under my feet, I exclaimed sarcastically, "Whoops!" and dropped my cane down between the slots, hearing it plunk like a disarmed torpedo into the quagmire.

I became increasingly clever in finding malicious ways to destroy my canes, but I didn't count on Mrs. Mundy's perseverance. "I will lead you from class to class until you learn proper cane technique," she stated. In response, I twirled the cane around in my hand like a Harlem Globe Trotter performing ball tricks. She forced me to take her arm and led me down the hall in front of my classmates. I heard them step back, keeping their distance, allowing me to pass. I had gone to school with these kids since fifth grade, but I knew they looked at me as if I were a stranger, a fragile porcelain egg whose shell could easily crack and ooze vile yokey fluid all over their shoes. "I'm the same person," I wanted to scream out. "I'm still Erik. I may not be able to see you. I may be forced to hold an arm and swing this dorky cane, but I'm still the same person that you've always known." Although I seethed with humiliation, I continued to hold Mrs. Mundy's arm tightly, because more powerful than my anger was my fear of becoming lost in the surging swarm of students. I lowered my head and clutched her arm tighter, trying to block out the bustling life of the hallway and the friends I knew were watching. My muscles stayed tense; a continuous stab of embarrassment shot through my nerve endings, making me sweat.

Mrs. Mundy dropped me off at math class and picked an empty chair front and center. "This way the teacher can make sure you're following along," she said. I was lost anyway. My textbooks had been brailled, but my fingers weren't honed enough to decipher the information fast enough. Although the teacher tried to verbalize the equations she was writing on the board, I couldn't remember them. My concentration was made worse by the fact that, since the beginning of the school day, I had needed to use the bathroom. With Mrs. Mundy parading me around all morning, however, I refused to suffer the added humiliation of being led to the bathroom. I squirmed in my seat, constantly shifting positions. Finally, the intense pressure in my bladder outweighed my bruising pride. I raised my hand and said that I needed to use the restroom. The teacher asked me if I needed assistance. I quietly replied no. When I got up, a few kids rushed to help me to the door. I eluded their grasp, bounced off a chair, and finally found the exit. Wandering down the hallway, I didn't have a clue where the bathroom was. Finding lockers in front of me, I chose a random right, then a left, and then another right. After a while, I couldn't recall the order of the rights and lefts. I went back to where I thought I had made the last turn, but I reached out and touched a classroom door. Nothing around me was familiar, like those nights when I had sat up from a deep sleep and couldn't remember where I was. I became frantic, walking fast and recklessly through the halls. Mrs. Mundy found me running my hands along the wall of the hallway looking for the bathroom door. Apparently, my teacher had called the office on the intercom and the secretary had tracked her down. "What are you doing out of the classroom unsupervised?" her big voice boomed.

"This sucks," I mumbled, still running my hands along the wall, hoping the men's room would appear so I'd have an escape.

"Well, it's going to suck even worse if you leave the classroom unassisted again," she said. "Now take my arm and I'll take you to the bathroom and then back to class."

"I can't go back to class," I murmured.

"You can and you will," she replied firmly.

"No! I won't go back," I said again.

"And why not, young man?"

"Well," I said slowly, "I turned fifteen a week ago and I just peed in my pants because I couldn't find the bathroom. I haven't peed in my pants since I was three." Mrs. Mundy was quiet for a few seconds as if her mind was scanning the blindness manual for an appropriate response. Finally, she simply said, "Oh, honey." Then, she put her fleshy arms around my shoulders and pulled me against her, my head pressed against her massive bosom. I could hear her breaths catching in her throat. "Oh, honey."

The next day Mrs. Mundy was back to business. Like a major giving orders to a private, she informed me that I would learn Braille so that I could keep up with my classes. I wanted no part of this; I had already learned to read in first grade and now this lady was telling me that I would learn it again and this time with tiny splatters of dots and with fumbling fingers that couldn't decipher one word from another. The idea seemed ludicrous. Besides, Braille was only for blind people, and the only blind person I had ever heard of was Stevie Wonder, and his head bobbed around way too much for my liking. I purposely tried to obstruct any Braille lessons. One morning I brought in my brailled reading, assigned for homework the night before. "Did you read it last night?" she asked.

"Oh, yeah," I replied.

"Then, read it now." I positioned the paper in front of me, cracked my knuckles, and cleared my throat. Starting with my index finger on the upper left-hand corner of the paper, I scanned the top line, as if warming up. After a few minutes Mrs. Mundy jumped in. "First of all, sit up straight and square your shoulders. How do you expect to read Braille with your body slumped in that chair. Secondly, your paper is upside-down."

Seemingly frustrated, Mrs. Mundy left the room for a cup of coffee, a bad move altogether. While she was gone I placed my cane so it stuck out from my chair into the aisle. Returning, she kicked the cane, fumbled her coffee, recovered, and then stood in indignant silence.

"Oh, um, sorry," I said lamely. "I'll move that."

"Thank you," she replied, her jaw clenched.

Two days later she left the room again during reading time. I found a suitable word and, with my fingernail, scratched out a few dots, so that the perfectly innocent word she had typed now formed a dirty word. When she returned, I pointed out the word and asked, "What's this word, Mrs. Mundy? I don't think I've seen that word before." She studied the word carefully, leaning over the desk and craning her neck, and then a noise emanated from deep inside her chest and grew in volume. "I didn't type that!" she growled.

I don't think Mrs. Mundy had much faith in my abilities. So far, I hadn't really given her any reason to believe in me. Still, she persisted in teaching me all the blind skills she could think of: how to use a Braille typewriter, how to erase Braille dots with a stylus instead of my fingernail, how to do this and how to do that, and how to be a good little blind boy. One morning she said, "I would like to come to your house so I can set up your stove and oven with Braille labels. You should be able to function independently in the kitchen."

"Don't bother," I replied. "I've got it all covered. Just this morning I cooked myself up an omelet." It was the latest fad to separate the egg whites from the yolk to cut down on cholesterol, so I threw in a little flair. "Of course, I only used the whites."

"How did you separate them?" she asked.

"With an egg separator. It's pretty easy to feel the difference between the yolk and the white."

"I don't believe you," she said matter-of-factly.

"Why don't you believe me? Don't you believe a blind person can separate the yolk from the whites?"

"I didn't say that," she snipped. "I simply don't believe you can do it."

What infuriated me more than her not believing me was the fact that she was right. I had made up the whole story. But what did her quick and certain disbelief say about me, about my capabilities? How could she write me off so easily? In my mind, the story almost wasn't a lie, because I wanted so badly to be able to do things like this. I knew that I should be able to separate a yolk from the white. There was no reason why I couldn't, that is, if I chose to learn how.

At lunch I escaped from Mrs. Mundy's stern eye and entered the cafeteria on my own. The cafeteria was my worst fear. It had so much potential for disaster: an ever-shifting maze of tables and pushed-out chairs, and fast-moving bodies carrying loaded trays. If those hazards weren't enough to send me flailing, the insidiously scattered book bags surely were. The place was like the video games I played when I could still see, in which I was the tiny rocket ship, plunging through the galaxy to avoid asteroids, space junk, and lasers fired from alien spaceships. It's only a matter of time before I'm obliterated into a million tiny pieces. The first week of school, Mrs. Mundy led me through the lunch line, holding my tray and placing on it the various Styrofoam cartons of food. She always offered to bring my tray and me to a table full of boys, but I always asked her to bring me to an empty table instead. I couldn't be led to a table full of my friends. I'd rather be forgotten.

On this day, however, I was on my own. In the line, I tried not to whack my cane against the person's leg in front of me. I found the counter and slid my tray along it until I heard the ring of the cash register. I managed to pay the cashier and get out of line. My friends chattered away at a table far to the right. Mitch's loud challenging voice was my guide, but I had to get through the maze. I moved haltingly, my tray slanting to the right and then to the left and the food and drink cartons sliding around precariously. It wasn't graceful, and several times, weaving around tables and book bags brought me to a dead end, but I was definitely narrowing the distance. When I seemed almost on top of their loud boisterous voices, the table went suddenly silent, like someone had flicked off a switch. I knew, in a sense, someone had. I imagined Mitch giving the table of boys the hand signal for immediate silence. I stood with my tray, only inches away from their table. I didn't know what to do, where to go. I could have managed to find a chair and sit down despite them, but instead I backed away, carefully retracing my steps to an empty table a few feet away. As soon as I started to eat, Mitch must have flicked on the switch, because their voices abruptly exploded again. I was surrounded by the hustle and bustle of student life—food fights, dirty jokes being passed back and forth, favorite sports teams being debated—but I seemed to exist in a cocoon. The barrier between them and me was as real as an ocean filled with sea crocs, as tangible as the bars of a prison. In my mind's eye, I could still see. Through the bars I watched all the excitement, the adventure, and exhilaration passing me by. I sat at my empty table until I knew everyone else had left the room before I summoned the courage to make my way out of the maze.

That afternoon, my English literature class read and discussed *The Rainbow*, by D. H. Lawrence. My assignment was to read aloud a passage to which I personally related. Most of the class had already gone before me. I had tried to avoid being center stage because of my inexperience reading Braille. Now I had been called up and there was no escape. I could feel everyone's eyes on me as I tapped with my cane to the front of the room. I took out the passage that Mrs. Mundy had helped me to type in Braille. I lay the Braille paper flat on the desk, sat up straight, and squared my shoulders. My fingers found the top left corner of the page, moved down to the first line, and began to plod across the page. The words came haltingly:

> "He was in an agony of helplessness. He could do nothing. Vaguely he knew the huge powers of the world rolling and crashing together, darkly, clumsily, stupidly, yet colossal, so that one was brushed along almost as dust. Helpless, helpless, swirling like dust, yet he wanted so badly to rebel, to rage, to fight, but with what? Could he, with his hands, fight the face of the Earth, beat the hills in their places? Yet his heart wanted to fight, to fight the whole world. And these two small hands were all he had to do it with."

Afterwards, for the rest of class, I sat at my desk, thinking about the words and letting them penetrate through me. I was so tired of being led around school, and tired of my own bumbling incompetence; I was sick of teachers' protective watchfulness, their syrupy, do-gooder helpfulness; I couldn't stand my classmates looking down on me, and even worse, their discomfort. They didn't know how to act, what to say, how to reach out and, in return, I hadn't given them any help.

Freshman year in high school wasn't supposed to feel like a prison. It was a first chance to experience a touch of freedom and to make choices, even bad ones. It wasn't supposed to be like elementary school where teachers made decisions for you and you ate whatever they slapped on your tray in the cafeteria. In high school, you chose your own electives, and you picked out your own food in the cafeteria, cheeseburgers and French fries, and another order of fries if you wanted it. Other kids could go where they wanted, when they wanted. They could choose to skip class. They could read smut and sneak into R-rated movies. A part of me knew that by mastering all these new skills, I would foster my own freedom, but that would take forever or even longer. My body and mind had been growing and maturing, getting me ready for this moment, and with a bang, blindness had sent me skidding back to elementary school. My fifteen-year-old mind cried out for freedom. I was learning to read, to carry my own tray, to move around the hallway, all over again. My life seemed to be going in reverse.

I touched my hands together. They were puny and my fingers were skinny. They weren't hard and callused like Mitch's hands; they weren't big enough to palm a basketball like my brothers'; Mrs. Mundy's hands dwarfed them. But as insignificant as they were, as I was, I could feel a hardness gathering up inside me. Enough is enough, I resolved. I would not be forced to play by other people's rules. I wouldn't be stifled at a time in my life when I wanted to be shot out of a rocket. I had to escape from this box.

At my locker I jabbed Chris, who was rummaging in his locker, just below mine. "You want to get out of this prison?" I asked him. Chris was, by far, the smallest kid in school. He was the bigger kid's first and favorite candidate when they needed a guaranteed scapegoat. So, to combat the bigger boys, Chris became invisible. He even displayed invisibility to me. His voice projected softly from his short stature and often, in the middle of a conversation, he wouldn't respond. I'd reach out, and he'd be gone. But the devious little spark that bubbled up now and then defied the meekness. "I was going to skip this afternoon anyway," Chris replied without any hesitation.

Mrs. Roland, our vice principal, infamous for her massive squatty legs stuffed into green stretch pants, had sat me down a week before and told me, "We've never had a blind student. I've met with all the teachers, administrators, and local business owners near the school and told them to watch out for you. We want you to be safe and happy in your new environment. We've made a decision that you should not leave the building unsupervised."

"Other kids are allowed to go to their cars in the parking lot during free periods and are able to leave in the afternoon when they don't have any more classes," I protested.

"It's for your own safety," she ended.

"Forget her stinkin' helpfullness, and her stinkin' safety," I had said afterwards to Chris.

"Squeezing her big butt into stretch pants every morning is more of a safety hazard than you could ever be," Chris had said. I imagined her huge legs squeezed into combustible green tights, steaming and groaning under the building pressure until, finally, fat and gristle explode through the hallway like shrapnel.

Chris and I dashed out a side door and across the empty parking lot toward the woods. Chris saw my cane waving in front of me. "Ditch that thing," he said urgently. "You might as well wear a neon sign saying, 'I'm the lost blind boy. If found, please return to Mrs. Roland.' " I folded the cane up and followed Chris's pitter-pattering steps. Tripping over speed bumps and curbs and crashing into parked cars, I doubted I was drawing less attention. Chris had an unregistered motor scooter hidden in the woods not far away, so for the rest of the afternoon we cruised back roads, me freaking Chris out by putting my hands in front of his eyes. On the way home we heard a siren. Chris sped up and I slid back across the vinyl seat. He cut right down a dirt road, through the woods, and popped out at the bottom of my road. Puttering up toward my house, we scattered the younger kids playing basketball on the cul-de-sac. We bounced up my driveway and threw the bike into the garage while Chris ran into the house. Just as I slammed the garage door, a police car rolled up the driveway. I smiled innocently. The cop knew me. "Where's the driver of the moped, Erik?" he asked impatiently. "Let's hope you weren't driving. What a police report that would make." He laughed a big belly laugh and I pretended to laugh with him.

"I don't even know the guy's name. I just caught a ride from him. He and the bike are long gone."

"It's not that I don't want to believe you," he said politely, "but there's a whole lot of smoke pouring out the cracks of your garage. The bike wouldn't happen to be in your garage? Would it?"

"Oh, no! Definitely not."

"Why don't you check for me?"

"Don't you need a search warrant for that kind of thing?" I asked meekly.

He laughed his great belly laugh again. "You've obviously been watching too much *Hawaii Five-0.*" In slow motion, I bent over, pretending I was having trouble finding the garage handle. My body didn't want to work.

"Are you going to open it?" he asked, losing his laughing tone. I found the handle and rolled up the door. Both of us stood stock-still in front of the opening. Finally, I said, "Wow! That's really strange. It's in there after all. He must have put it in there without me knowing."

"So, you've gotten your sight back, I see. What a miracle!"

"No!" I replied, trying to keep the sympathy train rolling a little longer.

"Then how'd you know the bike was in there?"

"Ahhhh . . . I smelled the smoke?" The cop laughed again.

"What are you, braindead?" Chris sneered angrily, the next afternoon in detention. "You smelled the smoke? How could you be so stupid?"

Even though Chris and I were both grounded for a month, we'd sneak out at midnight. I felt protected by the darkness. At night along country roads or in the woods, we were all equal. I could run as fast as anyone, even faster. I could find a good hiding spot through the end of my cane. My fingers could line up a match with the fuse of a cherry bomb. On quiet sleeping streets, I could hear car engines approaching from a long way off; it was I who shouted the signal for us to dive into the bushes, before Chris could even see the headlights.

One night Chris and I stood in front of Mitch's house, just beyond the porch lights. I stealthily opened his mailbox, a huge roll of firecrackers trailing in my hand. I pressed the long fuse between my fingers, with a centimeter of fuse protruding, and struck the match with my other hand. With trembling fingers, I held the match where I thought the end of the fuse was. Testing to see if I was in the right location, I moved the match slowly toward my fingers, feeling the increasing heat of the small blaze before it burned them. When I heard the sizzle, I threw the firecrackers in, slammed the mailbox shut, and ran as if Mitch was right behind me—ready to kick my face down the hallway.

Lying in the woods, Chris dared me to moon a car. I was eager to contribute to the team effort, so soon I was standing on the grass beside the road, my hood pulled over my face and my scrawny bare rump pointed out to the oncoming cars. Two cars simply drove by. I tried to imagine their expressions: amused, grossed out, and horrified. I didn't want anyone to recognize me by my white cane with red glow-in-the-dark reflectors, so I hid it in front of my body. I didn't count on the next vehicle being a van full of high school seniors. They screeched to a halt, whooping and hollering, and piled out in hot pursuit. The peril of the situation sunk slowly into my brain, and heavy lead seemed to sink into my legs. I imagined a gang, beer cans in hand, each guy twice my weight barreling toward me, each vying to be the first to begin pummeling the blind pervert. My hands, holding up my pants, didn't seem to work. I dropped them and my jeans flooded down around my ankles. I could hear the fastest boy only a few feet away, and I broke from the trance and bolted forward and down the road. My pants, around my ankles, forced me to take tiny rapid steps, and my cane tapping in front of me fell into the same fast-motion rhythm. Even at this awkward stride, my pursuers fell behind and I wondered whether they had stopped because they were too busy laughing at the bizarre sight. I darted left, twenty feet down a trail, and then right, into the woods. I threw myself down in some bushes and lay there trying to silence my gasping breaths. The boys systematically combed the forest for an hour. One boy came within five feet of me. Any closer and he would have tripped over my leg. I heard his deep heavy breathing and then he yelled, "I bet these are the same little bastards that blew up my mailbox." I had forgotten about Mitch's three older, even tougher, brothers. I shuddered, hoping they didn't have flashlights, imagining the light reflecting off my pasty backside. When they finally left I got up shakily and whistled for Chris. A thousand points of pain stabbed the front of my body, and I realized I had been lying bare fleshed on a pricker bush. "What's that, Pricker Dick?" Chris said when I told him what I had been lying on, and he laughed at me for the next hour as I plucked prickers from my most sensitive of areas.

Chris and I had been serving after-school detention for the last two weeks. We were detained in a classroom, the supervising teacher often leaving altogether. I had been encouraged by my parents and teachers to listen to books on tape, and I finally got excited about reading when I discovered the words "strong descriptions of sex" next to some of the books listed in the Braille catalog. I ordered several. I brought one tape to detention and laid the tape recorder on the table. About ten boys were serving that day, and when I played the explicit section aloud, they all rushed to the table, gathering closely around. They urged me to play the best parts over and over again, and to turn the volume up as well. They all listened intently, hanging on every word, and at the juiciest parts they let out a muzzled cheer. Chris, still indirectly blaming me for the confiscation of his motor scooter, piped in, "That's nothing. You should see his Braille *Playboys*." Everyone in the room laughed, and for the rest of the afternoon I had to endure an endless series of jokes about Braille *Playboys*.

"Do they come with scratch and sniff?"

"That gives a whole new meaning to feeling up a girl."

"So that old wives' tale is true about how people go blind."

I couldn't help but laugh along too. Plenty of people wanted to help me. Lots of them wanted to keep me safe and happy. There were a few who sincerely cared about me and wanted me to gain the skills that would help me to succeed. Maybe, down the road, I would actually begin to appreciate some of those people and the things they offered. For now, though, I was looking for someone just like me, a little freak, full of anger, rebellion, and spark, who I could call my friend.

# 4
# Faint Recognition

After each day of high school, I waited for the special car for the handicapped students to pick me up. Although I fought the school system so that I could take the regular bus, the administrators stood by their decision. My defiance and unwillingness to learn mobility skills made me too unsafe. It didn't help the situation when a day after their ruling, I sped by the school bus lying belly down on the hood of a friend's car. The bus driver had relayed a frantic message through the dispatcher to the school principal. "That crazy blind kid's on top of a car flipping me the bird."

Waiting for the handicap car, I hid behind a Dumpster at the edge of the parking lot, hoping no one would see me. When I heard the engine of the car, I ran with my cane flailing, found the door handle, and ducked inside. I slouched down until the car rounded a corner and was out of sight.

"I don't belong in this stupid car. It's for cripples, people in wheelchairs, using leg braces, not for me," I'd complain to Jerry, the driver. He was a middle-aged black man who coached the middle school basketball team. I was constantly telling him that I didn't need anyone's help, and I'd never do all the stupid things that teachers were trying to push on me.

"How many fingers I got up?" Jerry'd ask.

"How the hell should I know?" I'd reply.

"Then, there ain't no denying that," he'd say. "You're handicapped. Why you wanna take the bus, when you can ride with a good-looking dude like me and a hot babe like Sacha? What do you care how you ride home anyway? Since you're blind, you can't see that you're in an old green station wagon. Just pretend I'm a door-to-door limo service." Sacha was a tiny waif of a girl, a few grades above me, who rode in the front seat of the car. Her legs were even tinier than the rest of her body, and she wore metal braces over them. On bad days, when her legs were weak, she would roll the hallways in a wheelchair. "Just because you're blind, don't mean you ain't a stud," the driver said one day, "and just because of those braces, don't mean you're not a foxy-looking lady. Neither of y'all have a date for the spring dance. Both y'all are handicapped. Why don't you go together?" Sacha and I winced. Sacha dealt the first blow. "He's not my type," she replied, "and I don't date underclassmen."

"Well, I don't date midgets," I shot back.

"Well, I don't date blind geeks." The conversation continued to regress.

"I'll push your wheelchair down a hill, right into traffic."

"I'll hit you upside your thick blind skull with a baseball bat."

One day when I was the last student in the car, we passed the school bus and the driver said, "Wave to all your friends." I thought of the bright sign above the car with the picture of a smiling child in a wheelchair and reading, CARRYING HANDICAPPED CHILDREN. I dropped to the floorboard. "Tell me when we're past them," I yelled up.

"You plain childish," he said. When I popped up again, I released a brand-new barrage of complaints. Jerry listened without a response and then screeched the car to a stop, heaving me against the back of his seat. "Get out!" he commanded. I knew we hadn't taken a sufficient number of lefts and rights to be near my house.

"Right here?" I asked, alarmed.

"Get your sorry, complaining ass out of my car," he said, and his voice had lost its playful glint and taken on a menacing tone. Without question, I swung open the door and scurried out, thinking he was going to leave me on the side of the road. I had finally done it, complained so much that he was kicking me out, refusing to drive me. I waited to hear the tires screech away, but instead felt something hard and rubber bounce jarringly off my head. My ears rang as I listened to the object bouncing off in another direction. A basketball. He had whacked me in the head with a basketball. I was stunned; no adult had ever done something like that to me before. Then, his door opened and I heard him retrieve the ball. "You're blind," he yelled bluntly.

"Bullshit!" I yelled back.

"You're blind!" he repeated. "Get used to it."

"I'm not," I said a little more weakly.

"Well! You can't catch a basketball."

My stunned feeling only increased.

"This time I'm gonna tell you when it's coming. I want you to put your hands out . . . Now!" The ball hit me in the chest and my hands easily scooped it up. The rubber ball felt good resting in my hands. "Erik," he said, "you may not want to be blind, but you are. The answer isn't always to fight. Let people in. Let 'em help you for a while. You might just learn to catch again."

Independence didn't come in leaping strides but in tiny successes, almost imperceptible. It came in the discovery that I could match my socks by putting safety pins in different locations, in the pride of an A paper written on my speech-adapted computer, and in the confidence that came from knowing my surroundings by the clues I felt through the end of a white cane. Although small, they gave me the courage to dream a little bigger.

During a free period, I sat in the cafeteria, thinking about my midnight outings with Chris and what Jerry had said about help. I had almost been thrashed by a vanful of angry drunken seniors, and the unbelievable part was that I hadn't been caught. I had been standing on the side of the road, my pale butt glowing in the dark like a second moon, when they had poured out after me. When I had finally waddled away, my pants around my ankles, my cane tapping in front of me, I had heard the fastest boy's breath behind me, but he hadn't caught me. My escape was a little unorthodox, but it had done the job. The cane was what had really saved me, and if it could save my hide from an almost unavoidable thrashing, then why couldn't it work right here in school? A week earlier, Mrs. Mundy had made a tactile map of the cafeteria and had forced me to carry it. I leafed through my notebook and found the map. It was still fresh and untouched. I studied it for a long time, then practiced maneuvering around the empty tables. My book served as a tray, balanced in one hand while the other tapped my cane along the floor.

When lunchtime came, I took my tray from the counter, turned right until my cane gently tapped the wall. Then I trailed the wall until I felt the soda machine protruding. I knew the gap between two tables was a few feet away. I turned left, using the light tap of metal chair legs as my guide. Then, in front of me, over the bustle, I recognized the voices of my friends. Working my way around the table, I subtly touched the back of each chair until I found one much lighter. Here, I carefully placed my tray, making sure it was fully resting on the table. Finally I sat down; a secret sigh escaped from my lips. Mitch, sitting in the next chair, grasped my cane. "Hey! That thing really works," he said.

"I guess it does," I replied smiling, beginning to believe it myself.

In Braille class, Mrs. Mundy brailled an article and told me to read it for homework. "You'll read it out loud for me tomorrow," she said. Of course, I didn't read it that night. The next day I stumbled through it aloud, reading it listlessly with the speed of a first grader. As I slowly began to understand the story under my fingers, I learned that it was about minor-league baseball players struggling to make it into the big leagues.

Since Little League, the characters had dedicated their lives to making it in the majors, despite their knowledge that their chances were less than minuscule: one in one hundred thousand. Their struggle was like salmon swimming upstream. Usually my frustration was directed toward Mrs. Mundy for forcing me to waste my time deciphering complicated patterns of dots, my brain hardly bothering to recognize the meaning of the words. Today, however, my frustration was directed at my own stumbling inept fingers. I pushed them along, wanting to know if they would make it. Mrs. Mundy had outsmarted me. How hard had she worked to find a subject I'd be interested in? She had presented me with articles about politics and science, but this one had taken hold. It was about people striving for something, and the fascinating part about it was that they knew what they were striving for. They were moving in a direction. I realized that there was more to Braille than just raised dots; there were stories about people dreaming, and those stories made the gigantic leap from my stumbling fingertips all the way to my brain.

In the winter, all the freshmen tried out for different teams. I didn't want to be left behind. Prior to my going blind, I wasn't allowed to participate in any contact sports; my weak retinas might break away faster. Now that I was totally blind, there were no limitations; there was no more risk of me losing my remaining sight. In a sordid way, going blind had set me free. I was finally allowed to try out for wrestling. As I tapped my cane down the empty hallway toward the wrestling room, I wondered if I would be any good. When informally wrestling my brother Eddi in the garage, by feeling an ankle or a wrist, I could intuitively sense where the rest of his body was positioned. And with that knowledge, I thought I could join the team. However, my five-foot-nine, 114-pound body worried me more than my blindness: not much of a wrestler's physique. Squeezing one bony biceps and then the other, I almost walked into a wall.

On the first day of wrestling practice, freshmen line up to face off against the captain, usually to be pinned in quick succession. I was third in line. "Ready, wrestle!" I heard, and then almost instantly, "Pinned, seven seconds," as the first freshman's squirming shoulders were forced to the mat. The second victim was pinned in nine seconds. Then I was up. My legs turned to Play-Doh, and I felt ready to puke. I didn't have to do much work because I felt the strong, callused hands of the captain closing on my wrists, dragging me weakly to the center of the mat. The next moments merged together into a frenzied blur. Immediately after shaking hands, my legs were swept from under me and I landed on my back. Miraculously, I fought to my side before I was driven back again. I flopped on the mat like a fish out of water, struggling futilely. Soon the weight of my opponent crushing the air out of my lungs was too much. I heard the coach slap his palm squarely on the mat and pronounce, "Pinned, twenty seconds!" Without a pause, the captain continued up the line, demolishing each gasping opponent. No other match lasted more than ten seconds. I got up and staggered off the mat.

Coming to the first practice, I had worried about my teammates babying me. Instead, the captain had done the greatest thing he could possibly do: he had shown me no mercy as he ground my spindly body into the mat. My ribs were bruised; it hurt to breathe, but through the pain was a proud sense of elation. For the first time since I had gone blind, I no longer felt like "the blind guy." I was the blind guy who stunk at wrestling, but stunk ten whole seconds better than any other freshman in the line.

An hour before the team's first match, our coach learned that the varsity wrestler at my weight, one of his stars, would not be able to wrestle due to injury. He asked me to fill in, even though, in private, he remarked that sending me out to wrestle was like throwing chum to a school of sharks. I sat on my team's side of the gym conjuring up ferocious images of my opponent. When my turn came, the captain took me by the arm and led me to the center of the mat. I shook my opponent's hand and noticed the grip. It was softer, unlike my captain's grip, which was hard, callused, sinewy, and could snap all the fragile bones in my hand.

The match was almost even, our two bodies flipping, driving, tumbling all over the mat. In the last few seconds of the final period, my tired opponent slowed down, enabling me to get out to his side and drive my arm under his armpit and over his neck in a half nelson. I got to my toes, chest driving into his side, my arm like a lever, cranking him up and over. When his body began to lift up and roll, I could hardly believe it. I expected him to suddenly reenergize, clamp down on my arm, and break my grip. Maybe, he would even spin around me and score two points for a reversal. But he kept on turning toward his back, and my arm, buried deep in his armpit and around his neck, kept cranking. My arm strained. It began to tingle and go numb. I could no longer feel if any force flowed through it. Then, he was on his back, and I was driving the full force of my weight on top of him. A second before the final buzzer, I heard the whop of the mat as the ref yelled, "Pinned!" The entire gym erupted in cheers. The applause filled the room and, over the roar, I picked out the excited screams of my parents. Even my mother, who found it so hard to watch her son being bloodied and slammed against a wrestling mat, was cheering. Afterwards she told me that she had been nervously chewing her long hair and squeezing her hands together so tightly, she had fingernail marks in her palms for a week. Enveloped by the cheer of the crowd and surrounded by the pungent sweat of my teammates, I knew without a doubt that I was on the right path. Maybe, I had found the person that I had been before blindness, but when I settled on that idea, the implications disturbed me. In order to reclaim that person, I felt I would have to go back through the past, through the pain, frustration, and loneliness. How could I go back through time and erase all of that? Maybe, it was better to follow the advice that my granddad had given my mother once, to look straight ahead and never look back. Maybe, the best course was simply to set myself in motion, to propel myself forward, and somewhere along the way, I might stumble upon a new person, or even many new people, who would take my soul, which still felt a bit empty, and cram it full of newness and full of joy.

In the first period of the match that day, I had been slammed against the mat on my face. That night, I lay next to my mom, in her bed, like I had as a little kid. My mom brought me an ice pack and laid it over my swollen nose and the knot that was beginning to form on my forehead. We had just gotten a VCR, and we watched our first movie on it: Arnold Schwarzenegger in *The Terminator*. When she had gone for the ice pack, she had even attempted an Arnold impression, "I'll be bok!"

Throughout the movie, I kept lifting the ice pack and running my fingers over my face. I had never done that before, but realized that I hadn't seen myself for almost a year. I couldn't really remember exactly what I looked like either, but as my fingers ran over my nose, which seemed huge and bulbous, my long forehead, which seemed to stretch forever, and my thick brow, which seemed to jut out and hang precariously over my small deep-set eyes, my brain kept assembling the image of a monster. My mom must have noticed my frantic fingers squeezing my nose and measuring the distance from my brow to my eyeballs, because she said, "You're getting handsomer every day," which was extremely embarrassing to hear from your mother, especially when my fingers had just shown me that I had the kind of face that only a mother could love. "I think you're a little biased," I said. "My nose is huge and my eyebrows hang over my eyes like a Neanderthal." Then she took my hand and placed it on her own face. "That's quite an insult, considering, out of all my children, you look the most like me." This confused me, knowing how beautiful she was. One of my hands I kept on my face, my other hand I kept on hers. I was shocked; our noses were both thin and sharp, turning slightly to the right; her forehead was smooth and high like mine; even our eyes were about the same size, set back from our foreheads.

Over the previous year, my mother had taken on some new challenges and enjoyed some new successes. She no longer slept all day, far from it. She was much too busy. She still looked back on her time spent traveling all over Asia with fondness and still adored her collection of keepsakes. When I came in from school in the afternoon, I could usually find her in the front room of our house, dusting and varnishing all the chests, screens, and carvings that she hadn't been able to squeeze into the rest of the house. In the room, there was hardly any space to move. Maneuvering with my cane through the narrow twisting aisles, surrounded by piles of small papier mâché boxes, ornate umbrellas, giant fans, oriental carpets, baskets full of polished wooden beads, tiny jade animals, mother of pearl, and black onyx, I feared that only one misplaced tap would bring the whole array crashing down around me. One day my mother stood in the entrance of her collection room, gazing over the different pieces and remembering the origin of each. Few of the pieces had come easy. She had traveled by foot, by camel, even by elephant, to remote villages where the black-haired children had never seen a Caucasian woman. They touched her long blonde hair as if she were an exotic goddess, and before she feared of running out of hair, she had even given a strand to each child. Once, in Pakistan, while bargaining for a long jeweled saber, the shopkeeper indicated that he would only trade the saber for the designer jeans my mother was wearing, which he wanted as a present for his wife. So, she had gone into the back of the stall, changed into a white traditional *shamir* camise, and struck the deal. It was while standing in her collection room that my mother seized upon the idea to bring the passion of her past into the present. In the summer of 1983, my mom opened a shop in nearby Westport. She named it Oriental Origins. From the contents of baskets full of miscellaneous items, she designed beautiful and unusual necklaces and bracelets. She couldn't make them fast enough to keep up with the surprising demand, so she made the front room of our house into a factory floor and hired neighborhood women to help her string them. Soon she was getting requests from Bloomingdale's and Saks Fifth Avenue to stock their stores. She traveled up and down the East Coast exhibiting her line. My mother was even invited to be a guest on a local talk show, featuring successful businesswomen. Eddi, my dad, my mother, and I, all gathered around the TV when it aired.

During Christmas break of my freshman year I accompanied my

mother on a trip to Boston for one of her exhibits. I helped her set up her counter and organize all her wares. All afternoon I sat nearby, proudly listening to the throngs of people as they openly admired the unusual gems and figures that comprised her line, and the beautiful patterns. Afterwards, when we were closing up, I waved my hand over the few remaining necklaces and asked her straight out, "Mom, has all of this helped you to find happiness?"

She laughed and said, "That's a serious question. I don't believe anymore that you find happiness; I think you have to make it for yourself."

I reached out and found her hand resting on the table and placed my hand on top of hers. "I just want you to be happy," I said. "Tell me you're happy."

"I am," she replied.

In the summer after freshman year I went off to wrestling camp. My first week was a blast. Although I was only a first-year wrestler, I managed to take a third in the midweek takedown tournament, which earned me early respect among the older kids. The guys at camp were tough, almost without exception dedicated to building their strength, endurance, and wrestling skills. By luck I got to work directly with Dan Gable, America's most famous coach, who was there for a day and a half. I was on the mat practicing moves when one of my cabin mates slipped up behind me and whacked me on the head. Soon it happened again, this time on the butt, and once more, back on the head. By now I listened extra carefully for the next strike. It was a cat and mouse game as I lowered my hips and crouched in good wrestler's position, listening to his soft muffled footsteps moving around me. When I felt a tap on my calf, I wheeled around and surprised the offender with a quick takedown, which I converted into a half nelson and a pin, right in front of Coach Gable. There were some hoots, whistles, and even a little applause. Gable walked over to me and congratulated me on a nice combination, then spent the next fifteen minutes working with me on the arm lever, a devastating move that I eventually learned to perfection and which, in my senior year, earned me thirty-three pins.

I was fortunate in winding up in the cabin that won the first-week tournament. It was a tough athletic group of boys, who fed off one another and pushed each other into even higher levels of dedication. Together, all ten of us decided to undertake the "intensive" program the second week: extra six A.M. calisthenics and runs, regular morning and afternoon sessions, and an extra evening wrestle-off followed by a film session. The biggest sacrifice, though, was that intensive participants—about ten percent of the camp—missed most of the Thursday night dance with a nearby cheerleading camp. My Sunday phone call home to my parents was full of excitement. The first week was reviewed in all its glorious detail, and I proudly revealed my decision to go intensive. I let my mom know that there would be no time to call the following week; I'd be too busy and tired. I promised, though, to tell her everything on Saturday, when she and my dad would come for the big camp-ending tournament.

It was Thursday afternoon, and I was totally exhausted but knew I had enough in reserve to make it through the week. I was in the midst of a takedown drill when a coach approached saying, "Erik, there's a phone call for you in the director's office." I followed him out of the gym, wondering what was going on. Who would call me in the middle of a wrestling drill? My dad and mom both knew I would wait to talk with them on Saturday. I got in his car and we drove across campus, the whole time wondering who would be calling. "Who's it from?" I asked the coach.

"I don't know, son," he said softly. A little sliver of worry ran through my body. The car stopped and I got out. "Hello Erik," the voice said, and I immediately recognized it as my father's.

"Hey, Dad! What are you guys doing here so early? The tournament's not until Saturday."

Listlessly, my dad said, "Erik, I'm sorry." His voice quavered. "There's no other way to tell you this. There's been a terrible car accident. Your mom's been killed."

"You must be joking," I said, but my father was silent. "It's not true!"

I shouted. "It couldn't be!" Then, knowing it was true, there was a stunned silence, followed by a rush of tears. My dad stood still. I stood still a few feet away, my body shuddering, the tears rolling down my face. Finally, the head of the camp grabbed me and pressed me against his sweatshirt. My face was buried in his huge, round potbelly. His sweatshirt smelled new and my tears and snot were soaking it, but he kept me pressed against him. My father, sapped by the toughest thing he ever had to do in his entire life, stood awkwardly trying to control his own breathing and the three of us sobbed together.

How can I explain the pain that surged through me? If I had gone blind a thousand times, the pain would have been nothing in comparison. If I could have died that day by only choosing it, I would have died instantly, but the human body is stubborn in its power to cling to life, even when its owner wants to die. How could it be, the person who had savagely protected me all my life was gone?

At the funeral I stood by the coffin and touched her arm folded over her chest. Her skin was cold and waxy like a clay dummy. I couldn't believe her warm moving body had gone to this, but to me, what had been her was not this clay statue that lay in front of me. After the funeral my brothers and I walked to the service station to see the white Saab she had been driving that night. I touched the windshield and ran my hand across the glass. On the driver's side, my hand felt a crushed head-shaped bulge. There was still dried blood on it, and I winced in agony as I thought about my mother's beautiful face hitting the windshield, her skin being cut by the sharp glass.

Summer ended, school began, and I struggled to keep myself upright. Her death was so abrupt, overwhelming, and final, I didn't know how to react. I told myself that just like the onslaught of blindness, it didn't matter how I reacted. Nothing would bring her back. The fact that she was not there kept hitting me over the head: when I was listening to a song on the radio, "Glory Days," by Bruce Springsteen, or pulling an old afghan, rich with her smell, from a cabinet. I kept convincing myself that she was gone forever, that I would never see her again for the rest of my life. She wouldn't pick me up from school or curl up on her bed after dinner to read aloud to me. When I woke up in the morning, for just a moment before becoming fully awake, my heart lifted with hope that her death was just a bad dream.

It seemed so unfair. My life had finally taken a turn for the better. I was getting pretty good at wrestling, making new friends, finally learning Braille. I was beginning to regain myself after blindness. I had begun to take what was left after the loss and reassemble the pieces, forcing them to fit together. Just as I began to know that blindness could not kill my hope or happiness, another blow, twice as devastating as the first, had slapped me down again. Maybe we were never supposed to be truly happy, I thought after her death. Maybe we were never meant to take control of our lives, to gain mastery over it. Maybe life is a perpetual series of losses. If there was a God, he must enjoy putting humans through a great cruel punishment, like he had done to Job in the Bible, an endless punishment, which forces us to scramble and find ways of living with less. God kills off a vital piece of our lives, one that we thought was most important, we scramble to make do with a little less, and then he takes that away too.

My brothers were in college, and it was only my father and I living in the big house. Dad would leave for work at 5:30 A.M., waking me up before he went. "There's a casserole on the counter. Heat it up at four hundred for an hour. I laid it out to thaw," he'd say. Sometimes after school, I'd come home to the big silent house and I'd crave her presence so badly, I'd have trouble breathing. I'd think: How could she not be here in this house with all her clothes and possessions and the people she loved? Sometimes the yearning would be so strong, it would tug at me, pulling at my insides, until I had to do something. Then I'd lay facedown on her side of the bed and smother my face in her sheets and pillows. Even though they had been washed, I could catch traces of her smell, of her creams and her skin. Other times, I'd sit in her closet surrounded by all her coats and dresses, trying to lose myself in the familiar fragrance, trying to pretend that if her smell was there, then she must be too, or at least somewhere near. I'd pick up all her shoes, one by one, seeing if I could sense her presence through them. I'd imagine that while I was touching them in the closet, she was touching them in some other world. I wanted to stay in there, to live there forever, buried in her coats and dresses and shoes. But then I'd hear the door swing open as my father came home from work and I'd rush out so I wouldn't be discovered.

Wrestling gave me a focus and a sense of purpose. I decided that my first match of the season would be dedicated to my mom. This was a personal decision. I shared it with no one, but drew great inspiration from it. With my mother's force guiding me, I felt invincible. I was driven and worked harder than ever. I couldn't wait for the season opener. Even when I finally settled into a weight class, at 142 pounds, and learned that my opponent was a runner-up in last year's state championships, I was not shaken. I had dedicated myself to this match, to her, and I couldn't lose. I knew I couldn't.

But I did. I was never really in the match, and lost 10–2. I was absolutely devastated. I hadn't wrestled my best, far from it. I had really let myself down, and my mom. I could hardly live with the feeling of guilt and failure.

That night was hot and sticky as I fell into a restless sleep, still reeling over the wrestling defeat, my mother's funeral, and the crushed car. I dreamed I was in the locker room of my school before a wrestling match. In the dream, I could see in vivid color, but it was an awful vision, the room lit by a cheap fluorescent bulb, casting twisted shadows across the room. It was a night match and the small high locker-room windows were black. Somehow we had made it to a state championship. The whole team was in the room, sitting on benches and talking softly and nervously as they geared up. I knew that everything was riding on this match. I also somehow knew that my opponent was a hulking presence; one I knew would crush me. The team talked too softly and nervously, as though they didn't want to disturb the silence. Then, I heard the beginning of a rumble, and next, the deafening crack of the wall as the white Saab came crashing through. Splinters of plaster and wood flew everywhere. Metal lockers flew through the room and the engine revved deeply. Benches cracked in half, sending wrestlers tumbling. I could see clearly through the rising smoke and windshield. There was no driver, and angry needles of metal jutted from the grill like teeth. I could see the cracked, blood-streaked bulge in the windshield, like one shattered eye, staring past me, to somewhere far in the distance or far into the past. The awful vision would haunt me like the most terrifying Stephen King novel. I knelt down in the shards of glass and debris, not even caring about my bare knees, and screamed, but it wasn't my voice. It was the hopeless, high-pitched wail of my mother that Christmas Day when my brothers and father had carried her off to the emergency room.

I woke up kneeling against my bedroom window, and I was smashing my own fists and face against the black glass, again and again. The tough storm-proof Plexiglas refused to shatter, however, but my own face gushed with blood and it ran down the glass. "Oh God! Oh God! Oh God!" I cried, tasting the familiar metallic liquid in my mouth. "Don't let it be true. Oh God! Please don't let it be true."

Once a week after school, Mr. Westervelt, the assistant principal, led discussions in a group of students and teachers who had lost a parent. In the group, there were two sisters who had lost their mom to breast cancer and a boy whose father had committed suicide. Mr. Westervelt's dad had recently died too.

Lately, especially after my dismal display on the wrestling mat, I'd thought a lot about God, mostly about whether he existed at all. I wanted to believe he was real, because that was the only way that something of my mom could still exist. But when I had looked for her on earth, I had only been left with an empty feeling of loss, and when I looked for her in heaven, the strength that I had gathered from her had been a lie. The wrestling match had proven that, shattering my fragile shell of faith. At the next meeting of those who had lost a parent, the local pastor was there to help students sort out their feelings. As he talked to the other students, I thought about the devastating match, and I decided to confront him about it and how it could possibly fit in with God's "divine purpose." I laughed grimly to myself, because I knew I was setting the pastor up for failure. I was presenting him with a test he could not possibly pass. I wanted to listen to him squirm in his seat as he muttered and mumbled his lame response, probably quoting from some arcane passage in the Bible. I told my story, going slowly, pausing frequently to take deep breaths. "How could I have possibly lost with the combined tag-team weight of God and my mother in my corner?" The pastor paused for just a second and then asked a question.

"Can you tell me what happens when you win a match?"

"It's great," I responded eagerly. I thought back to my first win. "The crowd goes nuts and your team rushes out onto the mat. You're surrounded by bodies. They slap you on the back and hug you."

"And where's your mother in all of this excitement?"

I paused. "I'm not sure. She's there somewhere, in the stands," I said, "but there's no way she can get to me through the crowd and my team."

Speaking very softly and slowly, he replied, "Isn't that true? There's just no room for her. Erik, when you win and you're surrounded by your team and the crowd, when all is well, when life is great, you don't need your mom, but when you're faced with difficulty, when you're discouraged, when you're struggling, and you don't know whether you will be able to summon enough strength to hang on, when you need her most, she'll be there. She's with you now. I know you feel her love and her strength." I sat back in my chair. The smooth even words had gotten inside me. Could I feel her? Could he be right? It made sense. I still didn't know why God had taken her away, why he had taken away my sight, why my life seemed to be filled with so much loss, with very little gain, but despite that, the pastor's words somehow gave me comfort.

We ended the day's meeting with an exercise. Mr. Westervelt said, "When you lose a parent, they live on inside you. They become a part of you." Mother's Day was coming up and he suggested that we write a card and read it to ourselves on Mother's Day. I wrote a Braille card and put it in my mailbox and, on Sunday, pulled it out and read it.

Dear Mom,
I've looked for you, Mom, in your pillow, in your coats, in your shoes. I've even looked for you in heaven, in God, but I can't seem to find you. The pastor says your spirit will guide me and give me strength in times of trouble. It's so confusing. I don't know where to look anymore. Mr. Westervelt says I should look for you inside of me. So, that's where I'll begin looking now, and I hope I find you there, and don't you worry, because wherever you are, I won't stop looking until I find you.
I love you.
Erik

# 5
# Blind Warriors

In the spring a lady from the state came to our house to convince my dad to send me to a month-long skills camp at the Carroll Center for the Blind in Massachusetts. When she left, I said, "Dad, you aren't going to make me hang out with a bunch of blind dorks for a month, are you?" I bobbed my head around in my best Stevie Wonder impression to make the point, but honestly one side of me was curious. I had been a little impressed by the pieces of equipment she had brought along to interest me in the program; she had shown us a machine that could scan the print in a book and read the words in a synthesized computer voice, another machine that identified money, and she promised that the Carroll Center boasted far more impressive gadgets than the ones she had brought. More enticing than this was the fact that I had never met other blind people my age, and I wondered if I would find them to be like me. My curiosity seemed to pull me. What sports did they play? What schools did they go to? How did they read, use their canes, and carry their lunch trays through the cafeteria?

"Do you want to go?" my dad asked.

"Maybe," I replied, and that was good enough for him. He signed me up.

When we arrived at the center, my dad and I carried my trunk through a gazebo, into a restored old house, and up a spiral staircase to my room. The supervisor gave us a campus tour, showing me how to stay on the walkways by sliding my cane along the border between the pavement and the grass. On the campus there were beeping basketball hoops, a wood shop with Braille measuring tools, and a fencing court. "Good luck," my dad said, shaking my hand.

In the entrance of the house I sat down on a bench next to some other arrivals. A girl to my left was speaking, but I couldn't figure out who she was speaking to. "I got a four-point-oh GPA. I'm the smartest in my class. All the teachers say I'm very smart." I couldn't hear anyone in front of us or to the far left, so I figured she must be talking to me. Strange introduction, I thought. "Four-point-oh, that's great," I responded, turning to shake her hand. She must have seen a little because she rested her big limp hand in mine and I did the shaking. "I'm Adrian," she said so softly I had to lean in. Another arrival sat to my right. "Hi, I'm Joey," he said; his throat vibrated as if warming up before his words leaped off his tongue. As he spoke, his fingers tapped my wrist and made little tugs on my sleeve. "Hi, I'm Joey," he repeated. "My name's Joey." His fingers tapped and tugged.

"Nice to meet you, Joey," I said, getting up to escape. Maybe coming here was a giant mistake, I thought.

That night everyone sat in a circle, and we were asked to say our names and a little about ourselves. I sat next to a girl named Jenny who seemed to have the scoop on everyone. A voice boasted, "I'm Scott, and I'm into ham radios. Once I picked up Hawaii and once I picked up the North Pole."

"Nerd!" Jenny whispered.

"I'm Tim, and I'm twelve and I like comic books and squirt guns." His shrill voice made him sound much younger.

"He's got a brain tumor," Jenny whispered. "That's what made him blind. They say he won't see thirteen."

Everyone spoke: Keith, who was into Black Sabbath; Alex, who lived near Niagara Falls and had played soccer before she started having eye trouble; Jenny, who was very popular and had lots of boyfriends; Rick, who was into professional wrestling and liked putting the cobra clutch on his little brother; Adrian, who talked about her 5.0 GPA; and Joey, who said, "Hi I'm Joey. My name's Joey." I wondered who he was tugging on.

After that we ordered a pizza and sat under the gazebo, waiting. Jenny wasted no time. "Does anyone want to know what I look like?"

"Sure." Keith gave her the go ahead.

"All the boys I date say I'm cute. I have long blonde hair, a gorgeous smile, and big green eyes."

"Sounds good to me," Keith said.

I mostly only date older boys," she went on. "You know, boys who can drive me places and buy me things."

"You're allowed to date?" Alex asked.

"Of course. Aren't you?" said Jenny.

"No way," Alex replied. "My parents are very religious. They say I can't date until I'm twenty-one."

"How do you get around and do things?" Jenny asked.

"I don't, really. I used to ride my bike to soccer, but I can't ride a bike anymore. It doesn't matter, though, because I can't play soccer either. In fact, my parents forbid me from ever saying the word, *blind* or even from using a cane," she added.

"That's great," I said. "My parents forced me to use one."

"When I started having trouble," Alex continued, "they thought I was tricking them. They said that God wouldn't do that to a family like ours. So, I walked around school, crashing into lockers and tripping over people's books. Then, when they finally started believing me, they said I must have done something so awful in the eyes of God that I was being punished."

"No offense," Keith interjected, "but your parents seem really weird." When the girls left, Keith and I immediately turned to Tim, the only partially seeing member of the group, for a rating. Despite her own claims, Jenny only got a "fair" rating, but Alex got a "babe" rating.

The next morning in computer class we sat in front of Braille tactile computer screens and voice synthesizers and learned how to create simple programs. We wrote one that would ask the subject his name, age, and birthday, and then would sing happy birthday, inserting the person's name. It would end by telling the person how many days until his next birthday and promising to send an E-mail birthday card.

During free time we could play special computer games that were all words and sound effects. One was a fantasy game called Eamon, in which you were the hero and could choose your weaponry to fight against the goblins and trolls who lurked in the deep passageways of the castle. Carl, our blind computer instructor, had altered the game's programming so that one of the weapons you could choose was a blind person's cane. I'd laugh each time the dry computer voice listed the selections, "Sword? Spear? Mace? Long white cane?" and when I'd type in, "cane," and it responded with, "The journey ahead is long and dangerous, but you are wise, blind warrior, made wise beyond your years."

The best computer game was one we played after hours. Keith had smuggled it in. "Soft Porn," he whispered, putting my finger on the Braille title atop the disk. "It's black market, designed by one of the world's most brilliant blind perverts." In the game, you wandered through a seedy, Las Vegas-like town trying to make the move on three "lusty lasses." Different characters would give you clues. A bum sitting on a garbage can would say, "Chicks likes flowas. Why don't you get 'er some?" Or a bathroom attendant would suggest, "Get my dates off the bathroom wall. Why don't you read a few?" Or a pawnshop owner, "How 'bout this ring, pal. Sell it to you cheap. Never know, it might come in handy." The game was full of perilous turns. For instance, if you didn't give one girl the ring and flowers before making your move, her muscle-bound brother would dash out of the next room and beat you to a pulp with a barbell. "You are dying now . . . you are not a gentleman . . . That will teach you not to treat a lady like a . . ."

A few boys and I stayed after class that afternoon, missing dinner, playing the game late into the night. Near midnight, we finally obtained the key we had been looking for from the doorman in the lobby of the Playboy Bunny Hotel. We had to bribe him with a special pack of smokes bought from a drugstore clerk with money stolen from an underworld casino. The key got us to the roof of the building, where, according to the computer, a beautiful Playboy Pet sat in a hot tub. "Get in the hot tub," I typed, and we all cracked up as we heard the monotone computer voice read, "Ooh aah, ooh aah, ooh baby ooh baby aah . . . game over."

The next day in class, Carl introduced what he called "systems." As he explained the concept, he took off his shoe and bizarrely requested each of us to feel his sock. When my fingers investigated, I noticed a safety pin running through the top of the sock. "The safety pin at the top means they're black; placed in the middle, they're blue, and placed at the toe, brown. Systems," he said again, "you won't survive without them." For the rest of class, we learned to perform a variety of tasks by creating systems. Sometimes, the systems were far from obvious, but when we all brainstormed, we usually came up with one. I learned to open a carton of milk from the correct side, by feeling for a tiny indentation. I practiced filling a glass with juice by hanging the tip of my pointer finger over the side of the glass until the juice touched it, and with a hot drink, which would scald my finger, I learned to judge the full cup by the weight.

At the end of class, Carl even showed us how to "hear" objects. He explained, "You may not believe this, but sound vibrations are constantly bouncing off objects and then moving back to us. It's called echolocation, or sonar. Bats have it; so do humans. Sighted people just never learn to use it." To prove the theory, Carl had each of us walk down an empty hallway. He had closed all but one of the doors along the side of the hall. "Tell me," he said, "when you reach the open door."

"That's ridiculous," I replied, but when I walked down the hallway, I couldn't believe it. I stopped in astonishment when the confined sound bouncing back at me, suddenly, on my right, changed to open sound. I reached my hand out right and felt the open frame of the door. "Don't take no for an answer when you're looking for your system," Carl ended class by saying. "You may have to look beyond the obvious, but you'll find it."

Carl would probably never know how important systems would become in every aspect of my life, particularly in the mountains, when trying things no blind person had ever done before. I would look for that secret system I hoped would make the adventure safer, easier, more efficient, and sometimes, simply possible.

In our afternoon class at the Carroll Center, we sat around a table, and Carl asked us to reflect on the sighted world's perceptions of the blind. Jenny started: "My friends didn't think I would be able to put on my own makeup. That's why I'm here, to prove them wrong. I can't wait for the 'Makeup Without Mirrors' class."

"Sometimes, when people find out I'm blind," Keith said next, "they start talking really loudly and slowly. I always talk back to them in the same way, 'READ . . . MY . . . LIPS . . . I'M . . . NOT . . . DEAF, . . . I'M . . . BLIND, . . . OK?' "

"I hate it when a waiter says, 'What will he be having?' " Tim said shrilly, and Scott jumped right in, "Or when you pay for something, and the cashier puts your change in your friend's hand."

"Isn't it interesting," Carl said, "that the problem isn't always blindness, but all the false assumptions surrounding blindness, and that includes your own. Once, a lady wanted to ask me how long I had been blind, but she was too afraid to use the word, *blind*. Maybe, she thought that blindness was a kind of demon and just the mere mention of the word might give it the power to rise up and crush my spirit. So, instead she asked, 'How long have you been a person of sightlessness?' For some of you, blindness is still a demon, waging a war inside you, but if you can accept blindness for what it is, and lay it to rest, if you give it a place and make it a part of you, like having brown hair or green eyes or being tall or short, then the demon will wither away and it will die."

At the end of class Carl told us that on weekends we'd make field trips to Boston museums and to a Red Sox game, sailing on the Charles River, tandem biking on Cape Cod, hiking and horseback riding in Vermont, and most intriguing to me, a rock-climbing weekend in North Conway, New Hampshire. The motivation behind the recreational program was clear. The lady who had first visited me at my house had asked me what my hobbies were, and I had told her that except for wrestling, I didn't have any. I had signed up for a school wood shop and an art elective, but the wood shop teacher was nervous because the class worked with saws and planers, and the art teacher was nervous because his class worked with X-Acto knives. So, I had been turned down for both, due to "liability issues." I was also restricted from PE because they mostly played ball sports. Fortunately, however, I had found wrestling, but I knew most blind kids my age weren't so fortunate. The Carroll Center teachers had wanted to create opportunities for blind teenagers to enjoy the outdoors, take some calculated risks, and to push themselves a little further than they might otherwise. Although these reasons alone would have been enough, I think their motives were even deeper. "The human circuitry is all connected," Carl said to us. "If you can learn to push your body, your brain isn't far behind."

For our first activity, we went swimming at the local YMCA. We played freeze tag, and I was constantly looking for a chance to free Alex. When I got near her, she whispered, "Over here." When I freed her, I touched her shoulder and felt her satiny swim strap against her skin and as she turned to escape, her long, thick, wet hair brushed against my face. Halfway through the game, Jenny changed the rules so that a person could only be freed by a teammate swimming through that person's legs. When I swam through Alex's legs, brushing by her smooth calves, I was close to sensory overload.

During the tag games, Keith would sit on the side of the pool, idly slapping his hands against the concrete.

"What's up?" Alex asked. "Don't you want to play with us?"

"It's kind of embarrassing," he admitted. "You see, my parents, they don't allow me to put my head under the water. They say that if I go under the water, I'll get disoriented and won't know which way is up."

"So, you'll drown?" I asked, confused.

"That's what they think," he replied.

"Well, what do you think?" Alex asked.

"How should I know?" he said. "I've never put my head under the water."

"Well, let's find out," she said, grabbing his arm and pushing off the wall with her leg. Keith laughed. "No, no, I can't!" but he was already falling into the water and splashing beside Alex. Their laughter became muted as their heads went under. When they emerged, Keith was still laughing. "It isn't true," he screamed. "It's a conspiracy. I've been lied to." And that started Alex laughing again. She could somehow fix things in such a natural way. Treading water nearby, I wished I had a phobia that Alex could help me overcome.

At meals, everyone hung their canes by the door of the cafeteria. I guess the staff felt that fifty blind people in a confined space, holding trays and swinging their canes, was a recipe for disaster. We stayed in the lunch line by trailing our feet along a tactile strip, but I got used to the gentle bump of a body against my back or the brush of a hand across my leg. In a sighted world, this might have been considered sexual harassment, but at a blind camp an occasional touch was a tolerated part of life. Even Alex would break the codes of the sighted world. She would lean in when she talked to me, far past boundaries of personal space, her nose only a few inches from mine. I knew she was just trying to see my face, and I was thankful her weak eyes could not detect a zit, or a possible piece of lettuce caught in my front teeth.

After lunch Keith broke out his big boom box and jammed Black Sabbath tunes. "Do you hear that awesome rhythm guitar underneath the base?" Keith shouted.

"Oh, yeah," the other boys replied enthusiastically.

"What about that incredible drum set under the electric guitar?"

"Definitely," they replied again. I seemed to be the only blind person in the room who couldn't hear anything he pointed out. I tried to discern one instrument from another, trying to separate the electric guitars from the bass, from the drums, but they all merged together in a hodgepodge of blaring sound. "I love these lyrics," Keith said. "He's singing about when he went through drug rehab in '72," and all the boys would listen intently.

"Wow! That's powerful."

"That's deep."

"Did you hear that?" Keith asked grandly. "It's a metaphor. He's really the caterpillar crawling up the tin can."

Being musically inclined was supposed to go hand and hand with blindness. It was supposed to be part of the package deal. You were born with the tragedy of blindness, but you were also given the gift of music to carry you through the sadness. You were supposed to play the piano or sing with perfect pitch, but someone had forgotten to bless me with the gift. I couldn't even appreciate music, the only blind guy in the world who had no idea why the caterpillar was crawling up the tin can.

The music seemed to work the boys into a frenzy. Tim jumped around playing the air guitar and boys competed against each other in elaborate drum solos. Keith pounded his hands furiously on the table, his hands getting faster and faster, working toward the climax. Then, with one last whap on the table, he ended, saying breathlessly, "Top that!" and another boy began even more furiously.

The next day we went on a field trip to a Boston Red Sox game. For the ride to the park, I squeezed into the back hatch of the camp station wagon between Rick and Scott, who were both partially sighted, or as the teachers at the center termed, "partials." Since I was totally blind, I was termed a "total." It seemed as though Scott and Rick's testosterone levels were linked in some way to their level of vision. How much they could see became a ferocious competition.

"Can you see the telephone pole?" Rick asked. "What color is it?"

"Black," Scott responded.

"No!" Rick shot back hotly. "It's gray, doofus."

"What about that pickup?" Scott asked.

"Where?" Rick asked.

"Right in front of your nose, bonehead," Scott replied fiercely.

It was like a blind version of Beavis and Butt-Head.

Rick—What color's that guy's hair on the sidewalk?

Scott—Brown?

Rick—You're lying, jerk-off. You just guessed.

When we finally arrived at Fenway Park, I was glad to escape from the two battling partials. One part of me laughed at their ridiculous rivalry, but another part of me envied them. They had both bought into the subtle messages that sight meant power, and I was forced to admit that I had too. I had noticed it even at a camp for the blind, the way a partial would lead a group of totals through the campus to class or the way a total girl would show immediate interest in a boy after learning he was a partial. I had even felt the hierarchy on a group hike when totals were forced to hold a section of a long thick rope, while partials were allowed to walk along the side. I felt like a dork, trailing along on a leash while Alex walked solo. I hadn't wanted to cause a scene, though, so I took a subtle approach, barely acknowledging the rope's existence by only brushing my fingertips against it and frequently lifting my arm to stretch or yawn. When one of the sighted teachers scolded me for letting go, I replied casually, "Oh! The rope! I'm having such a great time talking to Alex, I completely forgot about it."

Inside the park, I maneuvered myself next to Alex and managed to sit next to her in the stands. Thankfully, we were a few rows away from the others. Sitting next to her, though, I was consumed by the thought that she wouldn't like me because I couldn't see. I wouldn't be able to tell her how the batter looked as he whacked one out of the park with the bases loaded or what had happened on the giant stadium video screen to make everyone howl in hysterics. Then I had an idea, a surefire way to impress Alex, despite the fact that I was a total. In my backpack was my Walkman. Quietly I pulled it out and slid it into my front pocket, running the long cord of the headphones to my ear farthest from Alex. I subtly tuned the radio to the game play-by-play. I hoped Alex couldn't see the small plug protruding from my ear.

"This is silly," she said. "I can barely see the field."

"Don't worry," I said. "I'm a walking encyclopedia when it comes to baseball stats. Yep!" I said importantly. "What would we do without America's greatest pastime?"

"I don't believe you," Alex laughed.

"Oh, yeah!" I challenged, and then proceeded to parrot everything the radio announcers said, even if I had no idea what it meant. "Wade Boggs is first in the lineup today. He's batting three twelve and is second highest in the league in sacrifice bunts." For the entire game, I barraged Alex with a fantastic array of facts, all taken from the radio's commentary. "Wow!" I roared. "A bat-splitting grounder. It sounds like a worm burner. That's when the ball rolls all the way to the fence."

"How would you know that?" Alex asked.

"By the way the bat sounds. It takes years of practice to identify that sort of thing." Alex didn't respond. I knew she had to be impressed, but I worried she might be getting a little suspicious. I told myself to tone it down a little, but I couldn't resist. "Johnson loves to steal bases. I bet ya he'll try to steal second," and even before I finished my sentence, the crowd was standing and going wild, because, would you believe it, Johnson had just stolen second.

Near the end of the game, a strange thing happened. Out of the blue, a large beach ball landed in my arms. "What the . . . ?" I said.

"What a nice present," Alex said.

"What should I do with it?" I asked her.

"If a beach ball fell out of the heavens into my lap, I'd keep it," she replied.

On the field one of the players, an obstinate pitcher perhaps, must have been stalling, refusing to throw the ball, because a few fans, and then a few more, began screaming, "Throw the ball, jerk!"

"Why don't you throw it, stupid?"

As I found the plug in the beach ball and pulled it out, air whistling through the hole, the crowd was growing even angrier with the stubborn player on the field. The sound of their protests rose in an ear-splitting crescendo. I wouldn't want to be in that guy's shoes, I thought. Why didn't he just throw the ball? I imagined the cocky pitcher bounding up and down the field, holding the ball up smugly in his hands, taunting the jeering fans.

I laid the beach ball in my lap and leaned down on it with my chest. It whistled louder and began to sag. Maybe I'd give it to Alex after the game.

This lunatic on the field was about to be pummeled by fifty-thousand irate fans. Even the announcers, in my Walkman, were getting into it. "Who's this joker think he is?"

"I don't know, Rodge, but he seems to be making a real spectacle of himself." Then the person in the seat right behind me, yelled in my ear, "Throw it, moron!" and, with shrinking horror, it dawned on me, as fiery-hot needles shot through my skin. The joker, the spectacle, the moron were one and the same. They were all me. In times of trouble, we instinctively turn to the ones who we have faith will protect us. "Alex!" I pleaded.

"You better throw it!" is all she said.

The once round firm ball had become a jellyfish between my palms. I stood up and heaved it away to a cacophony of insults.

"Loser!"

"Freak!"

"Throw the little bum out!"

Escaping quickly down the handicap elevators, Alex, judging I had paid sufficiently for my trickery, explained the Boston tradition, "In the seventh inning stretch, someone throws out a beach ball and the fans pass it around the stadium. I thought everyone knew that, especially you, a walking encyclopedia."

"A baseball encyclopedia," I replied huffily, "not a beach ball encyclopedia."

That night, everyone crowded tightly into Alex's room to listen to a continuation of Stephen King's *Pet Sematary* on tape. Bodies lay on the beds, the chairs, and all over the floor. I was still smarting over the beach ball incident. During the most terrifying part, when the little devil child crept down the hallway toward his father's room, wielding a scalpel, I inched on my belly across the floor, moving slowly, so that the partials wouldn't pick up on the movement. I weaved through bodies, using their shuddering murmurs as a guide. Lying at the foot of Alex's bed, I waited for the little boy to lift the scalpel to his father's throat. Then I reached up, finding Alex's ankle dangling over the side of the bed, and locked on. I let out a fierce growl, and, in response, she let out a high-pitched screech. Her leg shot up and her body bounced around on the bed. Then everyone was screaming and the screams were compounding. I lay on my back on the floor smiling. Mission accomplished.

The next afternoon I was walking up the spiral staircase after class when I heard Alex's voice on the landing above me.

"Where's your scalpel, devil child?" she asked, her voice drifting between annoyance and playfulness.

"I left it in the throat of my last victim," I said, but as the words came out, I could feel a thick cool liquid dripping on my head and sliding down my forehead. My hands jumped to my head and touched shaving cream.

Alex giggled. "Oh, yeah, and I heard about the sick little game you boys were playing. Soft Porn," she scoffed, and then bounded up the stairs. I chased behind, but her head start was too great. I imagined her long muscular legs leaping away. I wandered up and down the hallway, listening for a rustling behind a door or a slight giggle, but heard nothing. Then, I knocked on Tim's door. "Want to be my first lieutenant?" I quickly asked.

"Yeah," he answered excitedly before even knowing his assignment. He followed me into the bathroom where we crumpled up toilet paper into balls and wet them under the sink. "They're called soggies," I said.

"Cool!" Tim replied as I plopped one in his hand.

"If you find her, don't let her know. Just come get me," I ordered. Prowling down the hall, I heard a noise in front of me. Not having time to react, I chucked the wet ball of paper and heard the splat. "Uh, gross! Totally gross!" I heard Jenny's whine. Adrian, behind her, peered over her shoulders, her dim eyes straining. "Erik? Erik?" A wad of paper shot past my shoulder and exploded on Adrian.

"They're called soggies!" I heard Tim yell shrilly from behind me.

Soon Jenny and Adrian were both prowling through the hallway, their hands crammed with gobs of sticky wet paper. Others opened their doors and were greeted with splatters, and the halls became filled with a barrage of speeding wet missiles. There seemed to be no strategies, goals, or teamwork. Any flicker of movement generated a half dozen gooey balls hurling in that direction. The fresh splat of toilet paper against bare flesh fed the participants. In the midst of the battle, Tim grabbed my arm. "I think I saw her in the closet. Over here." His voice was extra shrill with excitement. I filled a pitcher of water from the sink, softly stepped inside the room, and shut the door. I pretended to look around. Then, I moved to the closet, bent over, and felt through the empty shoes lying on the floor. Soon, my fingers felt a pair of sneakers that were more filled out, and running my hands up them, felt a pair of ankles. "If I didn't know any better I would think someone's standing in these." That made Alex giggle and she leaped over me, dashing toward the door. I was ready with the water. It splashed over the back of her head as she groped for the door handle. Then we were both laughing as she turned around to face me, grabbing for the pitcher. Then we were tumbling on the floor, both wrestling for the pitcher. I could smell the sweet clean fragrance of her soap and could feel her breath against my cheek.

Abruptly, the door slammed open and Carl's voice was bellowing, "What the blazes is going on up here?" and, "What is it that I've been stepping in?" Thank God, he was blind himself and couldn't see the two of us tussling around on the ground. We stood up quickly and were marched out into the hallway. Others were slowly emerging from their hiding places. For the next two hours as I, along with the others, scraped wet toilet paper bits off the floors, walls, and even the ceiling, I wore the whisper of her breath against my skin.

The last four days of camp were devoted to the anticipated rock-climbing outing. On the van ride to New Hampshire I tried to imagine myself scaling a vertical slab of rock. I pictured the granite surface as smooth and straight as the walls in my room. I wondered how my body could stay stuck to its surface. Climbing a rock face seemed dangerous and risky and defied reason, and because of these elements, I was immediately attracted. I would be doing something that normal people wrote off as crazy.

On the trail to the base of the climb I raced Alex, swinging my cane furiously in front of me, Alex running hard for a moment and then stopping to get her bearings. Her long legs won out in the end, and she touched the rock face first.

When everyone arrived, Nick, our instructor, gathered us around and fitted us with gear. The small clearing became a chaotic mass of tussling bodies with flying elbows and knees as each of us wrestled with harnesses, helmets, and climbing shoes.

"Is my harness on backwards?"

"These rock shoes are killing my feet."

"This helmet keeps falling over my eyes."

"What does that matter idiot?"

Then Nick familiarized us on how to belay our partner as he climbed by running the rope through a tiny metal device called an ATC and how to secure our harnesses to the rope with a special climbing knot called a figure eight. Finally we were ready. Nick explained, "When I climb, I scan the rock with my eyes. I look up, searching for potential holds, chalk marks, places to rest. I honestly don't know whether it will work, but your hands and feet and ears will have to become your eyes. You'll have to scan your hands across the rock and listen for instructions from your partner."

We sat on the ground, cheering each person on as they climbed. I got pretty nervous when Jenny only made it a few feet off the ground before she got freaked out and wanted to come down. When it was my turn, I stood up and tied the knot to my harness the way Nick had shown. I touched the rock. It wasn't quite as smooth and straight as I had imagined but it was still intimidating and thrilling to get off the ground. This first climb was what Nick called a "friction climb," sloping smoothly up at a sixty-degree angle. The holds were practically nonexistent, just rounded polished bulges and shallow concave dishes, but the angle was moderate enough that I could rest my palms against the curved holds for balance while I centered my weight over the sticky rubber soles of my climbing shoes, which enabled me to step gingerly up the face. As I worked higher, I gained momentum and confidence and toward the top, was practically running up the slab. Nick yelled up excitedly, "Alright, monkey boy!" My heart was pounding; the cool mountain air bit deep into my lungs. My calves, forearms, and fingertips were charged with life; most of my face was taken up by a giant toothy smile. Chuck Yeager could not have been more exhilarated when he broke through the sound barrier, and as Nick lowered me down on the rope, I was already anticipating, with nervous energy, moving to the next level.

For my second climb Nick said, "This is a steeper route than the last. Friction won't be enough to hold you to the rock." I found the angle of the first ten feet as moderate as the first, but then I stopped as the angle abruptly steepened, my legs, chest, and cheek pressed up against a sheer face, which wanted to shove my body over backwards. I had no clue how I would propel my body to the top, hanging by the strength of my fingers and toes; the idea of it was laughable. As Nick had said, my hands were my eyes, but at least on the ground, I was free to take time to feel around and investigate my world. On the wall, however, I felt trapped. My desperate grip was the only thing locking me to the rock face, and if I let go to feel around, I would surely fall.

Nick told me to move left and, as I inched delicately in that direction, my hands fell into a narrow vertical crack. I jammed a foot and hand into it and tried to pull myself up, but the rock in my face kept pushing me back. After a few tries I turned my body sideways and began moving up the crack painstakingly slow. Soon the crack narrowed even more, and I moved right onto the face. "There's a big knob a little above your left hand," Nick called.

My hand flopped around the rock frantically. No knob.

"Reach higher."

"Here?" I yelled, one foot turned sideways on a microscopic pebble, my other wedged painfully in a pocket.

"That's not a knob. Keep feeling left . . . Three inches more . . . That's more like three feet . . ."

"Here? . . . Here? . . . Here?" Eventually I made it to the top, but I spent the majority of the time resting on the rope with my burning forearms dangling at my sides.

By the end of the third day, I was finally learning to accurately locate the holds that Nick directed me toward. Nick's instructions seemed to be the only difference between panicking and finding a hold. So on the last day, when he stopped giving us directions, I was annoyed. Nick insisted though, "This sport is all about self-reliance, about moving upward under your own power. To be independent, you're going to have to find your own way up the rock."

That morning, I hung from a precarious finger pocket, with one foot slowly losing grip on a sloping ledge, knowing that if I didn't find the next hold within seconds, I would fall. I needed to find something, anything, but the face was so massive, a hold could be hiding anywhere. At first my hands and feet leaped and flailed around the face, just hoping to get lucky and find something. At least a dozen times, as I struggled up the face, I couldn't find anything and fell back against the secure rope. My arms were more exhausted than after a wrestling match. When I was about to fall, my natural reaction was to panic, but I forced myself to scan my hands and feet steadily and systematically across the rock face. I stretched my limbs as far as they would reach, scanning above, below, and beside me for that hidden "thank god" hold, just at the edge of my reach. As I got a few feet higher, I decided to work the face using a grid pattern, forcing my hand to slide and not to jump across, so that it would cover every inch of the rock. I also began to realize that if I could train my feet to find the holds that my hands just discarded, I'd save myself half the work. Toward the top, as my forearms burned and my fingers began to feel limp, just when I thought I couldn't hold on a second longer, I'd find a hold, maybe not the best one, but enough to keep me sticking to the face a few seconds longer, enabling me to claw my body up a few more inches.

Since I couldn't "see" beyond the reach of my hands, planning my route up the face seemed impossible. Earlier, I had reached dead ends where the face seemed to go suddenly blank. As I hung on, Nick coached, "Follow the clues in the rock. A rough broken section might lead to a crack, a shallow groove to a deeper groove. A crack might disappear and resume just an arm's length away." I was realizing that the beauty of climbing was to join the incongruent parts, to link the cracks, grooves, bowls, nubbins, knobs, edges, ledges, and pockets and convert all of it into a road map, etched in my mind.

So, by thrashing, groping, and bloodying the rock, I worked my way up the face, and despite the difficulty, I had powered my body up a piece of rock that seemed impossibly foreign to a horizontal world. At the top I sat on a pocket-shaped ledge with my palms flat against the rock and my legs dangling over the side. I was overwhelmed by the sensation of the mountain, by the wind at my back, by the brilliant textures in the rock, the intermittent patterns of coolness and heat under my touch. It was as though my senses had awakened. Every sound, smell, and touch was so vivid, so brilliant, it was almost painful. Blindness, I thought, was an incredible nuisance. It had definitely made climbing more difficult, forcing me to climb in a different way than most, but it hadn't stopped me from doing it, or even, loving it. Never again would I thunder down a basketball court on a fast break or jump a dirt bike over a ramp; the past was dead, and no matter how much I fought, there was no reclaiming the dead. But one hundred feet above tree line with the sun in my face and a sound of openness all around me, none of that seemed to matter as much, because, I had just discovered, I could climb.

After the long day of climbing we came home to the cabin we had been sharing in the woods. We played Braille Trivial Pursuit and talked about our experiences. It was unanimous: everyone had a blast, even Jenny, who at first was so freaked out, she had stopped talking for a while, a rarity for her. At the end of the day she had even rappelled down the side of the rock face, clutching the rope with what Nick had described as the "white-knuckle death grip," but she had done it. "That was like, so amazing. I can't believe it. I broke a fingernail, but I did it." Alex and I walked outside and climbed up on a sloping boulder. We sat silently for a while, and then Alex asked, "What do you miss the most now that you're blind?"

"Nothing!" I said at first, not wanting my mind to linger in the past.

"There must be something you miss," she persisted. Then, I gave into it and let my mind wander through my sighted life. Riding my bike to the reservoir and down along the Glen in the summer, sprinting full bore across a field—I weighed the possible responses. Then I came upon it: faces. "I miss people's faces," I said. "I miss looking into people's eyes, and I miss seeing their expressions change from sad to happy, from anger to laughter."

"Do you wonder what I look like?" she asked, and without waiting for me to respond, said, "You can feel my face."

I laughed. "Blind people only do that in movies," I said, but I reached out despite myself, tentatively touching her cheekbones, lips, nose, forehead; but my mind couldn't seem to assemble the pieces into a coherent picture. Her face kept coming out as a cartoon image. I couldn't tell whether she was visually beautiful anyway, so I gave up and clung to the things I could understand, the things I could touch and hear and smell. Those were enough. They were all I needed: the music of her laugh, the brush of her hair across my cheek, the fragrance of her clean skin, the whisper of her breath.

"I wish you could see me," she said again.

"I can," I uttered and leaned forward. She must have leaned forward too, because my lips touched hers. We kissed for a long time and, later, she lay with her head in my lap and we listened to the crickets and the faraway hoot of owls.

After I got home I made a tape for Alex. I had my friends tell jokes into the recorder. Some I had to edit, because I didn't think they'd go over too well with her religious parents. Then I made up little skits involving Keith, Jenny, Tim, and the others and performed all their voices. And lastly I took a chance and told her that her going blind wasn't her fault; that God wasn't punishing her, because I didn't think God worked like that. I had thought it too, that life was a punishment, made up of only losses. "Yeah, he takes things away," I said into the speaker, "but he gives other things back and, in a strange way, those new things can be just as good or even better. I think you just have to look for the new things a little harder."

# 6
# Wizard, the Chick Magnet

Later in the summer I received a Braille card from Fidelco, a guide-dog school near Hartford, which said I had been accepted to receive a guide dog. It had been my mother's suggestion to apply for a dog. She had seen a man walking with a sleek powerful German shepherd and had told me they looked graceful together. I held the card from Fidelco in my hand, missing my mom and missing the fact that she would never see my dog, whose name was written in Braille on the bottom of the card: "Wizard."

Usually guide dogs are given to blind students as they leave for college. People first have to be prepared to work the dog every day and be responsible enough to feed and groom it. I was only sixteen when I met Wizard, a sleek black and tan German shepherd. Ironically, Wizard was the youngest graduate of Fidelco's program and I was the youngest recipient in its history. He had a long smooth body with a long snout like a wolf's. His coat flowed all back in one direction and he had little tufts of hair like a cowlick where his leather harness rested. Dave Darr, my instructor, told me that Wizard had spent the first fifteen months living with a foster family, being housebroken, learning to heel, sit, and stay, and generally enjoying his puppyhood. I know it must have been hard for a family to give up a beautiful dog like Wizard, but perhaps they took solace in knowing that Wizard was going on to do very important work. Guiding for a German shepherd is about at the level of being the president of the United States for a human, except instead of protecting the population from foreign dictators, nuclear strikes, and inflation, Wizard would protect the life of one blind guy from collisions with fire hydrants, telephone poles, and overhanging tree branches.

For the first step in our training, Dave put an improvised harness and leash over his back. I walked around the neighborhood, feeling a little silly as I pretended Dave was the dog and told him right and left and halt. Next I walked with the harness around Wizard, with Dave about eight feet behind me, also connected to the harness by a long cord. If Wizard tried to bolt out of my grasp, he was ready to reign him in. On my first solo walk, Wizard, sensing immediately he was no longer connected to the safety line, ran my thigh squarely into a fire hydrant. It gave me such a charley horse I doubled up in pain, lying on the sidewalk, Wizard's bad breath steaming in my face. I imagined him saying, "Get up, tough guy, want to go for round two?"

Dogs aren't born with an inherent fear of traffic. At first, they aren't quite swift enough to associate a two-ton, moving vehicle with the unpleasant sensation of pain. So, Wizard had to be taught to fear the road. This was accomplished by Wizard and I standing on the edge of a curb, with Dave hiding around the corner in the Fidelco van. Then he whirled around the corner, and as he sped past me, only a foot away, I gave Wizard the signal to step off the curb. "Forward!" I said, and just as poor Wizard followed the command, I pulled him quickly back by his harness and scolded him by saying, "Bad dog." After a whole morning of Dave's squealing-tire near misses, with me yelling out, "Forward!" Wizard began to disobey me, and this was just the point. I needed to be the one to decide when to cross a street, but if blasting jackhammers or blaring sirens impaired my hearing, and I gave a "forward" as a car sped by, Wizard needed to know he could refuse my command.

Working with a guide dog was a lot harder than I originally thought. Getting where I wanted to go wasn't as easy as saying, "Wizard, take me to McDonald's, the one on First and Main." Wizard didn't possess a magical intuition, like a guide dog I had seen on a Sunday night Disney movie. The dog in the movie seemed to be smarter than the blind man he was guiding, and the two seemed to communicate through mental telepathy. Wizard was far from omniscient; we struggled to communicate. Dave told me, "You are the big picture guy and Wizard is the detail man." I had to know where I was going. In downtown Westport, when walking from the record store to the movie theater, I knew to walk down the hill, cross five streets, and soon after a sharp decline, to begin telling Wizard to, "Find left. Find inside," waving my hand in the direction I wanted Wizard to look. Wizard couldn't distinguish between the door to the movie theater and the door to anywhere else, so often I gave him the left command too early or too late and he would bring me to the door of the sub shop, or the bookstore, or the mini mart. From there, it was my job to notice the smell of books or bread baking, the ring of a cash register, and the absence of popcorn, assess my mistake and decide whether I needed to go farther or backtrack. The process involved a lot of trial and error and a lot of wrong doors, but it also opened up worlds of opportunity. When Wizard and I cruised around downtown streets with a group of guys, no longer did my heart beat with trepidation. Using a long white cane was perfectly respectable, but with the distracting noises of jackhammers, car horns, and other pedestrians, I couldn't hear my friends' footsteps well enough to follow. So this forced me to take an arm, which was OK if it was my brother's or dad's, but hanging on to the arm of a male buddy definitely cut down on the cool factor, especially if girls were around. In this scenario, however, Wizard was my secret weapon. All I had to do was to command Wizard to follow, and he would stick to a person like a bad odor.

During my guide-dog training, Dave tested Wizard's skill by trying to lose us in a shopping mall. For half an hour, he weaved crazily through a maze of clothes racks and glass counters, up and down escalators, and in and out of small stores. But Wizard wasn't even fazed. He simply lowered his head, flattened his ears, and it was obvious to me as I followed his zigzagging motions through the stiff metal and leather handle of his harness, he thrived on exactly this kind of challenge. He wasn't a dog; he was a following machine, a green beret in the ranks of guide dogs. Near the end of the exercise, Dave gave one last supreme effort to ditch me by darting left into a bathroom and hiding in a stall. I heard a nearby child ask, "Mommy, why is that guy running away from the blind man?"

Wizard couldn't be beaten, however. He made it to the bathroom door before it even swung shut, sat down very businesslike in front of the stall and pointed his nose in Dave's direction. Then he rolled his head up and let out a high-pitched yawn as if to let us know his following skills hadn't been remotely stretched. Dave was silent for a moment as he peeked through the crack in the stall and then, realizing he was found, began chuckling and speaking softly, almost to himself, "Good boy. That's a very good boy."

Wizard knew lots of other commands as well: find the stairs, find the curb, find the escalator, and my favorite, probably because I taught him this myself, find the chair. Coming into the school bus or into class, I always found it awkward to feel around for an empty chair. So, I set an empty chair in front of Wizard while we were home one day and said repeatedly, "Find the chair," and then gently pushed his head down so it lay on the seat. Now in the classroom, Wizard, spotting an empty chair across the room, would charge with purpose toward it and lay his head down, wagging his tail with gusto. My favorite pet trick was when he picked up spare change that I had dropped, by sliding it around with his nose until he was able to pop it up and get hold of it with his mouth. Then, he'd proudly hand it to me, all slobbered and slimy in my hand.

After long days of training, Wiz and I would play fetch in the cul-de-sac below my house. Even during downtime Wiz never took anything lightly. He played as intensely as he worked. My dad described to me his unblinking eyes, dark and wolflike, as they followed the tennis ball in my hand. Then I would throw the ball as far and high as I could, and Wiz would bound to the right spot beneath the falling ball and, like a professional outfielder, circle around, his burning eyes following its descent, and snatch the pop fly from the air with a quick leap and flick of his jaws. Afterwards, we wrestled in the driveway. Wiz and I faced off and he would spring in and out of my reach as I tried to catch his paws and roll his body to the ground. When I got hold of him, he'd escape with an explosion of writhing twisting movements, and we'd face off again, Wizard letting out little playful grunts and growls under his breath. Wiz's long snout would lunge menacingly at my wrists and hands and, only centimeters away, he would pull back enough that I would only feel the soft delicate pressure of his teeth and lips around my skin. When I finally held him fast, he still wouldn't give in, and I could feel his sinewy muscles wriggling and twitching beneath his fur. Then I'd pick him up in a fireman's carry, his belly resting on the back of my neck and his paws held in my hands. With Wiz still snapping and howling in delight, I'd spin us around and around, like a professional wrestler about to finish off his opponent with a body slam. After a few minutes of spinning, when we were both thoroughly dizzy and I felt ready to fall over, I'd lay him down gently on his back. Just as he felt my grip slacken, Wiz was up again, leaping, lunging, snapping, and barking. Often I was so into the game, I'd lose track of time, and afterwards, we'd both lie on the ground, panting and nearly lifeless. Sometimes I'd lie on my back with my head resting on Wiz's side as he licked the salty sweat off my hand.

Wizard accompanied me everywhere, through the hallways of my high school, to wrestling matches, and, a few months before high school graduation, on a Friday-night excursion to New York City. Wiz and I rode the train into the city with Chris and Bret, another friend, who both borrowed one of my extra long white canes so they could get the Metro-North handicap fare: $4.50 versus $8.00. They closed their eyes beneath dark sunglasses so their facial movements wouldn't give them away and swayed through the narrow aisle, clumsily swinging their canes and bumping their shins. The turbulence of the moving train kept bouncing Bret into people's laps, and at the end of each passenger car, where the aisle became wider, Chris would get disoriented, walking around in circles and careening into walls. Eventually, I got tired of waiting for them, so I had them form a line, each holding the shoulder of the person in front, with me like a mama duck, leading the procession. Imagining the commuters watching from their seats, I chuckled, a little chagrined, knowing we looked like a cross between the three blind mice and the three stooges.

After Wiz laid his head on an empty seat and we sat down, the conductor came by to sell us our tickets. Chris and Bret reached into their pockets and thrust out an unorganized wad of crumpled bills. The conductor plucked out the $4.50. "Here's your ticket," he said very slowly and a little too loudly. "Will you need any help off the train?"

"No, thanks," I replied. "I'll take care of 'em." The bills in my wallet were arranged in order from biggest to smallest, with twenties folded in half horizontally, tens folded in half vertically, fives folded in thirds, and ones not folded at all, so I was able to hand the conductor the exact change. Perhaps because I was the only one not wearing sunglasses and because I made a habit of facing a person when talking to them, the conductor asked me, "Are you wanting the handicap fare, too?"

I wanted to say, "Hey pal, if you haven't noticed yet, I'm the only one here who's actually blind," but instead I laughed, figuring I'd take it as a compliment.

In New York City we tried to get into a nightclub. The private cop at the door didn't question our poorly made fake IDs, but said bluntly, "No dogs." I tried to explain that the dog is not a pet but considered my eyes. I explained that Wizard would slip under a chair and wouldn't even be noticed, but this explanation had absolutely no effect. "The dog will scare customers," is all he replied. I even took out a small pamphlet that clearly stated the law that guide dogs are allowed into public establishments, but that just made him angry. "Don't show me the law. I'm an officer of the law, and if you give me any more lip, I'll throw you in jail. I don't care if you're blind." I desperately wanted to keep arguing the point but was afraid this approach would eventually lead him to taking a closer inspection of our puny seventeen-year-old frames and our lame IDs. We walked away, but then snuck around to the back door, knocked, and told a bouncer that the officer in front told me that it would be easier for the dog to get in this way. The bouncer escorted us to a table. On the way, women kept approaching me asking to pet the dog. When we sat down, Chris said, "Put Wizard a little in the aisle, so women'll see him. I know his job is to guide you around, but he's also a major chick magnet." The plan worked beautifully and we were seldom without admiring women, who, while walking by our table, found Wizard to be the perfect icebreaker. I suppose women figured anyone with a beautiful German shepherd at his side couldn't very well be an ax murderer.

"Oh, he's so precious."

"Oh, isn't he gorgeous."

"What a handsome boy."

As each new woman approached, I invented new responses. "Thanks for the compliment. The dog's pretty cute too. You can't pet him; he's on duty, but if you're cute, I might let you scratch me behind the ear."

My ego got a boost when one girl sat down with us and really seemed interested in me. "Most guys are just interested in how a girl looks, but beauty's only skin deep. You," she said with passion, "see through a girl's outward appearance. You see into the soul." I was pretty sure that being blind didn't give me special X-ray vision into the soul, but I didn't fight her assessment. Then she asked me to dance, and as her meaty hand clamped down on mine to lead me to the dance floor, I started getting suspicious as to why she was so interested in me not seeing her. The girl was inexhaustible, through a dozen songs of Madonna and The Culture Club, flinging me around the dance floor, even grinding and undulating with me against the wall, her squatty legs bent and midsection barreling forward like a sumo wrestler.

When she finally led me back to our table and left, I leaned across to Chris and whispered, "You're dead!"

Chris cracked up, high pitched and hysterical. "What was I supposed to do, say right in front of her, 'Dude, run and hide before it's too late'?"

"You've gotta give me a clue whether a girl's good looking or not, but it's gotta be subtle." I thought for a minute and then said, "When a girl comes over, you walk over and shake my hand like you're saying hello. If you shake my hand like this," I said, grasping his hand in a traditional handshake, "then it means she's average. If you shake my hand like this," I grabbed Chris's hand by interlocking our thumbs and wrapping my four fingers around the top of his hand, "it means she's hot."

"And what if she's a dog?" Chris asked.

"Then this." I curled my four fingers and hooked them around Chris's hooked fingers.

For the rest of the night, the handshake worked without a hitch. A girl would approach; Chris would interrupt, "Hey dude, how's it going?" while giving me the ugly shake. Then I'd say, "Yeah, the dog, he's great alright, except sometimes in really crowded situations, he just goes ballistic, snapping and biting. It gets kind of ugly. He's only done it a few times though," and magically she'd be gone in a few seconds. Another girl would approach; Chris interrupted with the same greeting while giving me the hot shake. Then I'd say, "One thing about being blind, looks just don't matter much to me. I try to see into the soul. So tell me. Where're you from?"

While I was buying a round of beers at the bar, some guys sitting nearby wanted to know how I could tell the difference between bills. They were clearly drunk, so I thought for a moment and said, "I can smell the difference. . . . Ones are made from pine trees, fives from oak, and tens from birch." I guess they weren't as drunk as I had thought and one said, "I don't believe that. You're gonna have to prove that one, buddy," already whipping out some bills. Chris and I excused ourselves for a moment to take a leak and when we returned, they handed me a bill. "Well," I said. "If you really don't think I can do it, how 'bout we bet a round of beers?" They agreed readily, handing me bill after bill, in no order or pattern. Some new, some old, some smooth, others wrinkled. Each time, I'd hold the bill flat up against my nose, taking in the deep aroma. Then, I'd roll it up into a tube and place it directly under my nostril, breathing in again, and finally, I'd take the bill and rub it vigorously up and down my cheek.

"Why's he rubbing it like that?" one of them asked challengingly. "I thought he smelled it."

"Shh," Chris commanded. "He's got his ways." Actually, Chris had no idea why, and I didn't either, except for thinking it might serve as a distraction for what was happening under the table. For each bill, Chris's foot tapped mine: once for a one, twice for a five, three times for a ten, et cetera. As I identified five different bills in a row, the group of guys grew more amazed and Chris and I got drunker. On the way out, we brazenly stumbled past the officer at the door who, no doubt, was wondering just how we had gotten in. "Don't worry, officer," I assured him. "I'm not driving."

I graduated from Weston High in June of 1987. I had been accepted to Boston College, a few miles down the road from the Carroll Center for the Blind. While at the Carroll Center, I had explored Boston and was enthralled by all the elevators with Braille numbers beside each button, the trolleys, called Ts for short, which could take me all over the city, and the thousands of other college students from over two hundred other universities. BC had an adaptive-technology center with computers that had Braille displays and voice synthesizers, powerful Braille printers, and Kurzweil machines that worked like scanners and converted printed text to synthesized voice.

On the evening of graduation, Mrs. Reddy, my guidance counselor, gave me an extra cap for Wizard. I put it on his head, but he constantly shook it off. I had rehearsed the walk from my seat in the audience to the steps of the stage, across it, and down the set of stairs on the other side, so that Wizard would do the route automatically. When I heard my name announced, I got up and said softly, "Forward, Wiz. Find the stairs." At the bottom Wiz stopped and positioned his body perpendicular to the stairs, so that my first step was lined up straight. At the top, we took three steps to where I heard the closed sound of a body to my left, reached out, and found the principal's hand. As I took my diploma, the audience clapped and cheered. The sound lasted for a long time, as long as it took Wiz and me to cross the stage and reach the other stairs, Wiz to pause and me to say, "forward," and us to carefully climb down and reach my open seat. When it was time for all the seniors to throw their caps in the air, I reached for Wizard's cap, but he had already flung it off again, becoming the first in our whole class to carry out the tradition.

# 7
# Flailing to Independence

In the fall my dad drove me up to Boston College. "This would have been a proud day for your mother," my dad said.

"Remember how she cried when Eddi left?" I asked, and suddenly I was jealous of Eddi, because at least she had been alive to see him graduate high school and cry when he left for college.

After my dad left, I surveyed my dorm room. Wizard and I had gotten the only single room on the first floor, a six-foot-by-twelve-foot handicap room, comprised of a single bed, small wooden desk, and sink. The strange and embarrassing part of the room, however, was the large stall and swinging door which housed an extra-tall wheelchair accessible toilet, as if I were going to be heading in there to do number two with a few friends hanging out on the other side. That afternoon as I unpacked my clothes and listened to other students getting settled and meeting roommates, I was filled by a blend of expectancy and loneliness. In high school my friends had known me when I was sighted. They had known my family, my mother, and about her death. They had known my past, my present, and the massive changes that had gone between, but now, I realized, I was beginning a new life as a blind person.

I was one of three blind students out of ten thousand, so I was easily identifiable, cruising around campus with Wiz, but the same distinction which drew people to me also kept me apart. Before class in the lecture hall, in the bookstore, at the student union, peers constantly stopped me to ask questions about Wiz and about being blind. I felt like a kind of blind ambassador. What they didn't know was that I had only been playing this role for five short years, and I didn't know many of the rules yet; nor was it a role I even wanted to play. It was so easy, however, to talk about Wiz, to make jokes about being blind, when I desperately wanted to move beyond this veneer and distinguish myself in some deeper way. Early into the year, I hit the weight room every day until I could bench-press 315 pounds, and I practiced the drinking game of "quarters" until I could roll the quarter off the bridge of my nose, have it bounce off the table and into the small cup of beer, but none of this felt like enough.

A few months into the school year, as I worked to learn my way around the huge campus and to acclimate to all my new classes, I began to feel a chronic ache in my left eye. Sometimes, after class, I lay on my bed with my palm pressed against my eye, rolling back and forth in pain. My left eye, which had gone blind years before my right, also began to turn grayish white and bulge out, with tiny blisters appearing on the surface. When the pain grew so bad it interfered with studying, working out, and even sitting through class, I finally went to see Dr. Brockhurst, who told me the eye had developed glaucoma. In a normal eye, internal fluid circulates through the eyeball, passing through the membrane of the eye's surface. The fluid gives pressure to the eye and gives it shape, but in my eye, cataracts had blocked the fluid's exit, trapping it inside the eyeball. Dr. Brockhurst tested the pressure in my eye with a small tube against the surface. The average eye has about eighteen pounds of internal fluid pressure; even though the numbers on the machine went to ninety pounds, the pressure in my left eye registered off the charts. He described my eye like a balloon that had been inflated as tightly as it would go. "Eventually," he said, "the walls of the balloon would become very thin and eventually a hole would appear which would collapse the balloon entirely." I grimly imagined my eye as a sun, expanding to a supernova and then collapsing in on itself, shrinking into a red dwarf. "The most logical course," he said, was to have my eye "enucleated," which meant to have it removed. After scheduling the surgery, that night I went out with some friends and sat at a bar drinking beers. Nobody but me knew the evening was a farewell party. I found myself reaching up and touching my eye through the lid and thinking about it no longer being there.

A week later I checked into Massachusetts Eye and Ear. As the nurse wheeled me into the operating room, my body shook. My father, who had driven up from Connecticut, walked beside us with his hand on my arm, as far as he was allowed to go, and afterwards, when I was rolled out again, I remember the vague sensation of his hand still on my arm. He later told me he was a little scared when he first saw my ghost-white face and the top of my head hidden by mounds of bandages and gauze. As I slowly drifted toward consciousness, I dreamed that the pain was so intense I wanted to cry, but discovered I couldn't because I had no eyes to cry from, and when I did awake, the pain was all-consuming, like a hot piece of coal jammed into my socket. I could sense my father's worry, so out of place compared to his normal gung-ho attitude, so I said in a dry hoarse whisper, "Don't worry. It'll get better."

Only a few days after the surgery Chris came up from Connecticut, where he was attending Fairfield University, to cheer me up. All I wanted to do was lie around, moan in pain, and pop my regimen of heavy narcotic painkillers, but in my drugged state, he somehow persuaded me to go out to a comedy club. Bouncing over Boston's cobblestone streets in Chris's car was an agonizing ordeal; I already wanted to go home. Reclining in the passenger seat, I felt the large bulky eye guard over my socket, held tight by a wad of bandages wrapped around the top half of my head like a mummy. "I feel a little self-conscious," I said to Chris.

"You'll be fine," he said, glancing over at me a couple of times, and I knew he was staring at my bandages. "I'm not letting this opportunity pass us by," he continued. "Not only do we have Wiz to attract the babes but now they'll love me too. At the club, if you could drool a little, we'll tell 'em that I'm the nice volunteer who's taken you out of the asylum for the weekend." At the comedy club Chris strategically sat us front row center. A few words into the comedian's routine, he stopped dead, looked straight at me, and in a disgusted voice, said over the microphone, "How do you expect me to do comedy with this mutant in the front row?" I imagined all the comedians talking in the back room. "Charley, it'll be an easy night. We've got a mutant in the front row." Chris practically choked, he laughed so hard, and for the next three acts, I provided glaringly obvious comic material.

Finally the patch came off and an ocularist fit me with a prosthetic eye. It wasn't glass, but a liquid plastic that he pushed into my eye socket, and when it hardened to the shape of the socket, he plucked it out. The eye was oval shaped: round in the front and concave in the back. The ocularist stared at my right eye for a half an hour and then painted the prosthetic eye to match the other. Then he layered the top with an acrylic to protect the color. When I left it felt like a giant heavy marble jammed tightly behind my lids, but over a few days, the foreign feeling went away and I didn't notice the prosthetic.

Since school began I had shied away from directly facing people, afraid they would gawk at my gray bulgy eye. I had even begun to wear sunglasses, an act I had once been adamantly against because I considered it a "blind thing," but now I jumped at the chance to stare down any passerby. I especially wanted to impress Sue, a girl who lived upstairs from me and on whom I had a major crush. My plan was to knock on her door and casually ask her out while trying to look her in the eyes with my brand-new, gleaming, vividly colorful eyeball. I took the elevator to her floor and moved through the winding hallway toward her door. As I turned the last corner, I touched my prosthetic to make sure it wasn't crooked, but must have rubbed it too hard, because it popped out, and to my horror, I heard it bounce somewhere on the floor. Then, like in a bad B-rated movie, I heard the elevator door open. People were talking and laughing. Even worse, among the voices was Sue's, drawing closer by the second. I was on my knees, my hand frantically scanning the floor for the small eye. As she rounded the corner, my hand touched the small plastic circle, snatched it up, and plugged it back into my socket. Just before rising, I heard Sue's very confused voice. "Erik! What are you doing on the floor? Are you okay?" It's probably unnecessary to mention that I never got a date with Sue.

With girls not working out to my satisfaction, I threw myself into my studies. I was fascinated by remote cultures around the world. My freshman history class was focusing on the Inca Empire, which had started around A.D. 1460 and had expanded rapidly out from Cuzco, Peru to over much of South America. In fewer than one hundred years, the empire had created a vast network of roads twisting through the jungles and mountains to transport goods and culture to over twelve million Incas. All this ended with the conquest of Spanish Conquistadors in the late fifteen hundreds, but one remote enclave, hidden on a high mountain saddle at eight thousand feet and protected on both sides by high peaks, was never discovered by the Spanish. Mysteriously abandoned by the Incas, it lay forgotten in the high jungle for three hundred years. This was the royal city of Machu Picchu.

Hiram Bingham, an anthropologist and adventurer, who must have been the inspiration behind the fictional character Indiana Jones, rediscovered the pre-Columbian ruins in 1911. With a small Quechua boy as a guide, he hiked over a mountain pass and stared down on mile after mile of stone ruins, built upon hundreds of terraces and linked by thousands of steps. It must have seemed to him as though he had stepped out of the forward motion of time and into a realm which stood magically still against the centuries.

Ever since my mom died, my dad had been looking to take a summer trip that would bring us closer together again, even though we were dispersed up and down the East Coast, from Maine to Florida. At

Christmas, when everyone was home, and after all the presents were opened, the conversation turned to the family vacation. "How 'bout a little hike?" I suggested.

"Where?" Mark asked suspiciously.

"I don't know . . . Peru maybe."

I pulled out the brochure I had ordered, and my dad leafed through it. "Inca Trail," I said. "It's on page twelve."

The brochure read, "A difficult physical challenge over seven days, moving amidst the still-existing remote and primitive culture of the Quechua Indians. We'll learn the facts and legends of the Incas and come across ruins of villages, temples, and messengers' rest stops that you can't see any other way except on foot."

There was a dialogue with Sobek, the adventure company organizing the trek, about the risks involved for a blind person. No blind person had ever trekked the Inca Trail, in the twentieth century at least, but after learning about my success with wrestling and rock climbing, Sobek made an affirmative decision. They would welcome me.

The Inca Trail begins at Cusco, the old Inca capital at eleven thousand feet, the oldest continuous city in the Americas. For the first few days we generally followed the fast-flowing Rio Urubamba, which sent cool mist sprays into the air. The trail rose up a thousand feet or more above the river before rolling back down again. Our group trekked eight to ten hours each day. At the higher altitudes, the mornings began cold, but by noon, the intense heat of the sun baked the trail, which then was churned into dust by passing trains of alpacas carrying loads.

My dad and I worked together. Dad walked a half step behind me, his left hand around my neck, with hand pressures steering me right or left between rocks and trees, around water, onto bridges, whatever. I used a thin white cane, which constantly probed the area directly in front of me. There was constant communication from my dad to me. "Giant rock on the left. Sharp right and over a tree limb. Big step up onto a rock. Gravel rocks, slippery." I had to take every step with utmost caution, bracing my legs and ankles for any slight incline or drop, or for a small rock or root on the rugged trail. And because the verbal instructions could only be a guide, when my foot landed, I had to totally rebalance it for the next step. It was an excruciatingly tiring way of moving. Recognizing the difficulty of trekking for long hours without being able to see what was ahead, Dad also flooded me with information, which broke the climb into mini goals. "Slight incline for the next hundred yards. Flat and easy, five minutes across a meadow. Climbing rocks, maybe fifteen feet up. Rest place ten minutes ahead. I can see it from here."

Meanwhile Mark and Eddi wanted to move faster than my dad and me. When the trail was clear, they often ran to the top of the next ridge, then sat and waited for us to catch up; their way of signaling that the climb was a piece of cake for them. Naturally, I wanted to move fast and be carefree with my older brothers, instead of inching and floundering along with my dad's hand around my neck. At a rest stop, with my dad off filling water bottles, Mark gave me a rather unflattering description of my dad's hiking attire. This new image of Dad didn't much help the partnership. To cover miles of difficult mountainous terrain, my dad wore white tennis shoes with smooth bald treads and cotton crew socks pulled up high around his calves. When it rained, he was prepared with a see-through plastic poncho, purchased for $2.99 at Kmart. To combat the heat, grime, and dust of the day, he wore a patriotic red, white, and blue bandana around his neck. And to eliminate a bad burn on his rather shiny scalp, Dad wore a canvas hat with a wide, floppy brim. He also stopped frequently to film the scenery around us: children selling Inca Soda along the way, grazing alpacas, and crumbling ruins beside the trail. While filming, he'd speak in a slow deliberate voice. "We are viewing the remains of a rock tower on which Inca warriors stood watch for the approaching enemy. The local people call this structure 'the Watching Tower.' " The worst was when he'd scamper a few yards ahead of me and film me approaching. "We are watching Erik negotiate his way down the rocky trail. Notice his excellent cane technique and his careful footwork as he positions each new foot for maximum balance."

When I heard the hum of the camera filming, with each step, I pointed my toes, lifted them high in the air, and twirled them gracefully before setting them down.

I was constantly pushing my dad to go faster, but his role was a tiring one too. He was often half off the trail, one arm stretching up or down to reach my neck, the other holding his trusty video camera. He moved at his limit, especially when we left the river and climbed onto higher ground. The trail became steeper, more narrow, and with a severe drop-off on one side or the other. At the end of one particularly long day, when our legs were tired and footing was not so sure, my dad, watching my feet, stepped on a loose rock and tumbled down the side of the trail. I heard bellowing noises as he fell, like a cow might sound when stuck in the mud. When he finally stopped, he brushed himself off and trudged, huffing and puffing, up the embankment to the trail. Realizing he wasn't hurt, I laughed and said, "Dad, you're kind of a klutz." But a few minutes later it was my turn. In a narrow section, I stepped on loose, sloping gravel and bounced down the side embankment, my dad bouncing on his belly behind me, his one hand clutching a wad of my T-shirt, the other still holding his video camera high in the air. Mark and Eddi, with a plain view of us from their vantage point atop the next rise, laughed and slapped their knees. Since Dad and I were already tired, the slow steep crawl up to the trail, with the sound of mocking applause in the distance, was anything but funny.

As the day wore on, cuts and bruises compounded our tiredness, and our patience waned. After the next tumble, I said angrily, "Dad, you pulled me right off the trail."

"Erik, do you know I can't even get one foot on the trail?"

"Fine!" I said. "Let's just keep going."

"Fine with me," my dad said.

For the rest of the afternoon my dad gave crisp directions and I followed them carefully but silently.

When the day was finally through, and we'd washed in a nearby stream, satisfied our thirst, and replenished our bellies, I sat alone feeling terrible. My dad had eagerly gone along with my idea to come to Peru. He could have been ambling along at his own pace, enjoying the beautiful scenery and filming every child, alpaca, and rock tower to his heart's content, but instead he had done his best to steer me and talk me through a maze of unending obstacles. I almost cried when I thought about how selfish I had been and how I had made his already difficult job even more difficult. Before retiring into our tents, I shuffled around in the dirt near my dad and then said haltingly, "Sorry about this afternoon. I know you were doing your best."

"I'm sorry I got angry," my dad replied. "I was just a little tired."

As I knelt down in front of my tent and unzipped the door, I could still hear my dad's breathing nearby. "I hope you're having a good time," I said.

"A great time," he answered happily. "I think I got some real good footage today."

The next morning, in the early warmth of the sun, my dad woke us all up with his typical "Wake up, boys, and smell that fresh air. Rise and shine like the morning sun!"

Mark responded grumpily with, "Rise and shine like an alpaca's butt."

My dad's bravado rested a little shy of the pretend bugle playing of our childhood. We were older now, Eddi and I young men, and Mark in his late twenties. My dad figured, rightly so, his bugle playing might prompt Mark to back up his wise-crack responses with a flying pile of alpaca dung.

Eventually, after completing three mountain passes in five days, the highest at almost fourteen thousand feet, we descended the thousands of stone steps into Machu Picchu. Some steps, laid by the Incas so many years ago, were so steep and broken up, I sat down on my butt and crab-walked down. From this entranceway, a gap in the mountain called the Gate of the Sun, I could hear the huge valley open below me and, to my surprise, some two thousand feet away, I actually heard the laughter and yells of tourists exploring the slopes below. We spent the day at the ruins, appreciating the Incas' sophisticated ideas and technology. The temples were built so soundly, I couldn't squeeze a fingernail in-between the granite stones. Machu Picchu was an explorer's paradise, and I thought of my mother, of Hong Kong and other romantic, exotic places that had inspired those who had stumbled upon them for the first time.

The Inca Trail began a tradition in my family. Each summer we continued to visit remote parts of the world, usually in the mountains, where local people are still relatively untouched by modern civilization. Sadly for my dad, the baton as my trekking partner passed to Mark for reasons of his amazing agility and much greater endurance. Mark and I quickly developed into an efficient team. We could now push on much faster, as Mark gave me the smooth middle trail to walk on while he took the steep edge of the mountain, never faltering. Since our first trip to Machu Picchu, the treks became even more difficult; we crossed the several-mile-wide Boltera Glacier in the Karakoram range in Pakistan, the largest glacier in Asia, leaping from one huge boulder to another, with black ice creating an extra hazard for us the whole way. Often it was Mark's jumping ability that helped get us to our next rock, and his strong hold on me that kept us there. Together we developed our own hiking language; "baby goat trail" meant a trail with a drop-off on one or both sides, in which I had to place one foot directly in front of the other. "Shin-buster" meant protruding rock in the trail; and different balls—football, basketball—described the size of the rocks ahead.

Although our days were spent trekking over some of the most beautiful and remote regions of the world, the nights often rivaled the mountain experience. In the remote villages of northern Spain, Mark, Eddi, and I visited the local cantinas. Late into the night and after several samples of the local spiced wine, I watched Mark make himself at home at a table of villagers. Soon Mark and the local patrons were all singing and laughing and swaying back and forth with their arms around shoulders as if they had been friends for decades. After several more toasts, my two bodybuilder brothers, who dwarfed me and everyone else, began dancing to the exotic local music, with me in the middle, swinging my entire body back and forth. First Mark would hook my elbow with his, spin me around, and catapult me across the dance floor to Eddi, whose elbow would catch me, spin me around, and catapult me back. Their so-called dance with their little brother continued through a dozen songs, and I felt like I was the victim of a midget-tossing contest, bouncing from Eddi to Mark, and Mark to Eddi. It was well into the early morning before I found myself stumbling into bed, my dad rolling over and grumbling something about the day's hard trek ahead.

Mark stayed up even later than Eddi and me, and at dawn, from my window, I heard our guides dragging my stumbling, boisterous brother into the refugio. Mark's loud voice echoed through the quiet streets. The guides had found Mark in the bar hitting on a local's girlfriend. They had brought him home before it was too late. "Americano loco," they said, rolling their eyes.

While in the mountains, after seeing me hike, local villagers and shepherds wondered, often aloud, why a blind person would choose to subject himself to such misery, and thought me an oddity. The guides who watched Mark and me work day after day marveled at our teamwork, but they were most impressed by Mark's incredible attention and patience. "The blind man is very good," one porter said with respect and puzzlement, "but the brother's love is more good. The brother is loco in village," he continued, rolling his eyes and circling his pointer finger around his temple, "but his love makes him a gentleman of the mountains."

Several years after we began our trips, we decided to travel to the remote highlands of Irian Jaya, a huge island near Australia. A territory of Indonesia, Irian Jaya was inhabited by Yali tribesmen, all cannibals up until the midsixties, and I had heard one of the Rockefellers had disappeared there, most likely winding up in a stew. Before flying Cessna planes from the last outpost, Wamena, Mark and I walked into the market. Much of it was roofed by a large thatch, with the insides dark enough to make Mark wonder just what things were. He turned to me and described the scene in a hushed tone. Small dark women and men squatted in the dirt selling pineapples and bananas. Strips of dried pork hung from the ceiling, resting places for flies. On one table lay a series of tools: axes and hoes with wooden handles and stone blades, the items looked over by Indonesians and a few western trekkers. Wamena was a place where two very different times in history met, and I wondered if this clash of cultures would benefit the local people or ultimately destroy them. The men were barefoot, the pads of their feet flat and as thick as the soles of our shoes. They wore nothing but long hollow gourds strapped over their penises. The women went topless, wearing six-inch grass flaps, placed over front and rear. For thirty years, Christian missionaries had been hard at work, persuading the people against cannibalism, but also drawing them away from their traditional dress. Every tenth local, instead of grass skirt or penis gourd, wore western shorts and T-shirts with pictures of Mickey Mouse and Pepsi logos. The Indonesians were also hard at work selling the Yali's sacred land to giant foreign companies interested in ripping old growth timber from the area and cutting the tops off of mountains to extract copper.

Our small plane bounced down on a grass airstrip on the outskirts of the small mountain village of Koserack. Mark's first words outside of the plane worried me. "Wow, this is freaking me out. They're all staring at us and they don't look very friendly. Holy shit. This could be it. Maybe we only think this is a family vacation, but really we're the main course." In the village, we were greeted by the chief, who wore a three-foot penis gourd, much longer than anyone else's. That set off an endless string of gourd jokes from Mark that lasted the entire trip. "Hey Erik, careful, that little dude behind you's trying to poke you with his gourd."

"Erik, this guy's gourd's so long, it's dangling over the campfire."

He even nicknamed our porters, Gordy, Gordon, and Gordo, according to the length of their gourds.

For the next two weeks we crossed the high rain forest, over rushing rivers on fallen tree-limb bridges, and descended steep cliffs on hundred-foot rickety trellises used by the Yali. When the path was easy,

Mark would say, "Easy cruiser ahead as far as I can see," and I'd forget concentrating for a while and we'd just amble along.

"So, if these people decided to become cannibals again," I asked Mark, "who out of our family would they catch first?"

At some earlier point, Mark must have taken time to ponder this very subject, because, with no hesitation, he launched right in. "You'd definitely go first. They'd catch you in about two seconds, you stumble-bumbling along. Dad wouldn't last much longer than you, bumble-clodding along. They'd catch him in about five seconds. Next, Eddi. He's too big and muscley to run very fast. He'd wear out quick. I'd give him about ten seconds. And me . . . well, I'd probably make it. Eddi'd feed the whole village for a month, and that'd give me time to haul ass. I'd hide in trees, live off the land. It would only be a matter of time before I'd become the leader of the tribe, because I've got the biggest gourd."

One day we had been traveling over a rolling trail on which the topsoil had been washed away by the spring rains. The trail now consisted of exposed roots with radically different shapes and sizes, jutting out at different angles, all slippery with rain. At least twenty times an hour, I would take a step and slip several feet through the network of roots, landing on the uneven forest floor or squishing knee deep in mud. Only occasionally would I land squarely on my feet. Usually, my twisting flailing body, trying desperately to recover, would crash down, perhaps a foot touching first but then knees and shins, and sometimes elbows. I was scraped and gashed from ankles to thighs, and my arms weren't much better. At moments like these, and these were most moments in the mountains, I hated hiking. I couldn't imagine anything worse or more difficult. I was mostly mad at myself for agreeing to come on the trip in the first place. After hiking all day, I was sure if I could see, I probably could have looked back and seen where I had left from that morning. For others, this was a vacation, but for me it was miserable, unforgiving labor. The hunters we encountered along the way, who ran across sharp rocks in their bare feet and climbed seventy-five-foot trees as quickly as a panther, must have puzzled over this young blind foreigner clumsily stumbling and crashing down the rough trail. When I'd hear them nearby, I'd force myself to smile and hide my misery.

Late in the afternoon, without too much progress, I asked Mark, who was trying to guide me through the impossible maze of roots and mud, "Is it really hard to guide me?"

Mark was almost ten years older than me. He owned an aquatic lakescaping business in Orlando, Florida, which meant frequent twelve-hour days of back-breaking work, standing waist deep in murky lakes and retention ponds, hauling away huge loads of imported plant life carelessly set free into the lake system and now choking off native species. "I could do this all day long," he replied. "Compared to hauling a thousand pounds of Maluka trees, guiding you's a breeze. Actually, wait a minute. What the hell am I saying? . . . I have done this all day long, and I did it all day yesterday too, and the day before. That's it. I'm ditching your sorry ass." His voice revved into high animation as he shook my shoulders roughly.

Then as we struggled silently forward, I sensed Mark was in deep thought. Softly, Mark said, "You know, Erik, if there was some kind of operation to get your sight back, I swear to God, I'd give you one of my eyes. I wouldn't think twice. Then, I'd have one and you'd have one. We'd walk side by side. You'd check out the topless babes on the right, and I'd check 'em out on the left. But, if they're cute, I get first dibs." I knew Mark meant what he said, on both counts.

An hour later Mark and I realized at our present slow pace, we would not make it into camp before dark. Mark asked our guide, Rudy, "Any problem with hiking in the dark?"

"Panthers hunt at night," he responded. "I will help." He blew into a horn and the deep sound echoed through the jungle. Soon, Yali porters were running up the trail toward us. I felt like I was in a Tarzan movie. They took out knives and began cutting down small bamboo trees and lashing large elephant leaves and vines through them. Before long, they had erected a makeshift hammock. "They want me to get in that thing?"

I laughed in shock. "They might drop me." Rudy translated my concern and a Yali replied, "He will be easy to carry. He is much lighter than a large sack of yams."

As the Yali team lifted me up on their shoulders and began to chatter back and forth in high, quick voices, Mark said, "Erik, I'm serious. These aren't our guides. I don't recognize a single one."

"Come on, Mark," I pleaded, "I know you're just joking around."

"These guys are total strangers," Mark insisted, allowing his voice to grow frantic. "I think this was all a ploy to get you tied up."

"Shut up, jerk!" I shot back, trying unsuccessfully to free my arms from the tightly lashed vines.

As the Yali began running with me on their shoulders, Mark called out behind me, "As long as I live, I won't forget you, little brother." From my hammock, I could feel we were flying at breakneck speed over the treacherous trail. Many times I heard crashing, foaming rivers churning below and knew they were carrying me over slippery tree-limb bridges. Please don't let them drop me, especially in the crocodile-infested river, I thought. Mark scampered along behind us, barely keeping up, snapping pictures and singing a parody to "She'll be Coming Round the Mountain." His version went, "They'll be carrying him over the mountain, when he comes."

A few days later, as we approached Anganook, horns blared and villagers ran hours from far distant places to gather under a large thatched roof, two hundred people in all. The women sat on one side, clad only in their grass "flaps"; their children beside them, bellies extended by undernourishment and disease. The men sat opposite, bedecked only in penis gourds, some a mere eight inches but others a curved, rather exotic three feet. My family, Rudy, and I sat very quietly in the back, wearing shorts and hiking boots, and not knowing at all what to expect. A high priest, brilliantly bedazzled in body paint and with colorful bird feathers in his hair, spoke in local dialect while Rudy translated: "Today we sit proudly with a blind man who has come many days across our mountains. We would never have thought such a journey was possible. The blind people of our villages sit in their huts and weave baskets. Maybe we have something to learn from this blind man. Maybe there is a better way for the blind people of the Yali."

Listening intently to the words, I realized that scrambling over boulder fields and sludging across glaciers took on a greater meaning than I had originally thought. That although I was blind, and probably would be forever, I had the ability to teach those around me, not by my words or my intentions, but by my actions. Afterwards, I smiled sheepishly as the village priest presented me with an honorary penis gourd. It was much longer than I needed.

# 8
# Perceptions

After graduating from college, I made the big move across the Charles River to Cambridge. I was completing a masters program in education at night and working as an assistant teacher during the day. My last year in Cambridge had been lonely. My college friends had all moved away to take jobs, so I filled my life with teaching, going to school, guitar lessons, kung fu—anything that kept me busy. I only noticed my loneliness when I didn't have something to do, particularly at night, if I was eating dinner alone or when the building would grow silent on a Friday night. It became clear to me that something was wrong when I had been dating a girl from my class for a few weeks and I invited her to my dad's home in Connecticut for the weekend. "I'd go with you," she said, "but it's not me you want; it's just anyone." She was right. I was just tired of having no one to share things with.

Besides being lonely, I was broke. My dad was paying for my schooling and apartment, and I felt like a sponge. I was twenty-two years old, and it was high time I became self-sufficient and began making a contribution to society. So, I decided to look for a weekend job. Not only would a job give me some spending money, but it would also help me to meet new people. A friend told me about a fancy hotel in Harvard Square that was looking for weekend help, and I promptly sent off a resume: Boston College, 3.1 grade point, double major, wrestling team, writer of articles for BC's literary magazine, certified scuba diver, officer of BC's Freshman Assistance Program. I got a quick response by phone. The supervisor had a front-desk job for me, and she wanted me to start the next Friday evening. I had landed my first real paying job on my own, and I called my dad excitedly to let him know. On Friday night I went with Wizard to the hotel to meet the manager. I was greeted by the desk clerk, who then disappeared for a long time, and finally returned with the manager. Before they approached me, they stood together thirty feet away, mumbling back and forth. The manager asked me to come into her office, where she nervously explained that the job was no longer open, that the previous desk clerk had unexpectedly decided to stay. I didn't really believe her. There was a jumpiness in her voice, and she was almost too apologetic. "Is there anything else I could do?" I asked, "like be a bellboy or a cleanup person?" But despite her apologies, she didn't think I'd be able to do anything that was available. At the end of our short conversation, she said, "By the way—that was a little unfair of you to not tell me you were blind. You put us all on the spot."

"Honestly," I replied, "I didn't think it mattered. I could have done the job." What was the point of telling her I had spent three hundred dollars on a machine that would read me people's credit card numbers? A few days later, my classmate and I walked by the hotel, and he told me about the help-wanted sign still posted on the door.

For the next two weeks I looked for work at dozens of local businesses, with no success. Most people were nice, but no job materialized. Discouraged, I finally resolved that I would take a dishwasher job, something I was sure I could easily do. It was hot work, the pay was lousy, and kids were quitting all the time for better opportunities. On Saturday, I woke up early and walked up and down Harvard Square with a Braille list of restaurants with their addresses. The first place I tried was a big restaurant with a large kitchen. The owner was polite but explained that the kitchen was too big. "You'd lose your way," he said. "There are dozens of cupboards. You'd never remember where to put things away." Next, I tried a small pizza parlor, where I had eaten two days before. The manager felt the kitchen was so cramped that I would just bump into things and cause confusion as servers hurried through the kitchen, carrying large heavy trays. Sitting on a brick wall outside the pizza place, I put my hand on my chin and thought about their worries. My gut told me they were unfounded, but how could I be completely positive? I had never been a dishwasher. I did know that there were plenty of people with few skills and no education who wouldn't even take a dishwasher's job because they felt it was beneath them. I, on the other hand, was willing and eager for the chance to work, for the opportunity to sponge off people's dirty dishes. Wasn't it something I could learn, like I had learned in high school to navigate with my tray through the cafeteria and learned to give tours of the Boston College campus with Wizard, even pointing out specific landmarks to the astonishment of my groups? As I walked toward a third restaurant, I told myself the last two restaurants were flukes and this would be the one. I made sure to try a medium-sized restaurant this time, but the owner brought me into the kitchen and showed me the belt that moved dishes into the washing area. "It's very easy to break those dishes as they come off the tray, and besides, you might burn your hand on a hot pan." Then I knew he wasn't going to offer me a job and must have shown disappointment on my face, because he said, "I'm sorry, son, but sometimes, you just have to realize your limitations."

Too big, too small, too fast, too hot, like a twisted version of the three bears—the story repeated itself again and again. I had thought somehow, that with my force of will, with my ingenuity, with my tenacity, I could eventually win people over and get what I wanted out of life. I hadn't realized there were doors that would remain locked in front of me. I wanted so badly to break through, to take a battering ram to them, to bash them into a million splinters, but the doors were locked too securely and their surfaces were impenetrable. I never got a dishwasher job that year in Cambridge, but I did choke down an important lesson, that people's perceptions of our limitations are more damaging than those limitations themselves, and it was the hardest lesson I ever had to swallow.

A few weeks later, while walking to the store, I heard the jingle of a dog collar in front of me and then heard a lady's strained voice. "Left! Straight! No! I said straight!" She exhaled in frustration. I figured it was a blind lady walking with her guide dog. What were the chances, I wondered, of two blind people with their two guide dogs crossing the street at the same time and place? Their meeting is such a coincidence, a special connection exists before they even meet. I reached the top of the curb and Wizard stopped. The lady was already crossing, but something was wrong. I heard the jingling collar zigzagging around the road and could hear a car approaching fast. I thought about rushing out, and then I heard the screech of tires as a driver desperately lay on the brakes. Then it was silent, except for the slow hiss of exhaust escaping from the engine. I imagined the driver inside letting out a deep breath and sinking back into his seat, knowing that he had narrowly escaped splattering a blind lady all over the road. Then he opened his door and rushed to her side. "Can I help you?" the driver asked, and before hearing her response, rushed her across the street. When the car had driven away and the street was silent, I darted across and caught up to her.

"Hello!" I said, extending a hand. Two blind people shaking hands is a little tricky. You can't see each other's hands hovering in front, so I put my hand out and lightly poked. When she felt my hand, she grabbed it and softly shook it. Then I blurted out, "I live in the neighborhood. I'm blind too. I have a German shepherd guide dog." She told me her name was Laura and we talked about our guide dogs for a while and she told me that hers was not working out. "First of all, she doesn't cross streets very well."

The next time I came across Laura, she was heading to the grocery store and wasn't sure how to get there, so I walked with her. This time, Laura walked with a tall white cane. We had to cross one major highway. Cars were merging from many strange directions. It was a typical Boston road, twisting and turning and overlapping with other roads. Only the first section had a traffic light. I had had trouble crossing it once before. Now I had to get both of us across safely. When I heard the cars stopping, Laura took my arm and we started walking. I imagined the amused stares of the drivers stopped at the light and I knew we were providing them with a convenient joke to tell the guys at the office about the blind leading the blind. When Laura and I got to the island, Wizard weaved us around a shrub and a pole and we crossed the next section, stopping and starting as cars whizzed by in front and behind. When we finally reached the last curb, Wizard, sensing the end to his extra responsibility, paused for a second before leaping up onto the unusually tall curb. I felt his leap and barely managed to clear the curb with my foot, but Laura wasn't so fortunate. She tripped and sprawled on her belly, half on the road, half on the curb. Her cane flailed out of her hand and clattered down the street. My mind was screaming out in misdirected pain, not for Laura, who I knew was OK, but for my knowledge of all the people who were surely witnessing this display. As I pulled her up, I prayed no Good Samaritan would rush out to save us. Luckily her cane was not too far away and I found it accidentally by stepping on it, bending it slightly. I felt like I had set the blind movement back fifty years. The beauty of being blind, however, is that since you can't see anyone, it's possible to convince yourself that they can't see you either.

Periodically I would come out of my apartment and hear Laura arguing with her dog. Laura's guide dog was a cute little golden retriever, but she would do her own thing—sniff crotches, eat banquet wieners off buffet tables, run off down the street when she was supposed to be "getting busy." Once Laura asked me to join her for lunch at the local Chinese restaurant. The owner was flustered, seeing two blind people with guide dogs walking toward his restaurant. He was somehow convinced that we and our dogs could not fit through the front door or down the four stairs which led into the restaurant, so he led us around to the side of the restaurant and pulled open a huge garage door used for grocery trucks. Hearing the giant door rolling up, I couldn't erase the mortified grin off my face. The owner, an older Chinese man, was so friendly and sincere that I just didn't have the heart to straighten out his misperceptions about blindness. He wanted to help, he just had no idea how. There are times when a person needs to stand up and assert his rights, but there are also times when it just isn't worth it, when an amused smile and a shrug are enough for the time being. I knew the next time I came in, I would simply walk through the door and down the stairs before he could react. That would accomplish more than a lecture.

"Much better for you," the owner said graciously as he proudly ushered us inside. He had a waitress read us the menu. Mindy, Laura's guide dog, must have shown great interest in the plates of food passing near us, because the owner returned and said happily, "Dog look hungry. He like chicken wing? Good chicken wing." Laura replied emphatically "No. He's a guide dog, a working dog." But the language barrier must have been too much for the overly anxious man. Ten minutes later, as Laura and I enjoyed a great meal, I heard chomping and slurping from under the table. I was pretty sure it wasn't Laura. I bent over and reached under the table. I felt Wizard's head lying obediently against the wall, but a few feet to the left I felt a heaping plate of chicken wings with Mindy's head attached. She was quietly chomping away at the wings, enjoying her own feast. She licked my hand, imploring me to keep her secret.

After several outings, Laura invited me over for a night of Braille board games. She had Braille Monopoly, Braille backgammon, Braille Yahtzee, and Braille Scrabble. We played a lot of scrabble. While it was her turn, I'd sneak in letters on the board to form dirty words. I thought she didn't notice but later her fingers would come across my extra additions, and she'd laugh. During one game she told me that she wanted to be the first blind talk-show host. "The first blind Oprah," she joked. I didn't see it as a joke, however. I had heard she was beautiful, was well-dressed; she had a smooth TV voice and was articulate. I thought she had a good shot at it. She had earned an internship at a major talk show, but the host was worried that Laura's big guide dog would scare her own little dog who often sat in her lap on the set. The producer had told Laura that the job was hers as long as she didn't bring her dog, but Laura had quietly turned down the internship. She seemed satisfied to wait for her big break. "I'm just waiting for a few more weeks," she said. "A friend of mine might have a job for me at a radio station, and there's a cable TV job I'm waiting on." I couldn't fathom why she didn't choose to fight for the internship that seemed so vital to what she wanted out of her life.

I knew, though, Laura was a fighter. She'd told me how she began to go blind when she was eighteen. The doctors were baffled because her eyes seemed to be working perfectly and, then, when it was almost too late, they discovered the problem was in her brain. She had had a massive brain tumor that was destroying the part of her brain that processed vision. In removing the tumor, they had to remove a part of her brain. Laura had to learn how to walk and talk all over again. Although I didn't notice, she told me she still slurred her speech a little bit. Laura had fought and won the battle for her life, but she didn't know how to wage this new kind of battle when the enemy was not as obvious as a brain tumor, when the enemy was elusive.

Weeks went by and Laura was still waiting for her big break. She was on social security and her apartment was paid for by the state, but she didn't have enough money to go places and do things. Most Friday nights, I'd head to the Chinese restaurant for takeout, next door to the bakery for cheesecake, and then to Laura's house for an evening of Scrabble. Laura would keep the window open, and I could hear the sound of traffic and people walking to restaurants and bars in Harvard Square. I felt like I was missing something, like there was something beyond cheesecake and Chinese takeout, and Braille Scrabble on Friday nights. I didn't want my life to be a waiting game, hoping for the right circumstances that would propel my life into fulfillment. I was ready for a change.

* * *

I was about to graduate and my teaching job was ending for the year. It was a perfect time for a move. A change in location doesn't necessarily change your life, but the excitement of it gives the mind some extra motivation. As I took a train to the New York City school job fair, I knew that if offered a job someplace new and exciting, I would take it. At the conference, independent schools from all around the country were recruiting graduates from East Coast schools. Many of my interviewers felt like my blindness created insurmountable problems. One such interviewer asked a series of questions: "How would you keep up with grading papers?"

"I could have my students read me their essays aloud, and I could speak my comments on a tape, or they could hand me a computer disk."

"Well, what about textbooks and all the literature you have to read?"

"I'd read them in Braille or on tape."

"How would you keep classroom management?"

"When kids are fooling around, usually they're just talking, and who better than a blind person to hear talking?"

"How would you . . . ? How would you . . . ?" I tried to stay positive, but no matter how I responded, he kept repeating, "I don't know. I just don't know." As soon as the interview ended, he rushed over to my chair, hauled me up under the armpit with his forearm, and began dragging me toward the door. "Really," I tried to mutter. "I can walk," but I probably wasn't forceful enough, because I really wanted the job. Wizard was puzzled, trailing along behind us on his leash. I was practically walking on my tiptoes, with his strong arm hiking me up and pressing me against his shoulder. Toward the end of the interview, he had been strangely silent. Now I realize he probably wasn't even listening to what I was saying but, rather, racking his brain over the problem of how he would get me to the door and rescue me from tripping over a chair. How did he think I had gotten to the interview in the first place? How did he think I had gotten to New York? How did he think I had gotten from my friend's apartment, where I was staying, to the lobby of the hotel, or did he think someone had hiked me under the armpit all the way from Boston to the threshold of his cubicle? Outside his door, I shook his hand, a little bewildered, rubbed my armpit that had gone numb from his forearm pressure, took Wizard's harness, and walked down the hallway to my next interview.

A handful of interviewers thought my blindness could perhaps be an asset. "What an interesting proposition," one principal said. "You're definitely qualified, and besides teaching English and math, I can imagine all the extras you can teach our students." When the conference was over, surprisingly, I had five job offers, more than most of my sighted classmates.

I visited several schools. One school was in Charlotte. It was located on a huge, green campus with beautiful fields, old Victorian buildings, and an indoor swimming pool where the Olympic team had practiced. It seemed perfect, but I needed an adventure. I had lived on the East Coast nearly all my life. I wanted to go to a place I knew little about, a place so different that even simple things like finding the grocery store or the barbershop would be an adventure. By forcing myself to step out of my comfort zone, I'd enable my mind to learn and grow. I sensed that a new exploration would make my life exciting again. I wanted to go west.

I had a friend who had gone to school in Phoenix. He'd come home for Christmas talking about sunshine and an apartment complex with a giant pool surrounded by women in thongs. I imagined the raging Colorado River, the Grand Canyon, the amazing volcanic pinnacles jutting out of the desert floor.

I was offered a job at a tiny but prestigious school called Phoenix Country Day School. Peg Madden, the head of the school and the one who hired me, later shared with me the reason why I was offered the job. "Your resume was excellent. Your grades were excellent. You were articulate and you had good ideas for your classroom, but I still had reservations," she told me. "A teacher has to do more than look good on paper. They have to be able to handle the responsibility of a classroom full of kids. What really sold me was something that happened after the

New York interview was over. I had asked you if you needed help to the lobby door, but you had replied no. I was doubtful that you could find it. You had to go up the conference stairs, past the elevators, down a hallway to the left, to the front desk and down some stairs. I had followed you because I thought you still might need help, but you and your dog found it beautifully. Wizard had even pointed his nose at the door handle. Your finding the door through that maze was more real for me than anything you could have said. That's when I knew you could do the job."

Everybody can look back at a few choices that they make in life, choices in the face of countless possibilities. Some of these choices, like my move to Phoenix, turn out to be catalysts that shape your life in ways you may not have expected.

# 9
# Thirty Sets of Eyes

On my first morning of school at the Phoenix Country Day School, I stood in my empty classroom, listening to the bustle of fifth graders congregating out in the hall and crowding in to look at their homeroom placements. I heard hands clap together and a student yell out excitedly, "Alright! I got the blind guy. Who'd you get?" Maybe, I thought, after I gave him his first homework assignment, I'd become just another mean teacher. I had been working in the classroom all weekend, hanging up posters, stacking the bookshelves with paperbacks and board games, and organizing teaching supplies. I had arranged desks into six groups of four, separated by little pathways crisscrossing between the clusters, so I could quickly and easily get to each student. As the bell rang and all the kids piled in, I called out their seat assignments.

"Do we have to sit in assigned seats?"

"Last year Mrs. Johnson didn't make us sit in assigned seats."

"Can I sit next to Billy? He's my best friend."

Each high prepubescent voice sounded exactly like the next. The students melded into an indistinguishable lump of chirping chipmunks. As I scanned over my Braille seating chart, trying to match voices to names, I didn't think I would ever be able to tell them apart. I couldn't even tell the boys from the girls. What an insult it would be if I said, "Tiffany, can you pass out those papers?" "I'm not Tiffany. Can't you tell I'm a boy?" I winced at the thought.

Mixing up genders wasn't my only worry. Throughout the whole spring and summer, I had lain awake at night with a dozen unanswered questions tumbling restlessly around in my head. During my interviews, I had talked a good game, because I knew it would have been suicide not to. I had bluffed solutions to every difficult question, but the bluffs had been like helium in a balloon, and now as I stood in front of a classroom full of living, breathing, chattering kids, the helium rushed out and the balloon came crashing down. My talking computers, Braille writers, and cassette tapes would handle the reading, writing, and researching part, but what about the teaching? How would I call on students without seeing them raise their hands? How would I be able to tell when kids were fooling around? How would I write on the blackboard? I had struggled for answers. Kids had dozens of questions about their schedules, classes, and school supplies, and for so many years they had been trained by other teachers to raise their hands. Theoretically, they knew I was blind, but couldn't seem to make the connection between their straining arm raised high in the air and the reason I hadn't called on them. "How many of you have your hand raised?" I asked. At least half the class said yes, and I heard the whoosh of air as a few raised their hands in the affirmative. "Put your hand down, stupid. He can't see it," I heard a voice whisper. "I'll make a promise to you," I said. "If you raise your hands, I won't call on you. So, I have an idea. Instead, if you want to speak, say your name and I'll call on you." Fifth graders are adaptable, so they charged eagerly ahead with this new plan, but I was battered by an uninterrupted explosion of screaming names. "Billy! Billy! Billy! Billy! Billy!" As soon as one student finished speaking, twenty other voices would begin firing. "Tiffany, Tiffany, Tiffany, Tiffany."

"Brian, Brian, Brian, Brian."

"Berry, Berry, Berry, Berry."

Well before the forty-minute class ended, I knew that little experiment had been a whopping failure.

A week before school started, I had gone to a toy store and bought bagfuls of two-inch-high Fisher-Price plastic letters with magnetic strips so they would stick to a blackboard: twenty-six sets of letters, ten sets of numbers, a variety of punctuation symbols, and mathematical symbols. On two desks near the board, I had forty-five plastic bins, one for each number, letter, and symbol. If I wanted to write a sentence or a mathematical equation on the board, I would select what I needed from the right bins, but in math I fumbled through the bins, trying to arrange an equation on the board. I couldn't seem to find the equal sign. Maybe it was on the other desk? I tried not to look frantic in front of all the eyes, as my fingers searched through the bins. There it was. It had somehow fallen into the plus symbol bin. And now, where was the six? Its bin wasn't where it was supposed to be, between the five and seven. Instead, I snatched up a nine and turned it upside down. I found the subtraction sign quickly and slapped it into the equation, but a student immediately called out, "Mr. Weihenmayer, that's not a minus sign. That's a number one." As I finally got the equation in place on the board, I heard a student yawn in the back of the room. When class ended, I flopped down in my desk chair, worn out from the demonstration of three equations. With all the time spent finding the right bin, how would I possibly have time to teach?

After class, I sat behind my desk, leaning back in my chair and recovering from the exhausting game of musical bins, when a student opened the door and stood in front of my desk. His voice was Guru Dharam's, a student whose family belonged to the Sikh religious community, a practice that had its start five hundred years ago in northern India. "I have a problem," he stated. "Don't get me wrong, I'm proud of my religion, but I'm a little embarrassed because I'm the only boy in the fifth grade who wears a turban."

"Well, let's help the other kids understand why," I replied. The next day, Guru held a Sikh show-and-tell. All the kids were fixated on the antique spears, swords, and artifacts possessed by powerful gurus of years past and used in the fierce holy wars. At the end of the demonstration, Guru stood up in front of his classmates, raised both hands to his head, and whipped off his turban. Brown wavy hair spilled down, down, down, and finally rested on the backs of his knees. One of the Sikh practices is never cutting the hair. The kids let out a collective gasp, followed by exclamations of "Cool," and "Awesome."

The next day at recess groups of boys, wearing toilet paper turbans, engaged in pretend sword battles, and throughout the fall, it became the trend to grow hair a little bit longer. Guru had pulled off an amazing feat. He had feared his differences would be viewed as weaknesses, so he had forged them into strengths. Blindness had always seemed to me like a weakness for which I was always compensating, but I wondered if Guru's lesson could be applied to my struggle.

The next morning before English class, I began fumbling through the bins to form some sentences on the board. Instead of having only ten numbers and a few symbols to contend with, now, I had twenty-six bins of letters, plus punctuation. As the kids rushed into the room, a little girl came right up to me and said, "Can I write on the board today? I have very neat handwriting. Plus, between you and me, those little plastic numbers, they aren't working out."

"OK," I replied. And as I began dictating a few sentences to her, I realized that the solution to the board problem and many others was right in front of me, but I had been blinded by my own preconceptions. When I wanted to accomplish a task, I first studied the way the sighted world accomplished that same task and then created a system, which resembled theirs as closely as possible. If a sighted teacher normally stood in front of the board independently writing out sentences and equations, then I would stand in front independently arranging ridiculous plastic symbols; if sighted teachers required students to raise their hands before being called on, then I would have them speak their names before being called on, even if their shrill cries blew holes in my eardrums. In order to transform blindness from a compensated weakness to an actual strength, I needed to take the next step and throw out—like Guru's turban—my preconditioned notions of the way classrooms are supposed to be run and launch myself into a radically new environment, built from the ground up.

Whenever I asked a question or needed something done, kids immediately responded with, "I'll get it!" "I'll do it!" "I see it!" In front of me were thirty sets of perfectly working eyes and hands, brains included. The kids could write on the board, hang posters, pass out papers, correct each other's quizzes, and if I grew really lazy, they could fill Wizard's water dish. None of my students ever saw these tasks as mundane but as special. When one of them stood in front of their classmates holding a piece of chalk, it immersed them in the learning process, gave them unprecedented responsibility, and helped them to become leaders. As far as raising hands or calling out their names, I threw these out too. In my class, kids would simply speak, with a few rules of course; they couldn't speak when others spoke and their ideas had to relate to our discussion.

After giving the students an overview of the year, I asked if anyone had questions, but their curiosity wasn't focused on English. First, they wanted to know all about Wiz, who throughout the day lay patiently against the classroom wall. I explained that when Wizard wore his leather harness, he was considered on duty, which meant the kids couldn't pet or play with him. "It's like the story of *Dr. Jekyll and Mr. Hyde*. While he's on duty, he shows his mature responsible side, but when that harness goes off," I paused and put a sinister edge on my voice, "he goes into dog mode."

More questions followed and some even caught me off guard. "How do you find your mouth with your fork?"

"How do you brush your teeth?"

"When you drive, does Wizard steer?" That one made everyone laugh.

Then one asked, "How do you play basketball?" I had answers for most, but this one stumped me. I hadn't played basketball since I had gone blind. In front of them I wanted to sound strong and confident, as if there was nothing I couldn't achieve, but I didn't want to lie either. So finally, I said, "I don't know." Then kids jumped in eagerly, giving their own solutions. "I have an idea! Put something in the ball, so it makes noise."

"And something that makes noise on the hoop."

"Wear a face mask, so the ball doesn't hit you in the face."

"And blindfold all the other players."

"Not bad," I responded. "Maybe this is the beginning of a professional blind basketball league."

Over the first two weeks, I strained bits of information from my students' voices and, slowly, individuals began to emerge from the homogeneity. Specific tones, inflections, and patterns in their speech, combined with the location of their voices in the room, gave me the clues I needed. I was actually surprised how much information I could gather from a voice, from its sound and texture, from its fluidity and inflection, from the words used and from the way a sentence is put together, from the subjects chosen to talk about and from the response to what others say. And as a teacher, I began to like it this way.

At lunch, I sat with a group of veteran fifth-grade teachers, chatting about students. I said, "Randy seems like a nice kid. He always asks me how my day is going and he helps the other kids with their work. Whenever he talks in class, his ideas are pretty sophisticated for a boy his age."

"Did you know he's a little chubby?" another teacher responded, as if she were filling me in on the complete picture, the missing pieces of the puzzle. "He has a bad habit of picking his nose in class. The other boys won't have anything to do with him."

"And what's with his T-shirts? They're about two sizes too small," another teacher added.

"The mother's no different. Her clothes look about ready for the

Goodwill pile. She never tucks in her blouse and her skirts are always wrinkled."

"Well, you know the apple doesn't fall far from the tree."

Their comments made me wonder if blindness impaired my judgments about students, but I refused to return to the concept of blindness as a weakness. If seeing my students meant they would go from charming, innocent, young people with promise and intelligence, to chubby, unfashionable nose pickers, then maybe I'd just remain blissfully ignorant. Maybe I wasn't getting the complete picture, but I would be happy to settle for only half, as long as it was the good half.

After that lunch, blindness was never again a weakness in my classroom. In a math unit, I incorporated Braille, using the spatial patterns of the dots to teach logical reasoning. To create bonding among classmates, I arranged the desks and chairs into an obstacle course and had each student, blindfolded and using a long white cane, navigate through, while others shouted out directions. A few months into the year, we even tried our hand at basketball using the ideas that my students had proposed. From a blindness catalog, I ordered a basketball with a jingling bell inside and a small beeping device to be hung from the basketball hoop. The students lay strips of tape over the painted lines of the court, so they could feel for themselves when they were in the key. Wearing fencing helmets and blindfolds made of long gym socks, they played game after game of one on one. Although fiercely competitive, I didn't think these games would ever rival the NBA, but as I stood on the sideline listening to the beeping hoop, jingling ball, and the jostling, colliding fifth-grade bodies at play, I knew proudly that they had become problem solvers, finding solutions to a real problem in a real world that does not offer up solutions very easily.

# 10
# Blind Faith

In the early winter I sat on a bar stool at the 40th Street Grill drinking a beer with Rob, another teacher at the Phoenix Country Day School, when he said, "You know who you should go after? Ellen Reeve. She's got the most beautiful blue eyes and a very athletic body. Did you know she coaches the boys' soccer team?" I had set up the conversation brilliantly by asking Rob who the good-looking teachers were, not letting on that I was really most interested in Ellen. Little did I know that Ellen would be at the top of his list.

Rob had gone through the teachers, first highlighting the ones who wore miniskirts barely covering their thighs, next the Ivory girls with wholesome good looks, and finally the older babes who still showed traces of their former beauty. I told him the ones who I thought had hot voices: some with a rough sexy purr, others high pitched and chirpy, and still others rumbling and spit-firing their words quickly and articulately; and Rob would confirm or dispute. Some think that blind people do not care about looks, that we are above assessing one's desirability through surface beauty, but if that's the case, I proudly break the stereotype. I am as much a pig as any sighted guy. In fact, I take offense at those who would assume that just because I am blind I am supposed to be asexual. Blindness has little to do with the virtue or villainy of one's character. I can be just as shallow, but my shallowness comes from the voluptuous hum of a sexy voice or the electrifying grasp of a smooth supple hand.

It is embarrassing the desperate lengths I have gone to learn what a woman looks like while trying to keep alive her angelic impression of me. Once I met a woman on the train back to Boston. We had talked and laughed together the whole way home. She had a clear pleasant voice, but although the connection between a sexy voice and a shapely body is often accurate, it is still a big risk to proceed by the sound of a voice alone. At the end of the ride I had gotten the courage to ask her out. When at last I met her for our date, I shook her hand and was a little worried. She had not passed the hand test: short, fat, stubby fingers nine times out of ten means a short, fat, stubby body; and, now standing, I was aware of her voice projecting from a long way down. I arranged for us to go have pizza at Geo's Pizza in Harvard Square where my friend conveniently worked behind the counter. I shook his hand as I introduced her and knew, instantly, my growing alarm was well justified. He had shaken my hand with his fingers curled and cupped together, forcing my hand to curl and cup in return. He had given me the ugly shake and there was nothing for me to do but to finish out the date.

So, in the bar with Rob it was comforting to hear his approval of Ellen. Before Rob's visual assessment, I had been working solo, as usual, with only Ellen's voice to guide me—but, oh, what a voice. When I had interviewed for a job at Phoenix Country Day School, the principal had taken me to observe his showcase teachers at work. Ellen's classroom was the first stop. I sat in the back of her room in an undersized chair as Ellen briefly set up the activity. Her voice was smooth and soft, and if I hadn't been paying attention, I would have missed the subtle, dancing spark behind the calm. Her words didn't leap out at the students in rapid-fire bursts or rambling diatribes, but seemed to roll out of her mouth like music, or even better, a musical roller coaster, soaring and swooping through the room, up and then down, up and then down. Before long, her voice would grow quieter and it would sound like doves' wings rising up together, or like the muffled whisper of a cascading waterfall through a deep hidden forest. I scooted my chair up to a table full of sixth graders, listening to them discuss their project, but I was a sufficient distraction and they began firing questions at me.

"Where did I come from? Where did Wizard come from? Was I married?"

When Ellen came over, instead of doing the typical teacherly thing like asking the children to get back on task, she began asking questions too. It turned out, we had gone to the same teacher's college in Cambridge, had lived in the same broken down apartments, had walked the same streets, and had eaten in the same restaurants. She was as curious about me as the children. It was obvious that she didn't see herself as the supreme leader, but just another learner in the discovery process. The question "Are you married?" from a student posed a major dilemma. A guy in my graduate class had advised me to tell all interviewers that I was engaged. He said it would make me sound more stable, as though I were ready to set down roots and become a pillar in the community. So, I decided to stick to the game plan and blurted out, "I'm not married, but I'm engaged." I figured if I were hired, later I could say that it just hadn't worked out. Besides, it might even work to my advantage. I could explain that I had grown more sensitive and vulnerable through the whole torturous affair. I had been hurt to the very core but, for the right woman, I might just be ready to take a chance again.

The last few minutes of class, Ellen walked to the front of the room, sat down and began reading a story she had started in a previous class. The story was *The Little Prince,* and she read a part where the prince talked about a rare flower that grew on his planet and was in danger of being eaten by a sheep. "If someone loves a flower, of which just one single blossom grows in all the millions and millions of stars, it is enough to make him happy just to look at the stars. He can say to himself: 'Somewhere, my flower is there . . .' But if the sheep eats the flower, in one moment all his stars will be darkened." Her voice made the story sound beautiful, sad and playful all at once. Soon into the story, it wasn't as though she were reading anymore, but had started a video and we could see the little prince and hear his proud, pleading voice. I sat in the classroom praying that Ellen's physical appearance was as stunning as her essence. Despite the obvious problems with the voice/body connection, and with no trusted handshake to guide my feelings, in the back of Ellen's classroom that day, squeezed into a sixth grader's plastic chair, I couldn't help but fall hopelessly in love with a teacher who at first, at least, was only a voice.

When I was offered a job teaching English and math to fifth graders, I took it, perhaps partly because of Ellen and her class. I wanted to be the kind of teacher that she was, and to create a classroom like hers. In graduate school, a professor had compared teachers to coffeemakers. "Some stand above the students letting their knowledge and ideas trickle down into the minds of the students, but then there are those rare situations where the teacher and students all brew and percolate in the same pot." It was an intriguing idea: teacher and students discovering and evolving together, the teacher not a pedagogue but simply a facilitator, students not empty vessels, but important resources, bursting with ideas to contribute to the classroom. It was revolutionary and I had wondered if it could truly work, but experiencing Ellen's class, I was convinced. Ellen's classroom was the rarer kind of coffeemaker, and I decided that Phoenix Country Day School was the place I could learn to percolate the minds of my students too, and maybe even my own.

Often, in those warm autumn months, I kept my classroom door open to the Arizona sun and would hear people walking back and forth down the sidewalk. Eventually, I could identify people by their footsteps, and each of their heels told a story. Principal John Crabb's gait verged on a run. His flat-footed steps pounded the pavement and spoke of a dozen unwritten memos and another dozen unanswered parent phone calls. Most of the women administrators clip-clopped down the sidewalk in a precise high-heeled power walk. Their heels screamed with purpose: student financial aid to handle, scholarships to grant, textbooks to buy. "Get out of my way," they commanded, " 'cause I'm walking and there ain't no stopping me." Ellen would visit my classroom from time to time, and I would never hear her coming until she was already inside the room, pattering across the carpet toward my desk and asking in her soft voice, "How's your day going?" I never had any time to react. If she had been a clip-clopper, I would have heard her coming with enough time to re-gel my hair, dab on a little cologne, and put on a tie, but she glided silently like a panther, her soft muffled sound materializing just inside the doorway of my room.

Sometimes, Ellen would offer to give me a ride home, and even though I only lived a five-minute walk away, I never turned her down. Once, we sat parked in front of my apartment complex talking for an hour before Ellen said, "Do you want to go get a beer?" So we walked across the street to the 40th Street Grill. In the bar I ordered the beer on tap, but Ellen ordered a vodka tonic and, with that, I figured I had no chance. No one sophisticated enough to drink vodka tonics could ever be interested in me. I was a little intimidated. With greyhound races blaring over a dozen television screens, Ellen asked, "So, when are you getting married?" Ellen's simple question hit me like a hammer. I had forgotten about my little white lie.

"Uh!" I stuttered. I should have known that one would come back and bite me, I thought.

"Aren't you engaged?"

I thought about my prepared lines. Could I tell her I had broken it off only two months into the school year? That might make me look more like a shallow loser than a vulnerable, sensitive guy. Besides, I wasn't sitting in a dorm room, trying to hook up with a college girl. I was sitting across from a sixth-grade English teacher. She lived in a cottage on a hill with a garden; she drove a Volvo; and at this very moment she was sitting across from me drinking a vodka tonic. Finally, I said, "Well, I wouldn't mind getting married, if I actually had a girlfriend." Ellen was silent, no doubt quickly losing faith in another standard-issue-male pig.

Then, I blurted out the whole truth, and ended with, "I really wanted the job." Ellen laughed hysterically, so I guess that meant she believed me. No cheating scum could make up a story that ridiculous.

Later we talked about the big adventures in our lives. I told her about packing up and moving to Arizona. "How did you know you'd like Phoenix?" Ellen asked. "I didn't know much. That's why I picked it. It seemed like an adventure," I answered, and actually Phoenix was like nothing I have ever experienced. Even my morning walk to school was refreshing, the feel of the cool desert air rising up to meet the hot rays of the sun and the pungent smell of the desert mixing with the sweet smell of orange blossoms. What still blew me away was plunging into the pool at my complex after teaching for the day. A few years ago, Ellen had felt her life was growing a little stale and was looking for an adventure to give her a jump start. So, she had applied to the Department of Defense Dependents' Schools, the wing of the government that contracted to educate the children of military people overseas. Out of an immense pool of applicants, they offered Ellen a job in Oppenheim, Germany, a small hamlet situated on the banks of the Rhine River. "I had never even been out of the country," Ellen told me. "When I waited for my plane, I was so nervous, I had to sneak away from my parents, who had come to see me off, to secretly puke in the bathroom." But it was the story of her first day in Germany that made me feel strangely connected to her. Alone in her hotel room, with no one there to escort her, she had decided not to eat in the boring hotel restaurant, but instead had taken a walk through narrow, twisting, cobblestone streets. "Everything was so strange," Ellen said. "The cars and trucks were strange with long license plates and stubby bumpers; the houses were strange. They had pointy tiled roofs and window boxes filled with bold, red flowers; the signs over the shops had strange sounding names like *Spielgefahrt* and *Schuhgeshaft;* even the trees were strange. They were so much taller and skinnier." Ellen had stumbled upon the town square, where drunken men in stockings and lederhosen and women in frilly blouses and long skirts celebrated the grape harvest by dancing arm in arm to an oompah-pah band. Above the square loomed a giant cathedral with a huge stained-glass window and an enormous bell that reverberated through the village every fifteen minutes. "Behind the cathedral," Ellen said, her voice almost a whisper in the loud bar, "I found a bone house."

"Bone house?" I repeated. "It sounds like a horror movie."

"No," Ellen replied, "just history." Behind us, in the bar, greyhound races were blaring over TV sets and someone was yelling out, "Go number six! Number six!" and banging his fists on his table. "It was a little house with a tiny square window," Ellen continued. "When I looked through, it was pitch black, but when I pushed a button, the room lit up and I could see ancient bones. They were stacked up like cordwood. One pile was for bones and the other for skulls. I was staring through the window wondering how all those bones got there when the town bell rang out. I almost leaped out of my skin."

Ellen finally found a tiny restaurant on the bank of the Rhine River where she sat down, alone, at a table on the porch. She looked out at long, flat-bottomed barges rolling down the river with plump tidy children swinging on squeaky rusted swing sets encased in chain-link boxes. With much trepidation, Ellen had ordered the only item on the German menu that she recognized, a chef *salat*, but even the salad came out strangely. Instead of being fresh, all the vegetables were pickled: pickled cauliflower, pickled zucchini, pickled beets. So, she sat there alone, eating her strange pickled vegetables and envisioning plump tidy children and men in weird leather shorts dancing arm in arm, stained-glass windows and houses filled with bones. She was a young American woman marveling at the strangeness of it all; the only thing familiar was the sparkling canvas of the German sky.

I have never been to Oppenheim; I have never even been to Germany; I have especially never eaten pickled vegetables, but somehow the scene had locked itself inside me. I could feel the nervous energy, the restlessness, the expectancy, the bare trace of loneliness, and I could feel the pulse of her heart as if it were my own heart, beating hope through her living body.

Now back in Phoenix for six years, Ellen had felt that stale feeling coming on again, and Germany had definitely been an exciting period of travel and adventure. Maybe, she thought, it was the answer again. She had reapplied and was offered a new job in the Netherlands. Ellen was seriously contemplating going, convinced that travel would be another jump start. The idea that there was no clamp holding her down to this place began to haunt her. No boyfriend. No friendship strong enough to keep her in Phoenix. She had felt like a drifter, a lofty balloon that had slipped away from a hand. Finally her father had given her the advice she needed. "Maybe," he said, "your adventure is right here. Maybe you don't have to go halfway around the world to find it. Maybe it's time to take a stand and find your happiness right here." So, she had stayed and only a month later, Wizard and I had walked into her classroom.

Just before winter break Ellen and I had talked about the plans each of us had made for vacation. Ellen was sticking around Phoenix, visiting her parents, who were retired south of town, and I was going to Florida to visit my brothers and dad. That afternoon I had packed up my bags and was rushing down the sidewalk to catch my plane when Ellen breathlessly ran up behind me and handed me a holiday card. I opened it up, beginning to hand it to Ellen to have her read it to me, when Ellen said, still panting, "No! You read it." Then my fingers explored the page and found the bumps protruding from the surface. "Merry Christmas," it read, "It's been very nice getting to know you." I read the Braille aloud, then lifted my face to Ellen and smiled. "Well," she admitted, "I had to keep it a little bland. Realize, I was dictating to an eighty-year-old blind man at the special needs center at the library." That morning, Ellen had put the card in my mailbox in the front office, but throughout the day she had repeatedly passed through the office and had seen the card poking out from the mailbox in the exact spot she had placed it. Moments before the closing bell it was still there. Without looking to see who was watching, Ellen had bent over, snatched up the card, and sprinted out the door toward my classroom. As my fingers ran over the

Braille note, I wanted to hug Ellen, but instead, I only slid the card into my bag and shook her hand. I felt her thin graceful fingers. They were strong, poised, and her smooth nails were cut straight across with no pretension. Faint lines crisscrossed her palms. They weren't deep but the lines of an athlete. To me they showed a blend of softness and competence. As I rushed off to the taxi that would take me to the airport, all I could think was that she had passed the test. Ellen had passed the hand test.

Two days after Christmas I had called Ellen from Florida and invited her out for New Year's Eve upon my return to Phoenix. I went all out, renting a limo to take us to dinner, dancing, and later a comedy club. After that night, we were seldom apart. Our first months together passed in a blur of excitement: long rides on my tandem bike and hikes in the desert where we encountered rattlesnakes and javelinas. Over a romantic dinner I asked Ellen what she wanted out of her future, and her response was quite miraculous. "Some girls dream of a fancy church wedding with rose petals carpeting the aisles and bells ringing. They want a big house with a white picket fence," she said, "but I've never dreamed of those things. I want to live a life that is extraordinary, never ordinary," and if extraordinary was what she truly wanted, she definitely got a healthy dose of it by dating me.

At first, I could tell Ellen especially struggled with the peculiarities of blindness. She was sort of a shy and private person, and she wasn't used to the attention I often received. Everyone is fascinated with the relationship of a blind man and his working dog and it often feels as though we are at the head of a parade. Ellen would watch as people lined up, crouching low, pointing, and staring. "Look, Mom, there's a dog in the supermarket. Can I pet him?"

"Honey, that's a working dog. He helps that nice blind man see."

"Why does he need a dog to help him see?"

"Because he's blind, honey."

"Then how does he know where he is? Does that lady tell him?"

I could almost hear Ellen's grimace. She knew, however, that people had good intentions, and they just wanted to let me know how wonderful they thought our partnership was. "Such a beauty! Is it your best friend?"

"It sure is," I replied, massaging Ellie's shoulder.

"What's its name?" And I replied, "Ellen."

In February I persuaded Ellen to go away with me to northern Arizona for a lovely romantic ski weekend. "We'll sit in the hot tub," I urged, "drinking wine with the snowflakes landing in our hair."

"And what about the skiing part?" Ellie asked innocently. "Have you skied before?"

"Plenty of times," I lied. Actually, I had only been once, five years ago in college, and the experience had ended with me lying spread-eagled on top of a bush, pulling burs out of my crotch. "Don't you worry!" I tried to set Ellie's mind at ease. "Guiding a blind person down a mountain is really easy. There's nothing to it."

Intuitively we had managed by Ellie skiing close behind me while calling out some simple commands like, "Turn—turn now! Oh, God I can't look!" and had managed to avoid any major trauma until the end of the day. We had chosen President's Day to embark on our maiden ski voyage, the most crowded day in the resort's history we later learned. So it was quite miraculous that we remained upright as long as we did. I found myself actually in sync with Ellie's commands and showed off my athletic ability by whipping aggressively from turn to turn in my best *Wide World of Sports* impression. Skiing down a blue run, we had just dropped over a steep, mogul-filled, icy section. Unknown to Ellie at the time, a woman had just wiped out ahead of us and she and her boyfriend were sitting at the worst possible place on the slope—just hidden below the lip. We were moving so fast and they were in such a bad spot that when Ellie saw them it was too late. I think she said something like, "Ughhshhtuh." The lady's boyfriend was right next to her, helping to sort out her skis, so when I connected, it was with two bodies, not just one. In this case, blindness worked to my advantage, because sight didn't cause me to tense up or to flail pointlessly. The whole thing was surprisingly painless. We were a contorted tangle of protruding arms, legs, heads, and skis, like a monstrously deformed octopus. I popped up, brushed myself off, and laughed off the whole incident, annoyed underneath, but not wanting to make Ellie feel guilty or cause her to lose her confidence.

On the campus of Phoenix Country Day School, Ellen and I tried to keep our relationship private from the snooping eyes and ears of students and, even worse, other teachers. At work, it was fun to be formal around Ellen. I never quite knew who might be listening. At break, I got a kick out of saying very properly, "Good morning, Ms. Reeve." With her responding, just as properly, "Well, good morning to you, Mr. Weihenmayer." But even with no exchange of words, when passing by her, I had a secret weapon to tell me she was near. If she was within range, Wizard would slow down and begin veering slightly toward her, panting a little harder and sometimes even making tiny high whimpers. Ellen and Wizard had become good friends, often playing a game of catch together after school in front of my apartment. If I was walking with a line of fifth graders behind me, I'd point in the direction of Wizard's subtle veer and call out confidently, "Hello, Ms. Reeve," to the complete amazement of the students. "Didn't you know all blind people have a bit of ESP?"

Each relationship has a transitional moment when two people begin to feel so comfortable with each other that they decide to share something embarrassing or let slip something a little less than appealing. It might come with a fart or belch in front of a partner for the first time. At this moment it might be argued that you are truly intimate. Our moment was a bit different from most people's. We were sitting on my bed when I took out my glass eye for Ellen. I had been warming her up to the idea by mentioning the possibility of a glass eye and then pretending to take it out by pulling down my lower lid and exaggeratedly popping the back of my head with my hand. But just to throw Ellen off, I'd perform the procedure on my right, real eye. Ellen would peer closely into the eye and proclaim, "It looks too real. It couldn't be fake." So, I would repeat the procedure on the left eye. "That one looks real too," she'd say. Then, sometimes, over an intimate dinner in the midst of a conversation, I would begin to casually tap one of my eyes with the nail of my forefinger, as if I were thinking really hard about what she was saying, except I would really be tapping the bottom of the table. I kept this up for a week, until Ellen was thoroughly confused. Behind all the joking, I was actually very sensitive about the loss of my left eye. I had never taken it out in front of anyone, even members of my own family.

Once in graduate school, with a relationship growing quickly sour, I had considered taking it out, but for less admirable reasons. We were on a ferry going to Nantucket Island for a girlfriend's birthday. My idea was to have her close her eyes while I placed something in her hand. "Honey," I would say gently, "it's a birthday surprise." And when she opened her eyes and peered excitedly down at her hand, something unexpected would be staring back at her. But I was scared that she would be so shocked, she might fling my eye overboard, and so the surprise gift only remained a fantasy.

With Ellen it was different. Even though I wasn't comfortable with the idea of a prosthetic eye, I wanted her to know me, even to know me with one less eyeball than I was supposed to have. So, while sitting on my bed, Ellen looked into my eyes and said, "Come on! Take it out." Her voice sounded like she had scrunched up her face, preparing for the gruesome sight. "Take it out! Take it out!" she chanted. "It won't gross you out?" I asked. "A little, but take it out anyway." She insisted. So I pulled down my lower lid, nodded my head forward and popped it out for real. Ellen let out a little puff of air. Since she was just a little grossed out, I decided to go the distance and fully gross her out. I stretched out my arms in front of me, palms up, the prosthetic eye lying on top of my palm like a crown jewel, and shuffled stiffly toward Ellen like a mummy. Ellen squealed and darted from the bed. As I chased her around the apartment, I moaned like I had just woken from the dead and opened my eyelids as wide as they would go. I heard her tucked down on the couch, trying desperately to quiet her breathing. When I came near her, she laughed and I collapsed on top of her. I laid my hand on her face and knew her eyes were squeezed tight, so I gently pried them open so she could see my one open socket and the pink flesh behind it as I kissed her. Ellen returned my kiss.

It was Wizard who finally gave our secret love affair away. One day, I was helping a student after school and was late for the faculty meeting. Out of breath, I rushed down the sidewalk, around the corner, and swung open the door. The meeting had already begun. Quietly, I told Wizard to find a chair. Customarily, he would walk us over to an empty chair and lay his head on it. When he stopped, I would slide my hand from his back, down to his head and muzzle, touch the empty chair and sit down. Wizard weaved through the crowded desks and lowered his head. My hand slid down his muzzle but instead of an empty chair, I felt knees and heard Ellen's giggle. Wizard laid his head on Ellen's lap, his big tail wagging. She whispered, "Wizard, Wizard, not here. Find another chair." Ellen had been waving him away, while stifling a giggle, but to no avail. The entire faculty erupted in laughter. Wizard's wagging tail and his bright eyes staring up into Ellen's shocked and laughing face had confirmed their every suspicion. The cat or, in this instance, the dog, was out of the bag.

# 11
# Preparation

Sam, my Phoenix climbing partner, and I were climbing a craggy volcanic peak which jutted sharply from the smooth desert floor. When near the top, Sam said dreamily, "Hey, what do you say we go try something a little bigger?"

"Like what?" I asked cautiously.

"How about Mount McKinley?"

"Don't you think there's a slight difference between one-pitch rock climbs in the desert and the tallest peak in North America?" I thought Sam was a lunatic. The treks I had done with my family hardly compared to the severity of McKinley. I didn't know about the gaping crevasses that lurked inches beneath the surface of the snow waiting to swallow climbers in their bottomless depths, or about the punishing cold that ripped through even a down jacket, or about the intense wind and sun that changed the human face into that of a reptile. And I certainly didn't know that when climbers approached the summit they only had one third of the oxygen at sea level to breathe. Covered with snow, McKinley rises to 20,320 feet. The people of Alaska call it by its Athabascan name, Denali, or The Big One. If I were magically able to fly straight up into the sky, I'd have to rocket up almost four straight miles to reach the summit. Despite my sketchy knowledge and questionable skill, over the next few weeks Sam's idea became like a greedy little tapeworm, burrowing into my brain and growing fat off my thoughts. Sam's unshattering optimism was contagious. It picked me up and carried me along. He believed so strongly that climbing McKinley was possible for us, soon I found myself believing it too. The whole radical plan was a huge untested leap of faith. I didn't yet know how I would pull it off, but I felt that, with the right preparation, ingenuity, team support, and mental toughness, there had to be a way.

In another sense, Denali was a perfect big peak with which to start. Much of a team's success would rely on a blessing from the mountain gods. With good weather, success was possible; without it, the strongest team didn't have a chance. This theory had been played out by relatively inexperienced teams who, by possessing strong legs and hearts and plenty of patience, reached the top; while elite, world-class teams have been sent scurrying back to base camp by a storm. With good weather rarely lasting more than a few days at a time and arctic storms commonly producing wind velocities of 150 miles per hour, shredding tents like paper bags, the key to reaching the top was to simply get lucky.

One night sitting at my kitchen table, Sam and I discussed how we could make this climb more than the dream of two climbers. Two years before, I had been contacted by the American Foundation for the Blind (AFB), a nonprofit advocacy and service group for the blind. They were putting together a major public-education campaign to inform America about the capabilities of blind people and wanted to dramatize those capabilities in a powerful way. Sam and I thought that a climb of Denali would fit perfectly with this message and could help open doors of opportunity for blind people in schools and in the workplace. After presenting the idea to AFB, they were ecstatic and supported us one hundred percent.

Sam and I had met while he was substituting at the Phoenix Country

Day School. Sam was a rock climber, and we had quickly become friends, working out together at the Phoenix Rock Gym a few nights a week. Our partnership, however, had not begun smoothly. Sam admitted to me on our first climbing outing at the rock gym that he suffered from ADD, attention-deficit disorder. That's great, I thought sarcastically, a guy who can't see and a guy who can't concentrate, teaming up to climb North America's highest and most dangerous peak. As we belayed each other up the walls, Sam and I talked about what inspired us to climb. Sam confessed that he didn't really enjoy school, sitting in the back of class, trying to concentrate on what the teachers were saying. Most kids seemed to be able to tune out everything but the teacher's voice, but he'd see and hear everything: the clock ticking on the wall, the kids laughing outside at recess, a fly crawling up the windowpane. He told me that if his mind were a radio, instead of hearing just one station, he'd hear all the stations at once. Sam had turned to climbing after a teacher proposed that climbing a rock face would help Sam develop focus. "He was dead-on," Sam admitted. "I was one hundred feet up, dangling from a crimper hold by my fingers, and you know something? For the first time in my life, I could totally concentrate. I wasn't thinking about how I hadn't studied for that algebra test; I wasn't thinking about my detention yesterday; I wasn't thinking about all the times I had screwed up. I was just thinking about getting to that next hold." Sam and I ended the night with a difficult overhanging route called The Monster. "Sam, this one's a little above my level," I admitted. "If I get into trouble and can't find the next hold on my own, bail me out with a little communication." Halfway up, as the face lunged out at a forty-five-degree angle, the holds got thin and my two fingers, which were jammed into a small pocket, were slowly slipping out. My other hand desperately slapped around for a positive hold, but I was losing energy, on the verge of falling. "Sam," I yelled, "what do I have?" Sam immediately screamed back, "Left hand, up two feet, left a foot." As I lunged up, my left hand slapping out for the hold, my feet losing contact with the rock, I heard Sam mutter apologetically, "Oh . . . sorry . . . I meant right hand." I dangled from the rope fuming under my labored breaths.

Sam's life always seemed a little discombobulated. For our first training session, we debated whether to go running or hiking, finally settling on running. But when Sam showed up at my apartment clunking around in hiking boots, I asked, "How you gonna run in those things?"

"Oh, I'll be fine," he said, and the angle at which his voice projected told me he was looking down at his boots, as if he was only then discovering his blunder. He hesitated and then said, "Umm, running doesn't really get climbers in shape. Let's go hiking."

If Sam was a little unorganized, I was a little pigheaded. After our hike, I said, "Tomorrow let's do a run in the desert."

"Will you be able to navigate through all those rocks and cactus?" Sam asked.

I gave Sam an annoyed look, as if to say, you just bring your running shoes. I'll take care of the rest. On the run, Sam was in the lead, with Wiz and I trotting along right behind. Wiz was doing a good job weaving me around cactuses and boulders and pausing for a moment to indicate small rocks to be jumped over. I was just starting to feel confident and stable on the uneven trail when I tripped over a cactus, soared through the air, and landed hard with my palm against a sharp rock. I took off my shirt and wrapped my hand as it pulsated with blood. I was hot, dripping with sweat, and angry with myself. The hand needed several stitches, so for the rest of the evening, Sam and I sat glumly in the emergency room. The next day, my fifth-grade class saw my bandaged hand and I told them what had happened. One very brave and precocious little girl stood up and asked, "Mr. W., if you fell down in the desert, how do you expect to climb that big mountain?" What worried me more than her question was that I didn't yet have a complete answer.

Over the weeks, we began to work the kinks out of our training. Neither Sam nor I could get to the mountains every day, so we got permission to run the back stairway of the tallest building in downtown Phoenix: fifty floors and about five hundred feet of elevation gain. Sam and I would meet every evening at the building with our seventy-pound packs to plod up the stairway. Soon we turned it into a competition, racing each other to the top. When one of us was feeling lazy or tired from a long day of teaching, the other would push him. It gave me extra energy when I'd hear Sam's feet thundering up behind me and Sam yelling, "You're slow tonight, Super Blind Guy. I'm going to shame you." That would give me enough energy to speed up, just enough to keep Sam at my heels. When I was feeling strong, there was nothing better than to race past Sam in the last ten flights, Sam laughing and grabbing the back of my heavy pack. Halfway up the stairway, we'd always stop to do twenty-five sit-ups and push-ups, but on our first night, after our first set, Sam yelled out as he hoisted his pack up, "Oh by the way—I did twenty-six. That would be one more than you did." So after that, the game was on. The next set, I did twenty-seven and then Sam twenty-eight, me twenty-nine, and Sam thirty. A month later, we were close to three digits.

When Sam couldn't join me, I found a way to compete against myself. I'd set my talking watch for twenty minutes and play a cruel little game. I'd say to myself, if you don't make it to the top before the alarm goes off, you won't summit. With that terrifying pressure, I'd never slacken my pace, no matter how tired I was. Sometimes, I'd push my watch halfway up and it would call back, "Six minutes remaining." I'd run with abandonment, ignoring my heavy leaden legs and my chest cavity suffocating, and touch the top landing only seconds before the alarm rang out. Countless times, I'd flop against the top railing, coughing and sputtering and gasping for air, with barely the energy remaining to lift my head. "OK," I'd say to myself. "You only squeaked by, but you deserve to summit." My training regimen wasn't very scientific; each night I only allowed myself to quit when, after four or five times to the top, I felt so nauseous and dehydrated I thought I was going to throw up.

Besides humping a heavy pack to the top of a building, I knew nothing could beat the physical benefits of pure running, but Wizard's and my desert running experience had been a disaster. Plus, Wiz had definite pacing issues; he'd drag me the first half mile and I'd wind up dragging him the next five and a half. Ellie wasn't a long-distance runner, but liked to ride her bike. I thought there might be a way to utilize Ellie's bike riding to help me run. Soon, an idea came to me, and I had a friend at the local hardware store help me realize it. The design consisted of two long wooden dowels, connected by a two-inch piece of bungee cord that wrapped around Ellie's bike seat. I held two loops of rope connected at the other end of the dowels, enabling me to jog comfortably behind Ellie's bike. The principle was similar to Wizard's harness. Through the two stiff dowels, I could feel Ellie turning left or right, slowing down or speeding up along the hard-packed dirt trail that stretched for miles just outside our house. Because the pace had to be maintained for a runner, Ellie often grew bored going so slowly on her bike. To entertain herself along the tedious miles, Ellie jammed to fast-paced rock 'n' roll with pounding drum solos on her Walkman. Inadvertently, she increased the pace until I was sprinting behind her. With her music blaring in her ears, she couldn't hear me sputtering and coughing out, "Ellie, slow down. Please slow down!" Eventually, when she felt the reverse tug of my body weight behind her, she got the idea and throttled back just enough to keep my lungs from exploding. Admittedly, dragging a blind guy mile after endless mile was very boring, so, a little frustrated, Ellie nicknamed my invention exactly that, The Blind Dragger.

Throughout the months I also poured through books in Braille and on tape about Denali. One book analyzed each of Denali's one hundred climbing fatalities: caught in a storm with no bivy gear, tripped on a crampon strap or a loop hanging from an ice ax, falling unroped through a snow bridge into a hidden crevasse. I didn't want to wind up a statistic in a book on climbing fatalities and figured a good way to learn what to do on Denali was to first become an expert on what *not* to do on Denali.

Sam had two friends in mind for our team whom he had met at an emergency medical technician class in Colorado. The first was Ryan Ludwig, a husky young climber from Wyoming, who had lived in the mountains all his life. The second was, as Sam described, a "free-wheeling, fair-haired pretty boy" who was as comfortable on an overhanging rock face as he was at a Grateful Dead concert or a Rainbow Gathering.

In the winter, Sam and I drove out to Joshua Tree, a vast high desert full of spectacular cliffs and crags, to meet the team. Late at night, when we reached the edge of J Tree, we pulled off the road and slept on our foam pads in the cold rocky scrub. Lying back under the stars, while anticipating meeting Jeff and Ryan, I listened to the massive openness of the sky, so sweeping and infinite, it was hard to conceptualize. Wizard was uneasy too, but for different reasons. He whimpered softly and snuggled closer to me as we both heard packs of coyotes yelping in the near distance.

In the morning, we met Ryan and Jeff and began a day of rock climbing. Moving up the steep slippery trails to the base of the climbs, I practiced my new and not-yet-perfected hiking system. Months before, Sam and I had gone to an outdoor retailers' show in Reno, Nevada, to beg free gear. Passing a booth, Sam stopped. "Check this out," he said casually and placed two long poles in my hand. At the time, neither of us fully imagined their implications. Just as Wizard had opened up worlds of opportunity traveling independently through city streets, subway stations, and airports, these two poles would revolutionize my ability to navigate in the mountains. They were LEKI trekking poles, amazingly light and so sturdy, that even by leaning my full weight on them and violently bouncing up and down, they wouldn't snap. They also gave me better balance; instead of only having two legs, now I had four. While hiking up the approach trail in J Tree, I thrust out a pole, scanning for a good foot placement. When I found one, I jabbed the sharp metal point in the ground, just past the placement, and leaning forward with all my weight on the pole, lowered my foot slowly down until it touched the trail. Often, the location was very uneven, which before would have caused me to twist my ankle, but now, with my full weight on the pole, I could reposition the foot onto flatter ground. I imagine all this scanning, jabbing, positioning, and frantic repositioning looked to a sighted person like a barely-under-control stumble and I can understand the panic that must have filled Ryan and Jeff when they watched me lurch up the trail beside a hundred-foot drop-off.

When scrambling up a steep rocky ramp to the base of the climb, Ryan kept his hands protectively around my ankles. I didn't know whether to drag Ryan's arms behind me or wait until his hands pushed my ankles forward. When I reached the flat section at the base, I had to tell him, nicely of course, "You can let go of my ankles now." I didn't worry too much about the extra help. I had been through this a thousand times when meeting new people. They don't know what to do, so they do everything. Ryan and Jeff would learn soon enough what help I needed and what help I did not.

That evening we built a campfire and sat around trading stories. Ryan had just completed a first winter ascent of a jagged thirteen-thousand-foot peak called Black Tooth situated in the Big Horn mountain range of Wyoming. Just hearing the feat made my hands go clammy, even in the cold desert night. With a partner, he had snowmobiled in for two days and then fought through chest-deep snow for five hours, just to reach the base of the rock. Near evening they found themselves on a five-hundred-foot steep rock face leading to the summit, but didn't have enough daylight to stay roped together and belay each other up each pitch. So the two had free-soloed to the top, with no safety line to stop a potential four-thousand-foot ride down into the valley. Ryan trained by taking long mountain runs over a thirteen-thousand-foot pass near his home. I had only been to thirteen thousand feet a few times in my life and once was in a car. I certainly couldn't imagine running at that altitude.

Jeff, although as hard-core as Ryan, chose to downplay his adventures. He was at home in the Rocky Mountains where he lived, so comfortable in fact, that he told us he made a yearly habit out of climbing Boulder's Third Flat Iron under the light of the moon, wearing nothing but his harness. "The harness actually chafed certain sensitive areas," Jeff admitted sheepishly, "so I had to put on a pair of boxers under the harness." Mountains were more important to Jeff than a home, a job, or security. He took jobs to be close to the mountains. Girlfriends had to be able to keep up with his high-altitude adventures. Although none of them could, a very large number had tried.

"I've never done a first ascent or gone climbing in the buff," Sam said, "but I'll bet ya I've been somewhere none of you have." Then Sam told us the story of his last summer's job, hanging off cliffs outside of Edgemont, South Dakota, drilling rock samples for the Bureau of Economic Geology. "I had nothing to do with geology or oil. I was just a hippie rock climber who found a paying job working with ropes way up off the ground." Sam had jumped at the opportunity, thinking it would be a good way to get out of Phoenix for the summer. Also, he was nursing a broken heart from a recent breakup with a girlfriend and thought the change would give him time to reassess his relationship, his life, his future, all of which felt transitory.

The new job and setting, however, didn't seem conducive to deep reflection on life. The town's only two businesses were its ramshackle bar and the county dump, and he slept on a cot in a garage that was constantly flooding in the violent thunderstorms of the northern plains. For ten hours a day, Sam hung from loose sandstone cliffs drilling thousands of core samples, amidst clouds of mosquitoes and biting flies. It was common for van-sized blocks of stone to come loose and tumble the hundreds of feet to the canyon floor, nearly taking Sam with them. As he hung, he listened to the only radio station on his Walkman—Lakota Indian death chants—and looked out over the vast empty prairie which, for Sam, held the ghosts of millions of buffalo and the Indians who hunted them. "I found myself wondering, what exactly was I being punished for?" Sam said, throwing another log on the fire. "Was it for some shameful act I had performed or a heartless thing I said or just for one of the many bad decisions I had made over the years?"

After a late night drinking binge, when Sam was particularly hungover, he found himself working alone on a distant mesa. Nothing was going right. In order to sample the cliff, he had to haul a few hundred pounds of equipment through the canyon bottom, over mud flats and boulder fields, and up a steep goat path to the top of the mesa. As soon as he would get his equipment organized and was prepared to rappel over the side of the cliff, he'd realize he forgot some vital piece of gear and have to descend back to his starting point. When he finally got suspended, inevitably he'd drop a wrench or screwdriver or drill bit and have to go all the way down again. In addition, his drill constantly needed to be filled with gas, causing him to go back up top again. This pattern kept up throughout the morning as the sun grew hotter, the insects thirstier and his hangover more fierce. The last straw was when the five-gallon water bag he had hauled up to the top of the cliff broke loose from its connections and emptied itself all over a cactus patch far below.

The story was vintage Sammy, I thought, as I reminisced on our first days training together. The fire had calmed now to just a sizzle as Sam continued, "After the water bag busted, I sank to my knees and began screaming and pounding the muddy ground with my fists. My vision went totally red and then I blacked out for a minute. When I opened my eyes, I sensed some movement, and after I found my glasses, which I'd thrown down and nearly stomped on in rage, I saw that two dung beetles were pushing a ball of shit up the hill, past me. The sight of it gave me a feeling of pure envy. Those two shit-bugs were succeeding where I had failed. Even worse than that, I was all alone. At least they had each other." Ryan, Jeff, and I could no longer hold back our laughter. It sputtered out and then exploded into convulsions, in spite of Sam's tragedy. He concluded, "I knew then that if the biggest thing I ever accomplished in life was pushing a huge wad of bullshit up a hill, I'd be satisfied, as long as I did it well."

"In a few months," I said, "you'll get your wish."

"Hold on there, home chicken," Jeff said. "Which of us is the pile of shit he's gonna be pushing?"

"Isn't it obvious?" Sam chuckled, poking me in the shoulder.

Over the winter and spring, we gained cohesiveness and skill as a team, meeting periodically for climbs of Mount Rainier in Washington and Long's Peak in Colorado. On Rainier, we worked on crevasse rescues, by lowering team members deep into open cavernous slots and having them climb the vertical ice walls to the top, using their mountaineering axes and the front points of their crampons. The bottoms of crevasses narrowed to only a foot wide in places, and I understood grimly how a real fall would inescapably wedge a climber between its icy jaws. No warming sunlight reached the frigid, dank bottom, so I always climbed fast and furiously until I felt its welcomed glow on my face. In case the victim was incapacitated, we also practiced pulling up team members by a complex rope system of ice ax anchors, ascenders, and pulleys.

On Long's Peak, we got our bodies used to pulling heavy sleds behind our equally heavy backpacks. After only an hour, the muscles in my hips were useless and patches of skin under my hip belt were rubbed raw. As we moved up the steepest sections, we practiced roping up, forming two rope teams of two, each of us connected to our partner by thirty feet. We practiced the technique of tying the back of our sleds to the climbers' rope with a prusik knot, which would tighten and lock off with any sudden movement. Many mountaineers have survived a crevasse fall, only to be killed by their fifty-pound sleds crashing down on top of them. With a prusik fall, however, the team members above the crevasse would self-arrest, throwing themselves down on their ice axes, which would anchor the climbers' rope; the prusik knot would lock off against the taught climbers' rope, preventing the sled from following the victim into the slot. Moving up a steep forty-five-degree snow slope, Jeff said, "Super Blind, I'm not gonna tell you when it's comin', but at some point, I'm gonna hurl my body down this slope, and you're gonna save my ass." Jeff was only emphasizing half the equation, since we were roped together. Climbing upward, I felt like I was marching into battle, every muscle in my body waiting for the enemy to strike. Then I felt the harsh jerk of the rope ripping me over backwards. I hit the slope on my back, head downward, with my large pack weighing me down like a turtle's shell. As I slid, I writhed and twisted my body onto my stomach and slammed my chest against the blunt side of my ax, which drove the sharp pick side into the glazed snow. With Jeff's heavy weight pulling us downward, at first the pick only sliced through the flimsy snow like a sharp knife through birthday cake. I kept my body stiff, also pushing my bent knees into the snow. I knew at this speed not to dig the front points of my crampons into the snow; the added pressure of these points combined with the powerful downward momentum would flip me over backwards again. Eventually, we came to a stop and without a word, started up again, only to have Jeff, a few minutes later, hurl himself down once more. By the end of the afternoon, my body ached from the dozens of falls and the sliding had pushed piles of snow under my GORE-TEX shell, soaking me through. That night as I slept in the tent, my body twitched and wriggled as the fierce pull of the rope and the vibrating motion of my ax cutting through snow crept into every dream. In a real rope fall, I knew my self-arrest had to be automatic. The action needed to be drilled into the involuntary circuitry of my muscle fibers. If I had to think about what to do during a fall, it would be too late.

Not all of my time leading up to the climb was spent on the mountain; as part of their public-education campaign, the AFB asked me to do some TV interviews. One was a cheesy daytime talk show, on which I was showcased among a group of blind people deemed "amazing and inspirational." All the blind people were led onto the stage, canes tapping and dogs' tails wagging, and seated in a row in front of the crowd. I was featured first, and the host opened with, "A blind mountain climber. Isn't that incredible? Even I, who can see just fine, wouldn't think of climbing a mountain." This wasn't the first time I had heard the "Even I" statement. It was always meant as a compliment, but it never failed to annoy me. There might be a dozen other factors that prevented the host from excelling in the sport of mountain climbing. She might be fifty pounds overweight, wheezing with every breath, and might never have even set foot on a mountain, but in her mind, success or failure was automatically attributed to one factor: sight or no sight.

The second panelist had "heroically saved another's life" during the recent San Francisco earthquake, but when the story was fleshed out, it seemed far less than heroic. Staying in a hotel during the earthquake and knowing a woman in a wheelchair roomed next door, the blind woman had yelled out her window for help. Two sturdy construction workers heard her yells, rushed in, and carried the wheelchair-bound woman to safety. I wondered why the construction workers weren't on this show. Next a blind comedian stood up and performed his act. He pointed to the audience and said, "Don't you all look lovely this afternoon." The audience erupted in laughter. "I've heard our host is a hot number," he said. "I'd like to feel her face. Hubba hubba." The audience erupted again. He told one blind joke after another, the kind I had told in middle school to gain acceptance, and even then, I had known the jokes weren't funny.

Throughout the rest of the segment, I squirmed in my seat. I should have been proud to be picked out as being "amazing and inspirational," but strangely, I felt more embarrassed and even a little sick. I was no more accomplished than the others. I was simply a blind person who planned to climb a mountain and nothing more. But people sensationalize the lives of blind people when, often, all they did was exhibit a semblance of normalcy. I had been receiving these accolades my whole life: give someone directions to my house—incredible. Make eye contact in a conversation—amazing. Pour a glass of milk without spilling it all over the table—inspiring. Each of us on the panel was being honored for our heroic tales, but the recognition spoke more loudly of low expectations than of accomplishment. My heart burned with the memory of my heroes, people like Helen Keller, who took the world's perceptions about the disabled and shattered them into a million pieces, people whose stories made me hunger for the courage to live in their image. For those who I exalted with the label of hero, their stories had to be truly heroic and not hollow.

The host ended the show with a demonstration of "beeper baseball," a game similar to baseball developed for blind people. With a dozen inspirational heroes on stage, I have no idea why I was selected as the representative batter. An audience member pitched me the beeping whiffle ball. I missed the first pitch, and the second. The third pitch was thrown with only a few seconds of air time left; the show's snappy theme song was starting to play, and the host had begun her ending monologue about how amazing and inspiring we all were, when I connected with the beep. I heard her monologue trail off as she spotted the ball rocketing toward her, then the clunk of the ball as it bounced off her head. Vindication, I thought later, when the amused pitcher told me what had happened. As I headed back to the airport to catch my plane home, I began to realize that when blind people could become stand-up comedians, organize an earthquake rescue, and plan to climb a mountain without being singled out as inspirational, that is when the world would be a perfect place.

# 12
# Zero Zero

Finally the day arrived. I was tired of training, tired of doing interviews. At least on the mountain we would have plenty of uninterrupted time to focus on one simple goal: reaching the top. But at the same time, the day of departure was one of the saddest of my life, because it was also the day I would say good-bye to Wizard. Wizard's retirement was well timed. In fact, he probably should have retired a year earlier, but I hadn't been ready to let him go from my life. Just like people, dogs' bodies eventually break down too. As Wizard passed age eleven, Ellen watched his muzzle go gray, and I noticed my once fast-paced, tireless companion now hobbling along, barely able to keep up. Wizard's bladder had reverted back to its days of puppyhood, because he would stop and pee in the middle of the sidewalk, in a crowd of pedestrians, or in front of families eating lunch at an outdoor café. In class, in the middle of a lesson, Wiz would whimper and I'd rush him outside, narrowly avoiding an accident. When I touched his coat, it had dulled and lost its smoothness, but none of that would have mattered, except for the fact that I thought it was time for Wiz to enjoy a carefree life, no responsibilities. Originally I wanted to keep Wiz as a pet, but Fidelco had warned that this would be too stressful on Wiz as he watched a younger dog take his place as my guide. So, my brother Eddi had offered to take him. Eddi lived in Pensacola, Florida, on several acres, with a river and a dock behind his house. Wiz loved to swim. In his younger days, we spent many Saturday afternoons playing fetch in the Charles River. I'd throw a tennis ball into the river and Wiz, in supreme athletic style, would sprint down the dock, leap off the edge, and swim back to shore, the ball locked proudly in his jaws. I imagined Wiz, leaping off my brother's dock, and his mind believing he was young once again. He would finally be able to fill himself with as much table food as his belly could handle: steak bones, pork chops, and apple pie under the table. He could run and sniff and bark to his heart's content. He could finally just be a dog.

In front of our gate, I knelt down in front of Wiz. He was never a lovey-dovey dog, always preferring to play fetch or wrestle in the grass, but this time, I put my arms around him and lay my cheek against his. "Everybody gets old," Ellie said, resting her hand on my back. "It'll happen to you and me someday."

"I know," I said, catching my breath, my tears dropping onto Wizard's fur, "but it doesn't make it any easier." For eleven years, Wizard had given me his life, beginning when I was only sixteen, and he had been a big part of opening up a world of opportunity for me. There was absolutely nothing I could say or do that would be enough to thank him. Throughout our whole time together, Wiz was constantly baffling me about the extent of his awareness, one minute running me squarely into a tree branch and, the next, finding the right entranceway to a doctor's office to which we had never been before. I could never totally predict what he knew, what he sensed, but with my arms around him, I hoped he could sense how much I loved him. I also wondered if Wiz could sense that something was changing. If so, he gave no indication, but just panted in the hot, June weather. It was better that he didn't know. Let him live in innocence and happiness, I prayed. I knew if Wiz was a human, he wouldn't be one for long syrupy good-byes, so I made myself stand up and ruffled his ears with my hand. "Good-bye, buddy. Have fun in Florida. Don't eat too much steak." Then I kissed Ellie, told her how much I'd miss her, and headed down the jetway. Wiz and I would never see each other again, because, sadly, he died only six months later of a massive stroke, but I can only hope that in those last six months of boundless freedom, he lived a lifetime, and that the stroke was caused, in part, from one too many leaps into the river from the end of my brother's dock.

My team and I flew into Anchorage and drove north to a small runway in Talkeetna, where we loaded a thousand pounds of gear into a stripped-out Cessna. We taxied by a wrecked plane, stuck in a ditch. It looked like a dead bird with its wings knocked off. Our pilot, Doug Geeting, said the pilot of the old plane had tried to land on the runway with his glacier skis still down. Changing from skis to wheels is not automatic and when landing on pavement, sometimes pilots forget to make the changeover. This was not the sort of place that would easily forgive mistakes, I thought. I would need to remember that when we dropped onto the Kahiltna Glacier.

Ten minutes later we were off, soaring over the Alaska Range, squeezed between overstuffed packs and sleds. The roar of the plane vibrated my body. It was an unstable feeling as the plane bumped and dropped sharply in sync with the air currents. "Going through One Shot Pass," the pilot warned, and the plane turned sideways. Five hundred pounds of gear squashed me against the door. A low-grade fear lay in the pit of my belly, like I had eaten ten pounds of dough. I knew the feeling well. It had been with me in the locker room before a big wrestling match and at the top of my driveway while catapulting my bike toward the orange blur of a ramp in the hazy distance.

The pilot cut the engine and we were blanketed in a weird silence. Then the plane was bouncing up the thirty-degree snow slope, engines revving again as the pilot whipped the plane into a 180-degree turn, preparing it for the next takeoff. For the second time he cut the engine and we were still. "Alright, let's unload this pig." Chris Morris, our husky-voiced Alaskan guide, was already swinging open the door and heaving bags into the snow. Immediately everyone erupted into action, dragging out gear and shuttling it to our tent site. Ryan showed himself to be a mule, as he hauled immense piles of gear 200 yards across the glacier to our campsite, dropped it off and, without pause, raced back for another load. My tiny load seemed pathetic in scale to Ryan's as I followed Jeff to camp. Chris was already at work, shoveling a flat space for the first tent. I approached him resolutely. I had prepared a little speech to set the right tone for the climb. "Chris," I said, "just because I'm blind, I don't want you to give me less work or to treat me any differently from the other team members. When there's work to be done, I want to be right in there."

"Wouldn't dream of shortchangin' ya," he replied briskly, slapping the shovel in my hand. "Start digging." As I heaved pile after pile of heavy wet snow over my shoulder, my back already beginning to cramp, I wondered if I had spoken a little too eagerly. Maybe I should have waited to see how things played out. Maybe I should have kept my big mouth shut.

I was sitting on a block of ice soaking in the crisp glacier air, when Ryan joined me. "Psyched to be here?" I asked, slapping my hand on Ryan's knee.

"This is all I've thought about for the last eight months," he replied.

"I'm glad you're here," I said.

"Erik," he said, looking out over the Alaska Range, "this has been my dream, ever since I can remember, to be sitting right here in the most beautiful place on the earth. I'm feeling so strong, I feel like I could carry us all up there. I want to be the anchor of this team." I knew Ryan meant it and I felt comforted by his words and his passion.

Our first night on the mountain began ominously. The tranquility of the mountain was constantly being interrupted by the whirl of Chinook helicopters overhead. Two situations were desperately unfolding on the upper mountain. A pair of Spanish climbers had fallen while attempting to descend the Orient Express, a steep chute at eighteen thousand feet. The rope connecting them had luckily gotten snagged on a rock. One climber was already dead from the fall and the other dangled helplessly, the warmth of his injured body quickly dissipating in the brutal arctic night. Higher up, a two-person Taiwanese party had become trapped on the Football Field, a flat exposed snowfield below the summit, by high wind and whiteout conditions. Without a tent they had huddled together, the one climber still conscious frantically calling out for help on his two-way radio. Before the night ended, one Taiwanese would be dead, the other's life saved by the highest-altitude helicopter rescue in history.

The next day, on our first carry, loaded down with sixty-pound packs and fifty-pound sleds, we roped up into two teams, and I used the traveling system I had developed on our training climbs. With multiple layers over my ears and with the steady wind that swept across the glacier, I wouldn't always be able to follow the climber in front of me by the crunch of his boots. But since we were constantly roped together because of crevasse danger, I was able to follow by looping the rope around my hand and creating just enough tension to sense the direction of movement. While my rope team of Chris at the lead, me in the middle, and Sam behind toiled up Ski Hill, I was accused of putting a little too much tension on the rope. I felt the rope go slack and Chris, in lead, screamed out, "Boys, I'm hauling tuna." I could feel his eyes burning into me, so I said the most logical thing that came to mind. "It's not me." I tried to look falsely accused. "It's him," pointing back at Sam. But from then on the word *tuna* was indelibly burned into my chest as a reminder of my slow pace. Whenever we'd begin a steep climb, I'd scream out to Chris, "Get your fishing boots on. You've got some tuna to haul."

With the rope looped around my wrist, both hands were free to use my trekking poles or ice ax, depending on the steepness of the terrain. It is important that climbers stay precisely behind the leader, stepping directly in his boot holes, to minimize the risk of stepping through an untested snow bridge into a hidden crevasse. I scanned the trail with a trekking pole, feeling Chris's boot marks, and by leaning on my second pole, gently lowered my foot into it. I tried to get into his brain, into his rhythm, so that my steps would automatically match his. For hours, I'd feel my feet sliding into target after target. Then, the distance between steps or the angle of the footprint would change, and it would take me ten minutes to figure out the new stride. I wondered if Chris, who usually led, was just getting bored and decided to make both our lives more interesting.

Coming out of my tent at eight thousand feet on our fifth day on the mountain, I could hear Chris and Ryan speaking in whispers, the tone of their conversation definitely serious. Approaching, I heard Chris asking, "You didn't sleep at all?"

"No, not for the last two nights," Ryan answered huskily. "I feel like my heart's gonna explode out of my chest."

"Have you ever had this before?" Chris asked, his EMT training kicking in.

"Yes, when I was a little kid. I had a leaky heart valve. I took medication for a while, but it's been so long, I'd almost forgotten about it."

"This ain't a place to be messin' around with leaky heart valves," Chris said.

"I know. If it wasn't serious, I never would have said anything. Honestly, I'm a little scared."

"You've gotta go down," Chris said, and Ryan knew that this was nothing he would say lightly. Chris knew as we all did how important this climb was to Ryan.

"I know," Ryan finally said, his voice cracking as he fought to hold back tears. It was crushing to see this proud young man defeated, barely after he had begun, by a leaky heart valve he hadn't felt in eighteen years. Ryan stood at the edge of camp organizing his gear. I came and sat next to him.

"Can I help?" I asked, not knowing what to say.

"No, I got it all," he replied, facing away from me. Then, he turned to me and knelt in the snow. He was crying, the tears shaking his large frame. "I've dreamed about this mountain," he said, his voice trembling. "I even went out and had this cross made. I thought it would bring me luck." He drew it out of his fleece. "See, feel it. It has the name of our team, HighSights '95 engraved on it." I touched the warm metal and could feel the outline of the letters. Then he took it off his neck and put it around mine. "If I can't wear it to the top, then I want you to. I want you to wear it for me. Please."

"I'll wear it," is all I could say, because I was crying too. I hugged him and we shook hands. Then he was up, buckling his pack and moving slowly down the mountain with a descending team. I don't know whether Ryan's condition was just incredibly bad luck or the result of the pressure he placed on himself, but perhaps it simply wasn't his time. Maybe if he got proper treatment and worked just as hard, he'd get here again someday, or maybe he wouldn't, but there was nothing I could do but hug him, wish him well, and carry his cross to the summit.

An hour from our eleven-thousand-foot camp, Chris had an idea. He knew his friend Rodrigo, the leader of another climbing team, would be camping ahead and Chris had told him about the blind climber whom he would be guiding. "Rodrigo doesn't know who the blind climber is. So Sam," he said, "when I introduce you, I want you to try to shake his hand but miss. You know what I mean?" Sam needed no more explanation. His devious mind was already clicking through the options. Soon we rolled into camp and Rodrigo came bounding over to us, curious about the blind climber. "Meet Erik," Chris said, amazingly keeping his voice in check. That was Sam's cue. He stepped forward and thrust out his hand. Then he began groping in the air feeling for a hand. When he found Rodrigo's body, he began feeling him up, leaving no part unexplored. Rodrigo, stunned by the spectacle, stood like a deer frozen by headlights. His large eyes locked on his friend Chris, pleading for a suggestion as to what to do. Then Chris could no longer hold it together. He burst into laughter. Sam stepped back and burst into laughter too, and then the rest of the team followed suit. Rodrigo's expression slowly changed from astonishment to the hint of a smile. He knew he had been burned and was just beginning to understand the joke. Then I stepped forward and shook his hand for real, and just for a finale, reached out for his groin. Rodrigo backed up and turned to Chris. "Oh, Chris," he said in his infamous Ricky Ricardo accent, "you're so crazy."

At eleven thousand feet we were socked in by a storm that dropped fat wet flakes as big as dimes. We spent hours in the megamid, an eight-foot-square room we had made by digging a hole, building snow block walls, and attaching a slanted nylon-framed roof on top. We'd swap stories and pass around an immense bag of little slimy sausages. Chris told us about moving to the wilds of Alaska and building his own log cabin house in Wasilla. "I stole the logs from a family of beavers," Chris said and then laughed, "and I stripped the bark with my own teeth." During his first winter, snowdrifts piled up to his roof and his favorite husky dog was eaten by a pack of wolves. When he told us his mailing address, swearing he wasn't lying, we all laughed.

Mile 12.2 Sourdough Lane
Third Dirt Road on Right
First Log House on Left
Wasilla, Alaska 99287

Throughout the day, different Alaskan guides whom Chris hadn't seen since last year in a similar storm would drop in and soon they'd be best friends again, laughing and telling large Alaskan tales. I loved listening to their stories, which expertly blurred the line between folklore and truth. "I was floating down the Aragatch when I rounded a corner and there they were, a herd of caribou, a thousand thick if there was one."

"Have you ever heard the story of Hue Glass? He was tore up by a grizzly and left for dead, but he crawled thirty miles with his guts falling out all over the ground and when he found that old cod who left him for dead, well . . ."

"Did you hear about that moose that gored that old boy up near Valdez? Stomped him flat and then damned if he didn't spit on the poor soul."

"I was up near Fairbanks last winter. It was so cold, my tires froze into squares. You ever try driving on square tires?"

"Ever poke around in the Chugatch Range? Rock ain't much. So soft, you can carve your name in it with your finger. Call it Chugatch crud, but there's enough unclimbed peaks to keep a fella busy for quite a spell."

Chris, by far, had the best Alaskan adventures. I loved listening to his rough twang, relating his narrow escapes of giant avalanches in the Talkeetna Range, his treacherous fordings of the McKinley River when he was swept, pack and all, down the churning rapids, and his isolated float trips, catching Dolly Varden and Arctic grayling above the Arctic Circle. I imagined Chris as a larger-than-life frontiersman, straight from the Alaskan bush, riding caribou across the tundra with Daniel Boone, together fighting grizzlies and taming the land. "You must be a burly dude," I said to Chris.

"How do you picture him?" Jeff interjected with a hint of a grin in his voice.

"About six foot two and maybe, two hundred fifty pounds, with a big bushy lumberjack's beard and arms of steel."

Jeff cracked up, rolling back and almost choking on one of the slimy sausages. "This time, Super Blind, your extrasensory perception is way off. Six foot two? Two hundred fifty pounds? Arms of steel? He's more like five foot eight and a hundred fifty pounds soaking wet. Picture a little weasely runt with a shiny bald head, and there's Chris Morris for ya." I couldn't believe it. My brain couldn't put together Chris's burly voice and Jeff's description. I felt the way Dorothy must have, when Toto pulled the curtain back and exposed the Wizard of Oz. Chris jumped up, deepening his already rumbling voice. "He's lying, Big E! He's just jealous. I'm six foot four if I'm an inch and at least two-eighty. I'm a big burly sucker, just like you pictured me, and don't you let anyone tell you otherwise." Needing to know for sure, I jumped up and grabbed out for Chris. My fingers swept across his bald scalp and then locked around his biceps, which, despite Chris flexing them as hard as he could, were well shy of burly.

Every so often, someone would poke his head out of the megamid and report, "Yep, it's still snowing." And once a friend of Chris's said, "Ain't gonna be no traveling today. It's zero, zero out there."

"Zero, zero?" I asked.

"Zero zero's what a climber gets when it's all socked in like it is now. The sky gets so gray and flat that you can't tell it from the snow. If you're caught out in it, you're in a mess of trouble. There's no tellin' whether you're walkin' on the sky or on the earth. You get so dizzy, you can't tell which way is up or down or sideways. Climbers'll walk right off a cliff, and won't even know they're fallin' till they hit the ground."

"Come to think of it," Chris said, turning to me and slapping me on the shoulder, "you're in zero zero all day long."

Finally after four days, the storm ended and we woke to clear skies and several feet of fresh snow. Soon we were off trudging up Motorcycle Hill toward our fourteen-thousand-foot camp. Periodically I would ask Chris how far we had to go, and he would reply, "We're getting pretty close. Just a little while longer." After the third cycle of me asking and Chris replying the identical lines, I began to grow suspicious. Finally I stopped abruptly, the rope going taught and Chris jerking to a stop. "Are you lying to me?" I asked, annoyed.

"Yessir!" he replied, laughing. "Now keep movin'." The rope tugged me forward. So, without a lot of options, I followed. That afternoon, we navigated a notorious section of Windy Corner. For three hours we did not stop moving as powerful winds, streaming straight from the Arctic Sea, pounded the ice wall and anything stupid enough to move across it. One section consisted of an eight-inch-wide trail, cut into the side of a glazed blue ice wall rising five thousand feet above us and dropping away five thousand feet below us to the Ruth Glacier. I concentrated on scanning with my trekking pole, finding the step and lowering my foot into it. The metal crampon blades strapped to the soles of my boots dug into the hard snow and prevented my feet from slipping. I leaned into the wall, working to offset my fifty-pound sled, which hung completely over the edge and threatened to pull me with it. When we rounded the corner the wind magically disappeared, replaced by sunshine. But the day was far from over. In front of us lay a vast maze of open crevasses. One crevasse was twenty feet across with Windex-blue walls plunging down to blackness. The only way across was a narrow two and a half foot snow bridge. "Stay directly behind me," Chris yelled. "Jeff, watch 'em." Farther up, Chris said, "Take three steps and then a real big one." I had been listening to Chris's frequent directions for two weeks, through thousands of steps for many hours each day, so I didn't pause to contemplate this one. When I took the "real big one" and my foot came down, I didn't feel the reassuring surface of the snow that usually greeted it. I pitched forward, swinging my ice ax wildly in front of me. It bit into firm snow. I had fallen up to my knees in a hole in the middle of the snow bridge. My knees dug into the opposite lip of the snow bridge and my feet dangled in space. If it hadn't been for the thin rigid poles extending from my waist to my sled, fifty pounds of gear would have slid on top of me. Straining, I pulled myself out carefully, shaking a little. Farther up the trail, I shook even more when Sam told me he had peered over the edge of the hole and couldn't see the bottom.

At fourteen thousand feet we took a rest day to acclimate. The day was sunny, although only a few hundred feet below us, clouds socked in the lower Kahiltna Glacier. Sam said, "It's like being in a lost world, cut off from the place you know—looking down at clouds when you should be looking up."

After the usual oatmeal, Chris walked around cautiously, placing wooden wands around the perimeter of a crevasse-free zone. Then, he brought out a stuff sack converted into a ball. "Pick your sides," he commanded. I got up lazily and chose Jeff. "Then I'll take Sam," Chris said. I heard the whoosh of Chris's ski pole as he swung it near my nose. "How's my swing?" he asked sarcastically.

"I bet a blind guy could strike you out," I shot back. Chris batted first, while Sam warmed up in the dugout; Jeff became catcher, and I pitched. Jeff squatted behind Chris, giving me the direction of my pitch by shouting, "Hey batter, hey batter, hmmm batter, batter." I rifled the first one.

"Whoa, young sportsman!" Chris yelled, jerking back his head to avoid a clocking. "That one clean near took off the hair on my head."

"What hair?" Jeff called out from behind him. "Ball one."

"Just seeing if you're awake," I said.

The second pitch was right on target, smoking right down the line. "Strike one!" Jeff yelled. I had found my aim. The next ripped past Chris without even a swing. "Strike two!" Jeff yelled, jumping up with visions of strike three in his head. On the next pitch, I must have lost my concentration, because I heard the whap of Chris's ski pole against the ball, and Chris strutted around the bases, each comprised of plastic freeze-dried food wrappers, making congratulatory statements like, "Who's your daddy? The crowd goes wild. Mark McGuire's got nothin' on me." With Chris distracted by self-praise, Jeff shot out of his catcher's position, snatched up the ball, and chased Chris around the bases, but Chris had too much of a head start and managed to just beat Jeff over the home-plate wrapper.

Getting three outs on Sam and Chris seemed to take forever, but finally I stepped up to bat, taking a few hard practice swings, and I noticed everyone quickly got out of my way. Chris lobbed a couple of easy pitches in my direction as Jeff coached, "Swing a little higher . . . too late." Chris clearly underestimated my ability, not having seen my rousing performance playing beeper baseball on TV. On the third lob, I felt the pole connect with the ball and heard Chris grumbling, "If he's not aiming for my crown, he's aiming for my crotch." As I ran the bases, Jeff kept ahead of me. When he got to first, he yelled out, "Over here. Over here. Over here." And just before I smashed into him, he leaped out of the way and ran to second. "Over here. Over here. Over here." Then I heard Chris behind me, gaining fast. I'll never be quite sure of the order of what happened next, but I think it went like this: Jeff tackled Chris who tackled me, and Sam piled on all of us, perhaps just for the fun of it. We rolled and tumbled through the snow in a cantankerous pile of GORE-TEX knees and elbows, and afterwards, everyone lay on their backs in the snow, gasping for air in the thin fourteen-thousand-foot atmosphere.

We ate lunch in the newly built megamid. Chris made his specialty, which he called "grease bombs," made of Spam and cheddar cheese between two halves of a bagel, fried in a pan, with an inordinate amount of grease. "My secret ingredient's the grease!" Chris said proudly, taking a big crunchy bite. "Well, . . . and the Spam, of course." After lunch, Chris asked about the American Foundation for the Blind, the organization we were supporting through our climb. "Over seventy percent of working-age blind people are unemployed, and many blind children are never taught Braille or taught to use a cane. I was one of the lucky ones," I said, remembering back to my struggles with Mrs. Mundy.

"Why are so many blind folks out of work?" Chris asked.

"I'm not sure," I said, thinking hard, "but I think it has a lot to do with people's low expectations about what blind people can do, and that rubs off on blind people themselves." I told them about my failure to get a dishwasher job in college. "Some guy told me I needed to realize my limitations. I think too many people sit around realizing their limitations when, maybe, they should spend more time realizing their potential. The AFB does a lot to combat those low expectations. Last year, they kicked off a public education campaign with a poster they hung up in libraries and schools all over the country. The poster showed pictures of blind people performing jobs you might not expect. There was a blind lawyer at a big firm, a blind systems analyst in the technology field, a blind paleontologist who can distinguish between different kinds of shells by touch, a blind color commentator for a minor league baseball team, who provided stats using a stack of Braille charts, and in the center, yours truly, appearing as a high school wrestling coach. The tag line above the pictures was designed for a little shock value. It read, 'Blind people—They don't just sell pencils!' "

"Can they say that?" Chris laughed.

"They did," I replied. I didn't know that by describing the shocking tag line, I had opened myself up to Chris's twisted humor. "I got a better one than that," he said excitedly. "Blind people—Everybody should own one!" Then, he repeated it, a little slower this time, enjoying it again in his brain. "Now that's catchy," he said and began patting his thigh and making kissing noises through puckered lips. "Come here, little buddy. Fetch Chris's slippers."

Later that afternoon, we took out the cellular phone CNN had given us to make periodic updates from the mountain. We had waited to use it until now, because fourteen thousand feet was the lowest elevation on the mountain we could get reception. We were now higher than most of the other peaks in the Alaska Range, nothing but air between us and the satellite receiver over Anchorage. At the end of the CNN interview, the reporter asked, "Now, can you reach the top between seven-fifteen and seven-thirty A.M. on June twenty-eighth, so we can do a live interview from the summit?" I explained that it didn't quite work that way, but promised we'd try. When I hung up, I thought about the phone call that I had been excited to make all week. It was Father's Day, and I wanted to surprise my dad with a call from the mountain. I tried to imagine a beam of sound waves streaking toward Anchorage, up to a satellite in space, and back down to my father's house in Connecticut. I knew that by now Ellie had arrived there too. His house was the launching point for my family's Alaskan vacation, a two week adventure of rafting, fishing, and camping in Denali National Park, before heading to Talkeetna, our meeting place after the climb.

Since leaving, I had missed Ellie terribly. She had made me a tape, filled with jokes, encouragement, and stories, and for the first few nights in the tent, I'd listened to her smooth dancing voice. Her reading selections fit her personality perfectly, pure innocence on the outside, combined with a little flair of devilishness. Between her selections from *Walt Disney's Winnie The Pooh and Tigger* and *The Corniest Jokes You've Ever Heard,* she had slipped in a few *Penthouse* "Forum" letters.

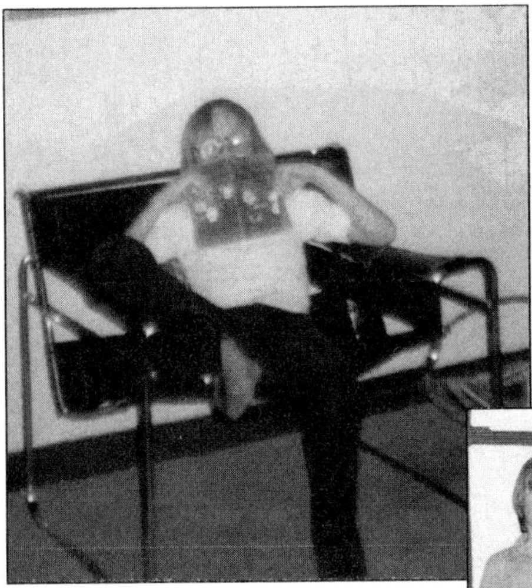

Me at age 10
wearing thick glasses
to read.

My family in
Hong Kong:
Eddi, Mark, Mom,
Dad, and me.

At age 16
with my first
guide dog,
Wizard.

My father and me hiking together on the Inca Trail.
(MARK WEIHENMAYER)

Me, my father, and my brothers, Eddi and Mark, eating spaghetti on the edge of the Boltera Glacier in Pakistan.
(ANWAR)

Yali tribesmen transport me to the village because "panthers hunt at night."
(MARK WEIHENMAYER)

Searching for a hold. (JAMIE BLOOMQUIST)

Using the tension of the rope and my ski poles to guide me on McKinley.
(Jamie Bloomquist)

Sam, Jeff, and me in an igloo at 17,200 feet on McKinley.
(Jamie Bloomquist)

Summit of Mount McKinley: Jeff, me, and Sam.
(Jamie Bloomquist)

Ellie and Seigo,
in El Capitan's Meadows.
(KIM JOHNSON)

Hans traces the route to
El Capitan's summit for me.
(JONATHAN CHESTER)

Me leading the second to last
pitch on El Capitan.
(JONATHAN CHESTER)

Me with Kilimanjaro in the background. (ELLIE WEIHENMAYER)

Ellie and me exchanging wedding vows on the Shira Plateau at 13,000 feet on Mount Kilimanjaro. (DANIEL FUNDI)

With Baltazar on the true summit of Kilimanjaro. (JOANNA STORM)

Penitentes on Aconcagua, just below base camp. (KEVIN CHERILLA)

On the summit of Aconcagua. (CHRIS MORRIS)

On one of the final pitches up Polar Circus—the 3,000-foot vertical ice wall in Alberta, Canada. (MIKE GIBBS)

Emma, me, and Ellie hiking near the summit of Chief Mountain, Colorado.
(BILL D'AMICO)

On the knife edge en route to the Hillary Step, Everest.
(DIDRICK JOHNCK, CORBIS/SYGMA)

Crossing a crevasse in the Khumbu Icefall, Everest.
(DIDRICK JOHNCK, CORBIS/SYGMA)

Listening to her voice, however, had filled me with a deep ache and such a sense of loneliness; I had to turn the tape recorder off.

Holding the cell phone in my hand, I considered not even calling Ellie, but I couldn't stop my fingers from dialing the numbers. "Hey Dad," I said loudly, his voice a little faint on the other side. "Happy Father's Day." We talked for just a moment before Ellie got on the line. "There are a lot of people rooting for you," she said, her voice upbeat. "Just today I received a bunch of letters from a class in Ohio. One little girl donated a dollar to the AFB. Everyone's proud of what you're doing, and I am too."

"This may sound strange," I said, "but the energy of all those people, it helps a lot. Oh, by the way, we've been listening to your stories," I said. "Chris, Sam, and Jeff really enjoyed them too. They keep borrowing your tape every night." Ellie laughed.

So much had happened already since I had last seen Ellen that it was hard to decide what to talk about. I told her about Ryan having to go down, I mentioned a few of Chris Morris's expressions, and described the baseball game and the grease bombs we had for lunch that day. Then it was time to say good-bye, and I knew there were no words that would give her a true grasp of this wild place. While her voice sounded clear, I felt she was a world away.

That evening after I was already in my sleeping bag, Sam, still outside, said, "Hey everyone, get out here." The urgency in his voice made me scramble to throw on my parka and inner boots. When I popped out of the tent and got to my feet, I could hear a crowd of voices murmuring heatedly like spectators at a golf match. "There's a guy with a snowboard way up there. He's probably four thousand feet above us. He looks like a speck to me but a guy over here has some binoculars." The speck turned out to be a thrill seeker who wanted to be the first person to snowboard down the Messner Couloir, a steep long snow gully that ran from twenty thousand feet to a few hundred feet up from us. As he picked up speed down the couloir, we heard a rumble. A deep jagged fracture line appeared in the snow above him. Then he was tumbling as he was swept down the couloir in the midst of a raging avalanche. A tremendous slab of snow the size of a football field tore down the slope and dropped over a thousand-foot serac, an immense wall of ice. When it hit, it shook the ground like dynamite. A tall plume of snow shot into the air. "Get down behind your tent," Chris shouted, and a second later we were blasted by a staggering gust of wind and stinging snow. Although we were hundreds of yards from the slide, the force was enough to cover us with an inch of displaced snow. "Where is he?" people were shouting. "I can't see him. Oh my god. There's no way he could have survived that."

"What's that?" Chris screamed. "That speck in the snow? Is that a rock?"

"I'm not sure. It could be." Soon the guides had mounted a rescue attempt. It was ten P.M., but still light under the Arctic sun. They were tired from the work of a long day, ready to head inside their tents, but instead they were throwing together a provision of sleeping bags, water, a sled, and medical equipment, and racing toward the dark speck in the snow. I admired their sense of duty. No matter how stupid some climber's act was, others would risk their lives to rescue him. Late that night, I heard them returning. A two-thousand-foot tumble, a thousand-foot fall, and an hour's imprisonment up to his neck in cementlike snow miraculously had not killed the snowboarder. If the guides had gotten there only a few minutes later, he would have died, but they had found him in time, wrapped him up in down bags, and dragged him in a sled down the slope to the fourteen-thousand-foot ranger's tent. A doctor, who was among a party of climbers, had driven a large needle into his chest to suck the air from his plural cavity and reinflate one of his lungs, which had been crushed by his own splintering ribs. I could hear the helicopter's propellers as it took off with the snowboarder inside. He had wanted to be the first person to snowboard the Messner Couloir, but instead he would live the rest of his life as a paraplegic.

Later I fell into a restless half sleep. All the layers of down, fleece, and nylon piled beneath me weren't enough to insulate me from the mile-thick ice of the glacier. I dreamed that I was the snowboarder, hurtling out of control down the five-thousand-foot couloir, riding the enormous slab that had ripped away above me. The earth rumbled around me as the gray rocks and sky shot by in shadowy swirls. Then I was tumbling over the ice serac in a massive sea of snow and debris, swimming, swimming as I had been taught, fighting to keep my head above the spill. In the morning I woke with a hollow nervous feeling in the pit of my stomach, and I was extra slow in gearing up, dreading the moment when I would emerge from the tent to face the elements. Entering the megamid, I heard Jeff asking Chris, "Did you feel it?"

"Better believe I felt it. Shook me out of my sleep. You boys just slept through a good old fashioned Alaskan earthquake."

"Did you check out the serac, the one the dude sailed over?" Jeff asked. Everyone looked out.

"It's gone. It's totally gone." The serac had been reduced to a splintered pile of ice fragments. In the last twenty-four hours, we had been reminded that we were operating in an environment oblivious to our presence, a place where avalanches and earthquakes could obliterate a thousand-ton tower of ice and the tiny humans in its wake overnight.

The first day above fourteen thousand feet seemed endless. Chris told us, "Everything up to fourteen's just a slog. Above it, you're really climbing." True to his word, the next two thousand feet hosted the steepest part of the mountain, the sixty-degree headwall of the buttress. I couldn't seem to catch my breath. "Pressure breathe!" Chris said. "You gotta find your rhythm." But I couldn't seem to find it. My pack felt heavier than it ever had. The weight seemed to compress my spine and squeeze my internal organs. My chest strap suffocated my labored breathing. The hip straps cut sharply into my sides and kept slipping, so that the shoulder straps weighed down on my traps. Earlier I heard about a woman who had made the summit of McKinley by sheer will, but in obtaining her goal, had crossed her threshold. Just below the summit, she collapsed and died, her frozen body slowly buried by falling snow. I wondered how far I could push myself before I collapsed in the snow. I feared that I had made a horrible mistake in coming here, and I seriously doubted I had the strength within me to reach the next camp, let alone the summit. I tried to concentrate on my breathing and the placement of each step. "Rhythm," I willed. "Find the rhythm." Throughout the five hours we toiled up the steep face, I never found my rhythm, and it never got any easier. Other days were hard, but this day had clearly been my greatest struggle, when I came closest to turning back. When it finally ended, and I collapsed into a dank snow cave at sixteen thousand feet, I was more exhausted than I had ever been. The day could, in no way, be described as fun. In fact, it was miserable, but in an unlikely way, the experience had also been a rare privilege. Every few moments, when I had thought I was at my absolute limit, I was able to push through it, and never once had I felt like collapsing in the snow as I had feared. Some limits were real, like the inability to climb a twenty-thousand-foot peak before acclimatizing to the thin oxygen. But many more limits were conceived and imposed in my mind, and there was a torturous beauty in crossing through them.

Living in a snow cave was grim. The ceilings were so low that you couldn't sit upright. Our body heat warmed the walls and they emitted a damp clingy atmosphere. We lay out our foam pads and lay head to toe, bickering constantly. "Your smelly sock is in my face."

"Your ass is on my mat, home chicken. Move over."

"I can't. Then I'll be on Sam's mat." We lay like that for hours arguing over who smelled the worst and who was the biggest dirtbag. Jeff pointed out that he had personally seen me stash my toothbrush and toothpaste in a pile of nonessentials left at fourteen thousand feet, and because of this information, felt I should win the prize. "Your breath," he said with conviction, "smells like my ass. Have you been brushing your teeth with toilet paper?"

"I wish your breath smelled as good as my ass," I replied. "That would be a big improvement."

A few days earlier we had heard about two guys wanting to paraglide off the summit. We had been laughing about all the things we wished they'd drop off for us on their way down. Jeff rebutted with, "I just wish those paragliders would glide over here and drop off a little toothpaste." In the midst of the volleying, Sam slipped over to the entranceway. "Hey guys," he interrupted. No one minded. "It looks like the weather's improved." He disappeared outside and reemerged a few minutes later. "I strongly advise everybody come out here right away," he said. Although the cave was miserable, the cold and hours of lying around had made me lethargic. Finally I scrambled out with the others. It was eleven P.M., but the first thing I felt was the Alaskan sun on the back of my neck. Everyone was quiet as they looked out over Mount Foraker, a seventeen-thousand-foot peak, second highest to Denali. "The sun is hitting the top of Foraker," Sam described. "Mount Foraker is popping out of a mass of white puffy clouds and the sun's making it rosy."

"The part above the clouds looks like a crown," Jeff added.

This day had run the gamut. Hardship and exhaustion had enveloped us like the billowing layer of clouds below a summit, but out of the suffering emerged a rare simple beauty. Strangely, the day came closest to capturing the essence of why I climb. Some people explain that they climb because it's fun, but for me, this word is misleading. Fun is floating in an inner tube down a lazy river on a warm summer's day with a six-pack of beer floating next to me, but there is simply no word in the English language to describe the experience of climbing mountains. The feeling is an inseparable blend of extremes and contradictions, from the misery of a sixty-pound pack crushing my spine to the ecstasy of the warm sun on my neck and a description of the evening sky over Mount Foraker.

On day fifteen we finally reached our seventeen-thousand-foot camp after a steep climb up an exposed ridge of snow and jagged rock. I was so tired, I felt like I was only partly conscious. Chris would look back and yell, "It's narrow around that rock band, so watch your step." I could only muster enough energy to grunt in response as I mechanically heeded his warning. When we came into camp, we discovered an abandoned igloo. There was just enough room inside for Chris to use it as our camp kitchen. We began to dig a flat space for the tents. Chris began shoveling but at this altitude even he was breathing hard after only a few minutes. So, we formed a line; each of us would shovel for a few minutes and then another would take over, while the person who just finished would go to the end of the line to recover.

The next day was definitely not a summit day. Lenticular clouds hung over the summit and huge plumes of snow were blowing around. The weather was good enough for us to hike out to a ledge that overlooked the Kahiltna base camp, ten thousand feet below. From here, a crusty old Alaskan once told us, you could see farther than any point on earth. Sam described the giant crevasse we had crossed, now only a dark spot against the gray and white landscape. It was hard to imagine that we had inched our way up that ten-thousand-foot expanse. We had already come a long way.

By the second day at high camp, the weather had not improved. Above us, near the summit, wind gusted at over a hundred miles per hour. We entertained ourselves by sitting in the igloo, trying to pull conversations out of each other that hadn't already been extracted throughout the last seventeen days. My technique was to let my mind go blank, allowing the events of the day to slip by with complete acceptance and little judgment. Every now and then, for his own entertainment, Sam would snap his fingers in front of my face and say, "Anyone home in there?" During such times of boredom Chris would amaze us with the curious little toys that he kept hidden away in his pack, saving them for just such an occasion. At eleven thousand feet it had been a hacky sack, at fourteen thousand feet, a ball made out of a stuff sack, and at seventeen thousand feet, it was a $2.99 Kmart-special kite. He took it gingerly from its bag and, laying it on his lap, checked the knots and ran his fingers over the wooden sticks like a mother inspecting her child before school. He was beaming, because anything that provided a day's entertainment on a storm day in the mountains was more valuable than gold. Instead of spending another day in the igloo eating sausages out of a bag, he would be enjoying the open spaces, flying his kite where most people fly a plane. As he excitedly pulled on his boots and gloves, he turned to us with a smile and said, "Don't wait up for me, boys." I heard his boots crunching away and imagined his little kite tucked carefully under his arm. Ten minutes later he was back. "Forget something?" I asked.

"Where's the kite?" Jeff asked. Chris pulled a spool of string from his jacket. The end of the string hung limply in front of him. "That's what you get when you try to fly a kite in sixty-mile-an-hour winds," Sam laughed.

On the third day, the bad weather had increased to a full-scale blizzard. Jeff or I would have to gear up every few hours to shovel away the snow that was creeping up the walls of the tent. Getting out of our warm bags and exposing ourselves to the full brunt of the blizzard was far more appealing than being crushed by accumulated snow. The worst part about nasty weather was visiting the "ice throne," an old sled converted into a latrine that sat a hundred yards down the hill. Jeff had tried to improve the experience by tacking a *Penthouse* centerfold to the side of the sled. In the midst of the storm I shook Sam, who was lying on his belly, his face buried in his down jacket pillow. "Dude, I gotta grump."

"Can't you wait?"

"No!" I replied urgently.

"Does anyone need to visit the grump station with Erik?" Sam yelled, not bothering to roll over. Chris was the first to respond from his tent. "I draw the line, boys. I'll haul 'em, but I won't grump 'em."

Sam lay still for another minute and then abruptly sat up. "OK! OK! I guess I could muster one up. You got bum rub?" We both suited up with our balaclavas covering our faces, three-layer mittens and down jackets, and postholed down through fresh snow. First Sam went, his boots standing on each side of the sled, crouched over bombardier style, while I tried to block the wind with my body.

"Hurry up," I said. "I'm freezing." Then it was my turn. And in the brief time it took me to take my mittens off, yank down my GORE-TEX bibs, locate the toilet paper, and wipe in crucial areas, my hands went completely numb. I couldn't feel the TP in my hand, but it didn't really matter, because I couldn't feel my exposed rump either. I managed to pull up my fleece and bibs with dead fish hands. Sam had started back for the tent ahead of me and I fought to catch him through thigh-deep snow and blistering wind. When I finally stumbled into the tent, I was gasping for breath and my freezing face had joined my hands, completely numb. When I plopped down onto my bag, I thought about the ordeal and could not imagine an experience being so utterly grim. If making it back alive from the ice throne was this hard, I thought, then making it to the summit would be downright impossible.

By the fourth day at high camp, we were running out of food and fuel. We only had three boxes of macaroni and cheese and a pile of old frozen candy bars we had found stashed in the igloo. The rest of our food was all the way down at fourteen thousand feet. Lying in the tent next to Sam, I could feel our opportunity, which was once so boundless, slipping away like a puny dwindling stack of old candy bars. "All this work, all our training," I said, "we're so close, and we still may not summit." I couldn't get over this conflict between my desire to summit and the cold reality of the mountains. Over the last year, we had put in so much effort, a part of me felt like it was our right to summit. All the running, the stair climbing, the practice climbs, the heavy-load carrying, had been a test which we had passed, but on Denali, you could receive a perfect score and still be turned back. Those who imposed their human rules over the natural laws of the mountain were extremely lucky if they lived to regret it. During our eighteen days on McKinley, three climbers had died while trying to reach the top. Just the day before, two climbers had left for the summit with storm clouds above and went missing for twenty-four hours. Few ever survived a night out on the upper mountain, and the consensus at high camp was that they were surely dead. Earlier this morning, however, Chris spotted them, staggering down the snow slope above the seventeen-thousand-foot basin; they would take a few flailing steps, fall down, slide a ways, struggle up, and take a few more steps. "Those two boys are the luckiest fools alive," Chris said matter-of-factly. Miraculously, the two, lost in a white-out only a few hours from camp, stumbled upon a snow cave, built by previous climbers, and had hunkered inside through the night. Chris and Jeff helped the two into their tent. While Jeff boiled water, Chris pulled off their boots, socks, and gloves, assessing quickly that they would both lose some toes and fingers.

That night we were silent as we heard Base Camp Annie, our only contact with the outside world, give the weather report for the next day. It called for a brief break in the storm before it resumed at full force. Chris turned to us and said firmly, "You don't decide when to climb a mountain. The mountain decides."

By the fifth day, however, Denali seemed to be showing its friendlier side. Miraculously the sky was clearer. Lenticular clouds hovered over the summit of Mount Foraker, but because we knew this might be our last shot, we decided to climb to as high as the saddle between the north and south summits, where we could reevaluate the weather. We left at six A.M., roped up into two teams and waded through a field of thigh-deep snow. It was a struggle placing my feet in the deep boot holes that Chris had made. Many times I would miss them and begin veering to the left or right of the trail. This was a horribly inefficient use of energy and I knew that continuously breaking my own trail above seventeen thousand feet would exhaust me quickly.

With my tight fleece hat and the thick elastic strap of my goggles over my ears, combined with the constant wind rolling down from the saddle, I was cut off from the outside world. The frigid stinging air even obliterated my sense of smell. My many layers of fleece and GORE-TEX, three-layer mittens, and huge plastic boots protected me from the forty-below-zero temperature, and felt like a cocoon around me. This environment was both awe-inspiring and inhospitable, clearly unsuitable for the delicate flickering warmth of a human life. Although Chris traveled only thirty feet in front of me and Sam thirty feet behind me, I felt as solitary as an astronaut exploring the landscape of the moon.

Next we reached the Autobahn, a steep traverse, which led one thousand feet to the saddle. Climbers, constantly surrounded by death, develop a sick sense of humor. The Autobahn was named for the large number of German parties who had pitched off the side of it to their deaths. Another nearby section of the mountain was named The Orient Express, for similar reasons. "We have to complete the Autobahn in at least two hours," Chris said, "or it means we're moving too slow." I tried to force my body to move more quickly so we wouldn't have to turn around. Internal monologues would continuously play in my head. "Quit being a baby. You're not so tired. We'll rest in forty minutes, tops." Eventually, after what seemed like hundreds of pep talks, I stepped off the traverse onto a flatter section and Chris told me that this was the saddle. We made it in one hour and fifty minutes.

The weather seemed to be holding, so we made the decision to keep going, traversing up an endlessly steep slope, with the snow consolidated into glacier ice, hard and windblown. With no boot holes to find and only the repetitive consistency of my eight crampon points digging and catching in the smooth hard ice, propelling my body upward, I began to feel the rhythm of clean, pure, internal movement. For the first time all morning, I dared to believe we had a chance.

Finally we came out onto the Football Field, a large gradual slope where nineteen days ago, our first on the mountain, one of two Taiwanese climbers had died and been buried somewhere nearby. "Not a place you want to get stuck on," Chris warned. I forced myself to hurry past, fearing, with every step, that I was trespassing on top of his grave.

Next was Pig Hill, a six-hundred-foot headwall that was the last grunt before the summit ridge. As we began to climb, Sam, Chris, and I were no longer three individual climbers, but were roped together, moving up the slope like a slithering snake. Each of the parts worked, neither pulling nor tugging, to move the unit forward. Then something very strange happened, something that has never happened to me since, while so near a summit; I began to feel stronger. Halfway up, Chris turned to me and paused for a few seconds. "I don't usually say this, Big E, because I don't want to jinx anything, but I think we're gonna make it."

When we crested Pig Hill, the summit seemed very close, but I didn't realize the hardest part was yet to come. Connecting Pig Hill to the summit was the summit ridge, just a quarter mile long, but only two feet wide, with a thousand-foot drop on one side and a nine-thousand-foot drop on the other. The good news in this bleak scenario was that, if I fell, it really wouldn't matter which side it was off of. Before the ridge Chris huddled us around him and spoke, his voice unusually calm. "Boys, listen carefully. If you fall here, we all fall. You'll drag us all off the side of the mountain. So, if I haven't explained myself plainly," he leaned in toward us as his voice gained momentum, "what I'm telling you boys is . . . DON'T FALL!" I was nervous, taking each step slowly and carefully. In my life off the mountain, I could stumble and fall and get up again, but I knew, on the ridge, the mountain wouldn't tolerate a mistake. Then I leaned on my pole and it must have been too close to the edge. The snow gave way under the weight, and I felt myself sway forward over the side. I quickly recovered and stepped back. "Damn it!" Chris yelled, his gruff voice masking his nervousness. "Test it first before you weight it."

I found my confidence again and slowly placed each step, testing each by gradually weighting my front foot while keeping tension on my back leg. After every step, I'd keep my bearings by tapping my ice ax against the left edge of the ridge, sliding the tip several inches inward across the slope until it bit firm solid snow, and finally plunging it in. My other hand used my pole to scan for boot holes and monitor the right edge. All my preparation, all my skills seemed to gather together into this moment. The process of scanning, stepping, and breathing was all-consuming, so that the extent of my life was reduced to moving slowly and rhythmically up the narrow ridge, as if there had never been anything more than the tug of the rope, my raw amplified breathing, and the careful crisp bite of my equipment in the firm snow. How beautiful it was in its severity, my whole being totally consolidated into one purpose. Step. Breathe, breathe, breathe. Step.

I was concentrating so fully, Chris's voice, right in front of me, yelling over the wind, seemed to emerge as if I were waking from a dream. "Congratulations, you're standing on the top of North America." It seems strange that the last step felt no different from the thousands and thousands of previous steps I had taken in the last nineteen days. It was just another step, and then I was there.

Immediately I sat down in the snow, suffering from a gurgling high-altitude cough. Then Sam was next to me. "We're not quite there yet, Big E," he said.

"You're joking," I begged. But before I could protest, everybody's arms were around me and I was being guided up a little embankment. I could hear their breathing and their GORE-TEX crackling in the wind. We all stood as a team on the three-foot-by-three-foot mound of snow, which marked the true summit of McKinley. Sadly, though, I could feel Ryan's absence, and I reached into my shirt and felt his HighSights cross warm against my skin. Then we unfurled the American Foundation for the Blind flag and posed for a few glory shots.

As the last photo clicked, I heard the tiny mechanical buzz of the Cessna plane circling above. An hour before summitting, we had radioed down to Base Camp Annie, who radioed out to a small airstrip in Talkeetna where my family waited. Now as I stood on the top, my dad, my two brothers, and Ellen were circling above me, sharing in this exhilarating moment. It was strange, knowing that they were only a few hundred yards away, yet I couldn't touch them or hear their voices. Later I learned that Mark had spotted us first, tiny red dots moving slowly against infinite white. He lifted his oxygen mask for a moment and tapped Ellie. "There they are!" he said, his words trembling with excitement and vibrating with the plane's engine. "There they are, Ellie!" Ellie was so nervous for us, she only managed a nod, the tears spilling down her face as she peered through the window.

My team all wore identical red GORE-TEX shells. And with our hats and goggles covering our faces, we were indistinguishable. As the plane swooped by, we all waved our ski poles and cheered. Then I asked Sam if he thought my family would know which one was me. "I think they will," he laughed. "You're the only one waving your ski pole in the wrong direction."

Chris's voice was still on edge when he cut into our celebration. "This ain't no place to be screwing the pooch. The weather's changing, boys, and we need to move. The summit's only the halfway point." My thirty seconds of carefree exhilaration were over. The others were still hugging and shouting, ice axes drawn toward the sky. I stood aside from the celebration, a flash of panic shooting through me like a lightning bolt. You've gotten up here. Great. Now what the hell do you do? I thought. How do you get down? How will you get down the ridge? Tripping on a crampon strap or losing my balance on the way up would probably mean falling into the slope, but falling on the way down would mean a nine-thousand-foot head-over-heals tumble, my entire rope team dragging along behind me. As I thought of that gruesome image, tears formed in my eyes and immediately froze to my eyelashes. Then Jeff noticed how quiet I was and asked me what was wrong. "I'm worried about getting down the ridge," I said. "I'm worried I'll do something stupid." Then everyone gathered around me, putting their hands on my shoulders. "We'll get down," Chris said, and something in his voice made me believe him instantly. The concentration game began again and I carefully lowered each foot into the frozen boot holes in front of me, knowing that all of our lives depended on an action so seemingly simple. The terrain began to flatten out, bringing me out of my trance. "How much farther until the end of the ridge?" I asked Chris. "Boy, you passed the ridge twenty minutes ago," he answered.

Six hours later we stumbled across the seventeen-thousand-foot basin at the foot of the Autobahn. I tripped in one of the deep boot holes and fell facefirst in the snow. Knowing we were so close to camp, I just lay there moaning and laughing. Jeff and Sam followed my lead, collapsing in the snow as well. We were all moaning and calling out in pathetic voices, "Chris, help us up. We can't go any farther. Chris, you're my hero." Chris, knowing we were out of danger, and feeling somehow relieved from the responsibility of leading, untied himself from the rope and raced energetically toward camp as if he had forgotten the fifteen hours of constant movement. "You boys are the sorriest excuse for climbers that I've ever seen," he yelled as he motored away. Twenty minutes later we staggered into camp. I lay on my belly in the snow, my body beyond exhaustion, not even feeling the temperature that had dropped forty degrees in the last hour.

Later, sitting in the igloo around a pot of freeze-dried spaghetti, Chris loaded our bowls. "Gotta eat," he said. "We've got a death march in the morning." As I piled the last spoonful into my mouth, my wasted body rejected it and I gave the whole meal back to the mountain gods. It lay in a pile in front of the entranceway, quickly freezing into a rock-hard mound in the snow. Sam was so tired, he only said, "Wow, look at all the colors in it." Because of the mound's location, each of my team would have to crawl through it to escape the igloo. Jeff was the bravest, or perhaps his exhaustion outweighed his revulsion. He crawled tiredly through and disappeared. Sam was next, taking a deep breath and scurrying quickly through it. Finally only Chris and I remained. "I'm sorry," I said. "First you drag me to the top and then I throw up in your igloo." Chris was silent, sitting a few feet across from me. Then he spoke as if he hadn't heard me. "You're all right, Big E."

"But still," I replied, kicking my boot against the crusty mound in the entranceway. Then Chris reached across the igloo and slapped his gloved hand against my shoulder. "Anyone," he said, "who stands on the top of North America, I'll crawl through his puke any day," and he dropped into the doorway and was gone. Then I was alone, the events of the day flooding into my tired brain. The igloo walls enveloped me in a muffled silence, and a feeling of such intensity swept over me that I could feel my body shaking. I had only stood on the summit for a few minutes, but the experience had forged itself into me, more powerful than any memory, fusing so tight that it was impossible to distinguish me from it. I could still feel the blasting wind, the storms, and the staggeringly long days. I could feel it all, from the bumpy plane ride in, to the immense openness of the summit, and it was all within me, changing my life forever, no longer a dream but flesh and bone and blood. I had never known, never truly known, that this awesome place could exist inside me.

It had taken us nineteen days to climb Denali, and just two days to descend. Chris was right; it was a death march. We descended through the next day and through the night and through the next day again, coming down the narrow ridge below our seventeen-thousand-foot camp, sliding down the fixed lines on the steep snow face of the buttress proper, through the crevasse fields below fourteen thousand feet, and around windy corner, down Motorcycle and Ski Hill and finally across the endless flats below base camp. The joy of starting a Denali climb is that you immediately cruise down a thousand foot hill called Heartbreak Hill. Ironically the misery of ending a Denali climb is that very same hill, the other way. "This doesn't seem like much of a hill," I said to Chris on the way down. He responded with a laugh and nothing more, as if the punch line was much too funny to waste on such a tenderfoot as me.

At the bottom of Heartbreak Hill, with my sixty-pound backpack grinding into my spleen, and another fifty pounds of trash dragging behind me on my sled, I finally understood Chris's secret and hopelessly tragic joke. In order to catch the Cessna plane, our heavenly link to civilization, in order to eat pepperoni pizza and drink beers, in order to take a hot bath and sleep under clean sheets, we'd have to climb that last hill. The whole team was spent, creeping painfully up the hill, except, of course, for Chris. "Boys, the last plane's at eight o'clock, and By God we're gonna be on it . . . or at least I will. We got a half an hour to make it up this pig, so, mush!" Shuffling forward, we heard a faint sound drifting down from a thousand feet above us. The last three weeks had prepared me for all sorts of weird sounds: distant avalanches, wind whistling across the upper mountain, even earthquakes, but this one didn't sound like any of those. In fact, it sounded human, and not just one or two humans, but a whole choir. They weren't exactly talking or yelling or even singing, but chanting something over and over. I was so curious to learn the source of the baffling human sound, I pushed my ravaged body a little faster up the hill. Halfway up, the voices became louder and clearer. A chorus of people chanted "Hip hip hurray! Hip hip hurray!" Then even the voices were familiar. It reminded me of my wrestling days, when my father would take the early train home from New York City, arriving in the gymnasium moments before my match. As I walked out onto the mat to face my opponent, I'd hear his deep ex-Marine voice calling out over the rest of the fans, "Good luck. Go get 'em!"

The voices floating down to me from the top of Heartbreak Hill were my family's. I couldn't pick out any one of them individually, but even together, they were as unmistakable to me as the thick metal ice ax I had been holding in my hand for the last three weeks. They must have made the death-defying flight across the Alaska Range to meet me at base camp. I was smiling now, pushing on even faster, ignoring the grinding pain in my back and thighs and the fact that I was sinking to my knees in soft snow. Then I heard Mark's voice ahead of me. "What the hell is it?" He was looking at twenty-one days of beard and filth. And Eddi replying, "I think it's the Sasquatch."

"Good job, little brother," Mark said.

"Yeah, awesome job, little bro," Eddi seconded. Then they were on both sides of me, and Mark said, "Grab his pack, Eddi. I'll get this side." Suddenly, my pack and sled were weightless; even my feet barely skimmed across the top of the snow, and we all moved forward, my two bodybuilder brothers lifting me up by my hip belt.

At base camp we all enjoyed a party of a lifetime. Everyone was handed a slushy beer, dug up from Chris's secret buried stash. Mark opened a bottle of champagne and sprayed it all over me, the sticky liquid just one more layer over the sweat and grime. Base Camp Annie shared her prized stash of grape Kool-Aid. The best part was hearing Ellie's soft footsteps through the snow and her voice, catching in her throat, and reaching out to take her thin hands, wrapped in fleece mittens. She had brought Oreo cookies and chocolate milk, better than anything else I've ever tasted. And when we returned home, Liz Greco, from the American Foundation for the Blind, told us the strange coincidence: our summit date of June 27th just happened to be Helen Keller's birthday.

# 13
# "Big" Changes

When I got back to Phoenix, my new Fidelco guide dog, Seigo, accompanied me. He was about thirty pounds heavier than Wizard, with a huge head, the size of a small bear's, gigantic paws, and a husky chest to match. When Ellie saw him for the first time as he barreled out of the jetway in the airport, she asked, "Are you sure they didn't give you a seeing-eye pony?"

John Byfield, the head of the Fidelco training program, told me that Seigo had been named after a famous German show dog, who he had seen on a previous trip to Germany, where Fidelco found breeding dogs. Seigo, the show dog, was huge, proud, and noble, perfect in every way, and my Seigo was practically perfect, except for one tiny physical flaw, a lazy ear which flopped down and folded over when he was excited. Seigo's slight imperfection didn't bother me in the slightest; in fact, I thought it gave him personality.

Seigo was like a bodybuilder who didn't know his own strength. As a puppy, none of the female dogs would play with him, because in happy-go-lucky playfulness, Seigo would bound through the dog run and shoulder tackle the other dogs, somersaulting them like bowling pins into the walls. I almost didn't get a chance to meet Seigo. A year earlier, when I had decided that it was time to retire Wizard, I had gone to the Fidelco kennel to see the new dog John had selected for me. She was a beautiful, short haired shepherd named Whitney, but she was tiny and dainty, only fifty pounds, and after managing a bruiser like Wizard for eleven years, I voiced to John that I would wait one more year. Plus, even though Wizard was slowing down, every morning he still wagged his tail and whimpered at the door, to show he had a little kick left in him.

"Last year," John said, "you felt Whitney was too small. So this year we have for you the largest, most rambunctious dog we've ever trained. But you climb mountains, so you two should be well matched."

The first time I walked with Seigo, he happily and innocently almost pulled my arm out of the socket. Suddenly my confidence wasn't as great as John's had been.

Our first month together, moving through the Phoenix Country Day School campus, Seigo bucked and charged like a wild stallion, and I felt like a brazen young cowboy attempting to break him. Students would scream out cheerfully, "Hello, Seigo!" and dive to the edge of the sidewalk as his gigantic frame rounded the corner, and next I popped into view, dragging along behind, my left arm extended, clutching his harness, my feet practically running to keep up. I thought Seigo's power might have been more suited for leading a one-dog sled team in the Alaskan Iditarod.

In the school cafeteria, before finding my empty chair, Seigo would stop at each teacher's chair to pant, wag, and sniff out the contents of each lunch tray. Seigo was as gentle as Wizard was intense, but he hadn't yet resigned himself to the rules of guidedoghood. Once, as I walked toward my table with my tray, a little boy began laughing. "Mr. Weihenmayer, Seigo just took a bite out of Bobby's bagel." If he hadn't told me, I would have never known, because Seigo had hardly broken stride as he nonchalantly stretched his head and took one massive chomp out of one side of the bagel, just as Bobby bit a small chunk out of the other side. That was it, I thought. Seigo's education was just beginning. If I had to take on the role of a rodeo cowboy in order to curb Seigo's lovable yet inappropriate tendencies, then that's what I would do. In front of all the curious little eyes, I sat Seigo down, pried open his massive jaws, and poked my fingers around in his mouth, looking for the bagel. He hadn't swallowed all of it, and soon, I withdrew a few soggy remnants. All the boys at Bobby's table let out a collective, "Ewww!" as I held the slimy globs of bagel out, palms up. "Bobby, Seigo gives you his most sincere apologies, and he wants to give you your bagel back."

"Uh, no thanks, Mr. Weihenmayer. Seigo can have it."

Throughout the school year, people who had seen the McKinley climb on TV called, asking me to speak to their various groups. One call was from the Texas Lions Camp, an hour south of San Antonio, requesting me to spend a couple of days with 250 disabled campers. The camp was free of charge to all the children accepted, and for each session, they swam, camped, and rock climbed on an artificial rock wall. I was there to help the camp run a high ropes course, adapted so that campers in their wheelchairs could complete it.

At the opening campfire ceremony, I met the Dane family. All three brothers were born blind and mentally disabled. The youngest, Nathan, who was the most severely disabled of the three, was constantly connected to an array of complicated and obtrusive equipment, which kept him alive. He wore heart monitors to keep track of his irregular heartbeat and a mist collar so his skin wouldn't dry out. He had to be fed through a gastric tube placed in his stomach, and at night, every half hour, a nurse used a tracheotomy tube to perform deep suction on his throat so he wouldn't choke. When I asked him what he wanted to be when he grew up, he replied boldly that he wanted to be an astronaut. I envisioned him, connected to his gastric and tracheotomy tubes, his heart monitors, and mist collar, blasting off into space. Unlikely, I honestly thought, but then I reconsidered. Who's to tell? I decided, except him. Standing away from her children, Nathan's mother told me, "A social worker once looked at my children and told me they would only be a burden on society and asked me why I didn't abort them when I had the chance. I'd told her, 'Come to my house. Spend a little time with the children; see how much love they have to give, and you'd understand.' "

During the opening ceremony and under the stars of a clear Texas sky, the camp director asked each camper to find a stick. "Now," he continued, "make a wish, something you want to accomplish this week. Maybe, it's making a new friend or overcoming a fear or trying something new. Your stick represents your wish. Hold it in your hand and feel your wish taking form." Then all the children were asked to line up, shuffle past the campfire, and throw their sticks into the blaze. I sat on a log, listening to the long line of children slowly moving forward. The clearing was too small for a straight line of 250 campers and a hundred more counselors, so it curved around in a massive, spiraling circle. The line represented disabilities of almost every kind: paras and quads, blind and deaf, birth defects and mental retardation, spina bifida and muscular dystrophy, cerebral palsy, and autism. Every child held their greatest hopes and dreams in their hands and then tossed them into the fire. The mountain of small sticks fueled the flames as the heat rose. "Now, your wishes have been ignited by the fire," the director said. "The great possibility of your lives has been unlocked and is rising up into the Texas sky, now, only to be realized." That night I cheated and threw two sticks into the fire. I didn't want to believe that life was an either/or, that if you chose one thing, you couldn't have the other. Then I sat back and listened to the fire crackle and roar, picturing the sky crowded with wishes, rising up over the earth, like Nathan's rocket ship.

My first wish was to climb a few more mountains. Actually I had a tick list of mountains a mile long. Mount Kilimanjaro, the tallest peak in Africa, would be a perfect climb for Ellie and my dad to experience the beauty of the mountains the way I had on McKinley. I thought Kilimanjaro would especially appeal to the explorer in Ellie, since from its base to summit is the only place in the world where one can pass so quickly through the earth's five distinct vegetation zones: the cultivated fields of the lower slopes, forest, heath and moorland, alpine, and finally, arctic. Plus, I might be able to bribe Ellie with a Serengeti safari afterwards.

I also wanted to try a technical rock climb. On McKinley, Sam and I had discussed the idea of El Capitan, a 3300-foot rock face in Yosemite Valley, California, the tallest exposed-granite monolith in the world. El Cap was a climber's dream. What a way to spend a summer, in a climber's Mecca, Yosemite Valley.

Down the road, I wanted to climb Aconcagua, the tallest peak in South America. Aconcagua straddles Chile and Argentina and is located at the southern tip of the Andes. At 22,850 feet, Aconcagua is a full half mile taller than McKinley, and the perfect next step. The only problem was that Aconcagua was typically climbed in the South American summer, the North American winter. Falling right smack in the middle of the school year, it would be unfair to my students for me to take an entire month off. I had also begun to get the attention of the outdoor gear industry, so with a few sponsorships and with the money coming in from my slide shows, I thought I could actually make a living.

I even dreamed about a greater challenge, one so immense, I didn't even speak it aloud, for fear of sounding ridiculous. Recently, I had read a book entitled, *Seven Summits*, by Dick Bass. In his fifties, with relatively little climbing experience, Bass had become the first person to climb the highest peak in each of the seven continents. Supposedly, McKinley was the second hardest, a far second, of course, to Mount Everest. I wondered if I really had the capability to climb them all. The rational side of me warned, "Hold on there, tiger. You've climbed one big mountain. Let's not get carried away." But when I thought about climbing mountains all over the world, meeting new people and experiencing new cultures, my life just one great adventure, I found it impossible not to get carried away. After Kilimanjaro and Aconcagua, there was Mount Elbrus, highest peak in Europe, Carstenz Pyramid, highest in Austral-Asia, Mount Vinson, highest in Antarctica, and finally, Everest, a word that made me nervous just thinking about it. I would need to gain a lot more experience in the mountains.

But I couldn't stop asking myself, What if I fail? What if I make it to the top of six but find that Everest's summit is simply beyond my reach? With failure, the sighted world would immediately point to blindness as the culprit. "Well, of course he didn't make all seven. The guy can't see." Although the failure might have come from a dozen other, more pertinent reasons: sickness, injury, or simply my limitations at high altitude or as an athlete in general. Pushing the world's assumptions aside, I felt determined to rise to the level of my own internal potential, and if my potential fell short of seven, then at least that would be a more honest path than being talked out of something before I even started.

If I was going to climb mountains, why not live in the mountains? The greatest mountains in the U.S., the Rocky Mountains. Colorado was the perfect setting for steep rocky crags, massive pillars of ice, and basins of fresh white powder, and the only state that could claim fifty-four peaks above fourteen thousand feet. Living and training in a true alpine setting would build an invaluable foundation for attempting high peaks all around the world.

My first wish, to climb mountains, however, would have been meaningless without the second. I decided to propose to Ellen. I had never known happiness like I had around Ellen. I had a tendency to live in the future, to make a long list of goals and then scheme and conspire about how I would get there, but when I was with Ellen, I existed fully in the present. With her, the past and the future seemed like distant abstractions. Whether we were snuggling on the couch on a Saturday night, or standing on the top of a mountain, I was filled up with the richness of the moment, and I couldn't imagine being anywhere other than with her. I asked her to marry me on a perfect, sunbaked, Arizona day atop the Praying Monk, a two-hundred-foot rock formation, overlooking the city of Phoenix. For several months, Ellen had expressed interest, in her subtle way, in getting married. Off on a great hike in the Grand Canyon, all of a sudden it struck me that Ellen had been very quiet for an hour. It was obvious something was wrong, even though Ellie stubbornly denied it. After an hour of detective work—false starts, dead-end leads, and a long series of haranguing questions—I finally got to the core of issue: throughout her long bout of silence, Ellen had been hearing the loud clang of wedding bells in her head. Then one day she started talking about a special ring she had seen in Santa Fe. "I just really like it," she said. "It's not like I'm asking you to get it for me, I just like the looks of it a lot."

It seemed fitting that we began our marriage plans on the Praying Monk. From Ellen's classroom window she had a perfect view of the formation, which apparently looks like a cloaked monk kneeling and praying to the larger mountain. I knew Ellen had always wanted to climb it and I wanted to be the one to lead her up the climb. Hidden in the bottom of my climbing pack along with the climbing gear were two plastic champagne glasses with snap-on stems, a small bottle of chilled Mumm Cuvée Napa Valley sparkling wine, a ring made out of candy, and two tickets to Santa Fe, for ring shopping.

Leading the Praying Monk entails clipping the rope into rusty metal bolts that have been drilled into the rock every ten feet or so. The route begins with a slight overhang, then moves around a corner onto an exposed face at which the ground has dropped away and you are suddenly situated hundreds of feet above the city of Phoenix and the expansive desert floor.

I planned to lead us up the route, but Ellie, who needed to spot the bolts for me to clip into, could only see the first three bolts, losing sight of the rest as the route rounded the corner. Worried that my plans for a memorable day were washed up and with our champagne losing its chill, I encouraged Ellie to give it a try. "I'll get us past the hard part, clip in, then you can lead the rest," I told her. Ellie and I had been rock climbing together for a year but she had never lead climbed before. I knew, trying it for the first time, she'd be a bit intimidated. I wouldn't blame her if she opted out.

Ellie took the lead, never faltered, and before long, she yelled a confident, "ON BELAY! You can climb now." I climbed the entire route with a proud expectant smile on my face.

It was my turn to be nervous, when faced with the proposal. The top surface of the climb, the head, shoulders, and upper back of the monk, is smoothed by time and wind. The sandstone has small pockets and flat platforms that are perfect for sitting and relaxing. Warmer wind passed us by, drifting down from another mountain, muffling the city sounds below. Ellen had asked to start her descent, and I encouraged her to sit with me a little bit longer. I think she sensed something was up because my voice cracked. Finally I drew her near me and told her how much she meant to me. "Ellen," I said, my voice becoming strong and sincere. "You are the most important thing in my life, more important than any mountain. I think back at all the fun we've had together and I can't imagine not being with you. I think from the first moment I met you, I knew I loved you then. I hope you haven't waited too long for me to tell you that I want you always in my life. I want to be with you forever." I had rehearsed all morning what I would say. Once I started, the words flowed easily. "I want you to be my wife," I said. "Will you marry me?"

It doesn't matter how much time actually passes between this type of question and the answer. For me it seemed an eternity. "Yes," she said softly, and I touched her face as I sometimes did when I thought she was crying. Her cheeks were moist. Then I took out the champagne and glasses. Ellen popped the cork and it sailed forever down. "There goes the tradition of keeping the cork," she said as she poured us each a glass.

For an hour Ellie and I sat back, basking in the midmorning sun and listening to the city noises that floated up from far below. At the Lions camp, I had made a wish to marry Ellen and to climb mountains, but I worried that I had taken on too much. Maybe I was greedy to expect so much out of life. My mind spun with the magnitude of change. Leaning back, I reached out and took Ellie's hand. I didn't want my life to be a conquest. Goals seemed like false summits; you reach what you thought was the top, only to discover a higher summit. So, you continue to climb higher and higher, always finding another summit a little higher, and you never find what you are looking for. The magic of life had to exist beyond a perpetual series of summits. How could I expand the breadth of my own life beyond the tops of mountains? I thought about something our Balti guide had said when I hiked in the Karakoram Range in Pakistan. One day we hiked to the top of a seventeen-thousand-foot peak, high for our standards, but in the Karakorams, so puny as to not even have a name. It was a mere bump on the massive landscape, and as we moved up the rolling terrain, my brother Eddi not seeing the top, asked, "When will we be on the mountain?"

"We are on the mountain!" the Balti replied, a little puzzled. "We have always been on the mountain." Why did people, including myself, envision a mountain as only a summit? It was like looking at an iceberg and only recognizing the part above the water's surface. I thought about all the wonderful moments I had experienced on mountains: hiking with my brother Mark through the high rain forest of Irian Jaya, playing baseball with ski poles and snowballs on Denali, and now, sitting with Ellie on the top of the Praying Monk, feeling the light buzz of champagne. These moments seemed frozen in time, and I could bring them up to the surface whenever I wanted. They were like snapshots, which defined the essence of who I was, what I wanted, whom I loved. Maybe the real beauty of life happened on the side of the mountain, not the top.

In a philosophy class at BC I had studied the work of the great mythologist, Joseph Campbell, who had given the advice, "Follow your bliss." Were these gigantic, sweeping changes in my life the quest to follow my bliss, or did they represent the inflated ambition of a Walter Mitty pipe dream? I honestly didn't know. So, instead of trying to predict the future, I would rely on two principles which had led me to this point, and one new principle I was just starting to recognize: I would set myself in motion, have faith in my vision, and never lose sight of those precious moments of bliss along the way.

A few weeks later my class was reviewing a dry grammar lesson in our English skills book when Sarah yelled out, "I know the answer to number seven."

"Go ahead, Sarah," I replied.

"May I ask a question first?" she asked and, not waiting for my answer, blurted, "Is the rumor true, that you're in love with Ms. Reeve and you asked her to marry you on the top of a mountain and she said yes and you're gonna get married and go live in the mountains?"

It took me a moment to analyze her questions and then I responded, amused, "That would all be true. . . . You have any ideas about where we should get married?"

"On a mountain," she replied plainly, as if I had just asked her the most obvious question in the world.

Both Ellen and I had played with the same thought. We wanted to avoid a big fancy wedding with rules for this and rules for that, like the precise way to throw your garters or feed each other cake. Simplicity is beauty, so we racked our brains to come up with a beautiful and memorable setting. Since my next continental summit would be Kilimanjaro in Africa, maybe we could get married there, we wondered, but who could marry us? Surprisingly, we discovered our Tanzanian guide, Daniel Fundi, was a lay minister in his church and his brother, Baltazar, who would be with us as well, was the choir director. "Let's get married on the summit," I proposed, but then we thought of how climbers usually feel at the top of mountains. It was a grand idea, but I didn't want to be puking and gasping for air on the most important day of my life. "Maybe, halfway up," Ellen suggested.

# 14
# Uhuru

Ellen and I were married at thirteen thousand feet on the Shira Plateau on Mount Kilimanjaro. The plateau was a huge expanse of rock and small mountain shrubs with constant wind and penetrating sun. Ellen described looking down into the moist deep green of the montane forests and beyond to the rich red soil of the lowlands.

It had taken us three days of hiking to get to this point. The first day was a narrow trail through the high rain forest over slippery exposed roots. Rosewood trees rose sixty feet and at the top, their canopy blocks the sun. Great strands of moss dangling from branches brushed against my face, and I could hear monkeys screeching above in the dense vegetation. The second day we had come out of the forest and into groves of giant heath trees with their small leaves and tiny delicate flowers. Elephants, leopards, buffalo, and eland, an animal like a small deer, had all been seen in these lower slopes. Then we passed through heather, only chest high. The air, once heavy in the dense forest, turned cool and misty. Finally it all gave way to a rocky moraine with an occasional shrub and clusters of abnormally large alpine plants. Buzzards and ravens could be heard overhead and Daniel, our guide, found the sun-washed skeleton of an eland just off our trail. The eland had probably died in a sudden storm, while searching for mosslike lichen found on the rocks. Large mammals can't live at this altitude of almost fifteen thousand feet, although a frozen leopard carcass was strangely found near the summit in 1926. I liked the openness of the moraine. I felt like I could hear the mass of the mountain and the sky around it, and somehow I was part of it all, if only in a tiny way.

We chose to take the mountaineers' route up Kili, referred to by the locals as the Whisky Route, versus the easier side of the mountain, referred to as the Coca-Cola Route. I knew summit day would be long and steep, with some fourth class scrambling. Even with that, I was able to convince Ellen and my dad to come along. My dad was a good athlete, and I knew he would rise to the occasion. Two years earlier, when my family had met me on the glacier at base camp after my McKinley climb, I remember my father putting his hand on my shoulder and saying, "What an accomplishment. Wow! What an accomplishment," and the faraway sound to his voice made me think that if he had been a few years younger, he would have wished to have been there with us. I didn't forget that. Kilimanjaro's reputation was a lot milder than McKinley's; it would take six days instead of twenty-one, and we could have most of our gear carried by porters, but it was still a big mountain, rising 19,340 feet out of the African plains. To climb it would be a major accomplishment for anyone.

Ellen's reasons were a little different. She loves new experiences, loves meeting new people, but I don't think you could say Ellen loves the mountains. Sometimes I feel that she climbed with me more out of her love for me than her love of them. But when she was convinced that some physical effort was worth the great sacrifice, she could push herself to an amazing level.

Earlier in the spring, we climbed Mount Rainier together. On summit day, we started for the top at two A.M. It was very cold. We were surrounded by ice and darkness; void of any heat. We had to jump over crevasses that opened like black gaping mouths. A few hours up, I still hadn't gotten warm. Each time we stopped, I began to shiver, not a good sign so far from the warmth of a tent. But Ellen seemed OK. I kept expecting her to say, "I've had enough. Let's go down now," but each time I asked her how she was doing, she replied, "OK. How are you doing?" At which the testosterone in me replied, "OK." I had a little speech prepared for when she gave up. I'd massage her shoulders and say, "Don't worry. We'll do it next year. It wasn't your fault." But Ellen had continued to move up the slope slowly, with concentrated effort as if everything inside her was focusing on each subsequent step. So, pride had kept me going, not the best motivator on a mountain, but it forced my body forward and to the top with Ellen.

Sometimes, though, she just couldn't see the importance of it all. Coming down from the summit of Rainier, after our twentieth hour of constant movement, our guide Craig had told us that the parking lot was no more than a half an hour away. Ellen was lagging far behind, so I fell back to see what was wrong. When only I was in clear earshot, she remarked emphatically, "Climbing is an endless nightmare." Her short but clearly stated commentary was meant just for me. I began laughing uncontrollably, with the laughter that comes after your sensitivity is stripped away by exhaustion. I think she laughed too but only for a second. The journey did seem endless for Ellen. She was proud of her summit of Mount Rainier, but it wasn't something that she'd needed. Ellen climbed Rainier to be with me and to enjoy my company while challenging herself physically. This is partly why I love her. "People won't love you for what you do, but for who you are and for the kindness inside you," she said, and I knew this was a message I needed to hear.

So now Ellen and I stood in the cold sun of the Shira Plateau in front of Daniel reading the Lord's Prayer in Swahili. Our fellow climbers had built an altar out of rocks and collected mountain flowers that we held in a bouquet. Ellen had looked at her grubby climbing fleece and grimaced. "This won't do." Then she noticed the orange, purple, and green Tanzanian cloth that we had been using as a table cover. She wrapped it around her like an Indian sari and, although I couldn't see her, in my heart she made the most beautiful bride in the world. Daniel took a piece of cloth and wrapped our wrists together in it. "What God has brought together," he said strongly, "no man can separate." And I felt his words, our wrists bound tightly as one. We had not brought our rings on the mountain in fear of losing them, so Baltazar took two blades of tussock grass and tied them around our fingers. I repeated Daniel's words, their power transcending his broken English. "I will love Ellen as my wife during sickness and health and only death can separate us. This I will do according to the ability of God. This ring will be the sign of my love and trustfulness to you throughout life." After Ellen recited her vows, she locked her arm in mine and we walked across the plateau with friends, guides, and porters making a path for us. As we passed through the gauntlet, the Tanzanians sang a traditional wedding song in Swahili. Ellie and I couldn't understand a word, except for our names plugged in at various points.

Afterwards we asked Daniel to translate the song. He thought for a long time and then began carefully, in his slow English, "Erik is a good man. Ellen saw him and Ellen loved him. Ellen is a good man. Erik saw him and Erik loved him." Our friends, gathering around, laughed heartily, but a few misplaced pronouns couldn't take away from the strength and hope of the music. With the celebration in full swing, I couldn't seem to allow myself to flow with it completely. I felt a vague longing hovering on the periphery, as if all the music and singing, the remarkable mountain setting, and even the magnitude of Ellen's love could not heal a tiny angry wound in my soul. My mother had deserved to live, to witness these landmark moments in her son's life, to know that she had done a good job and that I was happy. I couldn't envision, however, my mother's delicate human body climbing Kilimanjaro's steep slopes to stand in this place, so I tried to settle on the idea of her laughing spirit hiding behind a nearby rock or in the bouquet of flowers.

The ceremony ended with a friend of my dad's giving Ellie and I some marital advice. He used the metaphor of a wheel. "What if the spokes of a wheel are not even lengths?" he asked. "Each spoke of the wheel represents a facet of your lives. There's the intellectual, the emotional, the social, the physical, and the spiritual. They all must stay in balance or the wheel will spin out of control." I don't know how he had read my life so accurately. I could see my climbing goals so clearly in front of me, but sometimes more important parts of my life hovered fuzzily on the periphery. I didn't want my life with Ellen to be fuzzy; I wanted it to shine brighter than anything else I had ever known. I remember feeling Ellen's wrist wrapped against mine and it felt like we were one person instead of two. I hope some of Ellen's centeredness flowed into me, fusing into me the deep knowledge that there was more to life than just reaching summits.

Two days later, Ellen and I enjoyed our honeymoon, a twenty-four-hour summit day. We left Lava Tower at one A.M. after a nutritious breakfast of dried English biscuits and caffeinated tea. On previous days, we had the option of having porters carry our gear, but I had chosen to carry my own, to stay self-sufficient. On this day, though, because we were attempting to summit from the Machame side and then descend on the Marangu route, I had acquiesced and let the porters traverse with my gear, along with everyone else's, from our presummit camp to a camp on the other side at about twelve thousand feet. Climbing 5,000 feet to the summit, from 14,500 feet, would be challenge enough without a fifty-pound pack on my back. Instead, I carried normal summit fare and a little extra: a down jacket, a complete down suit in case of an emergency, extra layers of fleece, chocolate, a can of tuna, a Yoo-Hoo to share with Ellen at the top, four water bottles for Ellie and me, a rope, and sunscreen. My pack felt light compared to other days, and I started strongly, chipping away at the elevation. A few thousand feet higher, altitude was starting to get the best of me. On Kilimanjaro, our acclimatization time was only five days, versus nineteen on Denali. "Much oxygen on the summit, because of many trees below the mountain," Daniel assured us. Maybe for him, I thought. Also on Denali, I was able to keep a consistent pace by kicking my own steps into the snowy slope; Kilimanjaro was mostly loose rock and scree with patches of ice hiding above thousand-foot drops. I found it hard to get into a rhythm as we shimmied through narrow loose gullies, around boulders, and up exposed rock faces.

In the predawn darkness, while scrambling up a steep rock ramp, one of our climbers above knocked a large boulder loose. The darkness leveled the playing field, made it the same for all, and we lunged blindly in different directions. I threw myself to the left as I estimated the trajectory from the sound. In another second I heard the boulder bounce past a few feet to the right and away from the group, then down a thousand feet below. Lucky, I thought.

Around five A.M. I heard a yell from far above. It was Greg, a team member, whose group had been climbing at a faster pace than Ellen, my dad, and me. "My altimeter reads seventeen thousand feet," he shouted, and I felt my attitude plummet. Greg, at seventeen thousand feet, was still far above me, but that was still far below the summit. The night was colder than I had expected. Ironically, on a mountain, the moments before sunrise are by far the coldest of the night, so I was grateful for the equatorial sun that peeked over the mountain around seven A.M. I asked Ellie how she was doing. "Fine," she said impatiently. "Let's just get there." I could hear the frustration in her voice.

As I got higher, I began to feel like I was in a trance. My muscles and thoughts were moving through syrup. I could notice a distinct delay between my mind commanding an action and my body following the order. I lost track of Ellen and my dad climbing right behind me and focused on moving my sluggish body forward and upward. Baltazar continued to repeat, "Close now, very close."

"How long is close?" I asked.

"One hour," he replied.

An hour would go by and someone would ask again, "How far?"

"One hour," he'd say.

I began to wonder if African guides, having not grown up with watches strapped to their wrists like Westerners, had never developed an accurate sense of time. How do you judge one hour? I asked myself, if you've never watched it pass? I continued to trudge up the steep slippery scree. I had learned well on other climbs that you go until you get there. When guides say one hour, I simply multiply their time by two, so my brain is pleasantly surprised if we reach our destination in one hour and a half, and not crushed if we arrive in two and a half.

I scurried up through a long twisting gully and then felt the mountain open up in front of me. It felt wide and flat, immense openness that I had rarely experienced. I stepped up onto the flatness. Baltazar touched my arm. "Welcome to the top of Africa," he said softly. We were on the giant caldera, the mouth of an extinct volcano. The terrain still sunk inward, creating the shape of a massive shallow bowl. I felt a tingle of elation through my body, but then exhaustion overrode it and I sat down against a pile of rocks. Out of the wind, the warmth was beautiful. I could feel the sunlight heating my face through the chill of the air. It was so pleasant, I even nodded off for a few minutes. When I woke up, I forced myself to eat a chocolate bar, but with each swallow, my body was trying to reject it.

Only one more obstacle lay between the summit and our group: the one-thousand-foot scree slope called Uhuru Peak. It was another smaller peak perched atop the one we had just climbed. Many climbers call the caldera the summit, but my brain is too rigid to make that stretch. Finally it was time to move again. I stood up dizzily and felt lucky that the next section was a nontechnical trudge up loose scree, much of it powdery fine. Here at the base of Uhuru, I was in my own world, so Ellen's voice came as a surprise. "I'm going down," she said firmly. "I've had enough." I was shocked and wanted to persuade her to go on, but her statement had sounded articulated and definite. Her voice didn't seem overly exhausted. It simply sounded as though she had "had enough."

"Endless nightmare?" I asked.

"Endless nightmare!" she repeated with emphasis." I knew there was nothing I could say to change her mind. This point was simply where our paths diverged and would always diverge. Ellie had already experienced her summit through the entirety of this strange and wonderful adventure, yet mine was still to be reached. My dad, standing behind her, piped in, "I'm going down, too. I'm pretty dizzy and need to keep some energy for the seven-hour climb down." For a moment, I thought about going down with them, getting out of this foggy high altitude dreamworld and back into the world of oxygen, the world of humans, but the fear of waking up in the tent the next day mired in regret was stronger than my exhaustion. So, I decided to go on simply because I knew I could. In the 1920's when asked, "Why do you want to climb Mount Everest?" and George Mallory asserted, "Because it is there," he was only stating the less important half of the equation. The unspoken half is that we are here. Striving and achieving is part of our nature, built into our genetic makeup. The evidence of man's nature manifests itself in rocket ships to the moon, skyscrapers hundreds of stories high, and flags planted on summits all around the world. In a sense I understood this component was misdirected and needed to be kept in check, and I respected Ellie for defying hundreds of thousands of years of genetic imprinting. For me, however, with a perfect sunny sky above me and enough reserves to stay safe, turning back would go against my human nature. Then, to fly in the face of my infallibility, my stomach lurched and I dropped to a knee, splattering vomit all over the rocks. I sprang up to show that I was OK. "I feel great. Nothing like a little high-altitude projectile vomiting."

As I pulled myself up the last slope, I felt as though earth's gravity had increased tenfold. Baltazar and I would stop every twenty minutes so that I could take a few deep breaths, but when I did, it felt like oxygen was being sucked out of my lungs instead of into them. The air around me seemed to be stealing it from me. "Tell me we're getting close," I said to Baltazar. "Even if it isn't, give me one of those optimistic time estimates."

"*Hakuna matata.* No problem. Very close now." He grinned.

After an hour and a half we stopped. "Very close now," he promised. "I can see the top." And because I wanted to believe him, I kept moving. This is turning into an endless nightmare, I thought. Step, breathe, breathe, breathe. Step, breathe, breathe, breathe, step, rest, breathe. Finally the terrain leveled out and we crossed a field of broken snow, the surface brittle and cracking like ancient flesh. My boots stumbled into little divots and tripped over unexpected lumps. "Where is it?" I asked, quickly losing motivation.

"There!" Baltazar replied, pointing my finger to a place that was only a few feet higher than us. "I see the sign." In a few more minutes there was no place else to go. The ground dropped off on three sides. A thousand feet below us, I knew, the caldera stretched two miles and then dropped away again, this time into forests and then plains, and finally, hundreds of miles in the distance, the Indian Ocean. "You can see it curve. I don't know the word in English," Baltazar said, and I knew he meant the horizon. I had heard this before, that from the top of Kilimanjaro, you could see the curvature of the earth. Then I put my arms around Baltazar's small shoulders. "Thank you," I said.

"It is my honor," he replied. "My father, in the Swahili tradition, he is married to seven wives. So, my friend, you come back to the mountain next year and be married again."

The sign that marked the top read, YOU ARE NOW AT THE UHURU PEAK. THE HIGHEST POINT IN AFRICA—ALTITUDE 5859 METERS. Sitting on the summit, leaning forward with my head resting on my knees, I asked Baltazar, "What does Uhuru mean?" He thought for a minute. "Freedom," he replied.

Freedom. It was a word I didn't understand. Freedom from what? Freedom from the limits of my body? From pain? From disappointment? What did it mean? I wanted to believe that by standing atop mountains around the world, I was achieving this kind of freedom, or at least coming close, but when standing in these high places, the immense power of the mountains only served to magnify my own fragility, my human need for food, for oxygen, for the help that I received from my team, for the warmth of their bodies.

Then it came to me, the thought coming slowly alive and charging my oxygen-starved brain. Perhaps it was the freedom to make of my life what I wanted it to be, or at least the freedom to try, or to fail in the trying. Perhaps freedom itself was unobtainable and the goal was only to reach for it, strive for it, knowing all along that I would fall well short. Perhaps the importance was in the reaching out, and in the impossibility of it all, and in the reaching out through the impossibility, my body planted heavily on the earth but my spirit soaring up and coming impossibly close to its goal. Standing on the top of Kilimanjaro, I hugged Baltazar and reached out and touched the sign. I still didn't know whether it would be possible to breathe in all I wanted from my life, but I knew that I would try.

Two hours down from the summit, Baltazar and I stopped at the top of Gilman's Point, which I knew overlooked Kibo Hut 3,500 feet below us. Baltazar picked up a pile of sand and put it in my hand. I felt the fine powder slip through my fingers. "No rocks," he said excitedly. We were atop the world's longest high-altitude sand dune. "Do you trust me?" he asked.

"I don't understand," I replied.

He paused a second and asked again. "Do you trust me?"

"Of course!" I'd been relying on the sound of his footsteps and his verbal directions for fifteen hours.

"Take my arm," he said and I interlocked my arm with his. He was at least a foot shorter and fifty pounds lighter than me, but I could feel the strength of his small frame. Then he began running, with me beside him, our bodies locked together, our movements beginning to coincide. We started slowly, but then picked up speed, each step dropping us five feet and then another two with a slide. We ran at a slight traverse, our feet making ski turns in the soft scree. Every now and then, I would step on the occasional loose rock, throwing us out of rhythm and propelling us into fits of laughter. We would both totter as we fought our own momentum and tried to gain back our balance. Then we were running again, our feet plunging in giant strides down the slope, moving faster than I ever had on a mountain. Halfway down we stopped to catch our breaths. "Do you want to go faster or slower?" he asked.

"Faster," I gasped, my body alive with exhilaration. "Let's go faster."

# 15
# Moving Through Darkness

A week after returning home from Africa, Sam, Jeff, and I drove into Yosemite Valley. We stopped at El Cap Meadows, a large field at the base of the immense rock face of El Capitan. I could hear the echo of the towering granite slab looming above. Its solid bulk blocked out the open sound of sky. Hans, our climbing leader and the fastest climber in the world, stood next to me trailing my finger slowly up The Nose route, 3,300 feet and the "proudest line" up El Cap. "The bottom is a giant prow, sloping up like the bridge of a nose. It feels vertical when you're climbing it, but it's only seventy or eighty degrees. Then, there's a stellar crack running up three hundred feet or so. That's the Stove Legs. Perfect crack for you to lead. Just reach up, feel the crack, and pull up. It'll be radical. From there, we've gotta traverse around a corner. You're going to love it. The leader, who will be me, of course, climbs up and sets an anchor. Then, he climbs back down and swings around the corner to where the route continues. That's one of the perks of being the leader; I get the king swing. Halfway up is The Great Roof, a hundred-foot bulge on the face. It's barely visible from here, but when you're hanging underneath it, you'll know it's there. Then, you get to

Boot Flake, then Texas Flake, and then Pancake Flake. From there, it's all overhanging until the top." For the last fifteen minutes Hans had been lifting my arm, and with his powerful hand, dragging my pointing finger back and forth up the 3,300-foot face. When I was finally able to drop my arm to my side, I gave it a secret shake, trying to clear the burn in my shoulder muscle.

Months earlier, Hans's new-wave climbing partner, Steve Schneider, had been giving a slide show in Phoenix about Hans and his radical speed ascents of valley classics. Their foremost achievement was capturing three consecutive speed ascents of El Cap summits, eight thousand feet of vertical climbing in twenty-seven hours. I had approached Steve after the show. "I've heard of you," he said, his valley-boy accent loud and clear. "Call me Shipoopi. I did Denali a month before you. When I found out a blind dude smoked the same route, I was shamed. Now, I have to go do something radder." I asked him for a tip on a trustworthy climber who might be interested in leading us up The Nose on a second American Foundation for the Blind climbing project. We thought he might volunteer himself, but instead, without hesitation, he volunteered his buddy Hans.

Standing under El Capitan, I felt a little light-headed to know that in one month, Sam, Jeff, Hans, and I would all be thousands of feet up, suspended from little metal anchors wedged in tiny cracks. I had originally committed to this climb when there seemed only a hint of possibility. I had climbed five-hundred-foot rock faces in a day, but El Capitan, the standard by which all other rock climbs are measured, was a huge stretch. My inner voice told me it was possible, but how would I know if this voice was truly leading me toward my destiny or toward disaster? I had just finished a book on Himalayan climbing in which a man in the 1920's received a vision from God, commanding him to climb Mount Everest. To demonstrate the power of his faith, the man decided to climb Everest in his loafers. A little above base camp, he suffered frostbite and had to be rescued off the mountain. I knew there were those who thought a blind person trying to climb El Capitan was as crazy as trying to climb Everest in a pair of loafers. Maybe I was simply guilty of dreaming beyond my ability. Sometimes my doubt completely filled me up, but amidst these feelings emerged a more powerful surge of hope, flowing out through my fingertips, joining me to this place, to the jagged fields of talus and the sunbaked granite. In this place I knew that my hope would smack up against the cold bluntness of reality. I knew I had a long way to go, but if a way existed, I would find it.

That afternoon we had a party to christen our upcoming adventure. Hans invited some of his climbing friends, one of whom was Warren Harding, a living legend in Yosemite climbing history. Thirty-one years ago, Harding had been a wiry, energetic road surveyor with dreams so extreme, he was embarrassed to admit them to anyone. In the golden age of Yosemite climbing, he had put up the hardest routes in the world: The Leaning Tower, Dawn Wall, and finally, the culmination of his climbing career, The Nose on El Capitan. Completing this route had consumed a year of his life, and the ultimate story was splattered all over the pages of *Life* magazine.

Sam and I picked him up in a valley parking lot to bring him back to our cabin. "Just let me park, and I'll be right with you," he said, his voice ringing out like the typical grandpa.

"So, what's he look like?" I asked Sam when we were alone. "Is he a stud? Does he have forearms of steel?"

Sam hesitated, "Well, put it this way, he's aged a little in thirty-one years, but I'm sure there's still a tiger raging under that beer gut."

Later, on the porch of our cabin, everyone gathered around him, beers in hand, to listen to him spin tales of legendary feats around the valley. To a climber, it was better than listening to Neil Armstrong describe the Apollo mission. I instantly liked Warren's self-effacing manner. "Never could free climb more than a five-eight," he said proudly, "but put me on an aid ladder, and I could get by. On The Leaning Tower, a bashy"—a thin piece of gear—"popped out of the crack with me attached. The fall broke my nose and cracked a few ribs. It was a fantastic excuse to give up and go have a beer. Problem was that the bartender wouldn't serve me. He kept staring at my swollen face and telling me to go to the hospital.

"On Dawn Wall, some accused me of drilling too many bolts. There's a very obvious reason," he said, standing up and putting my hand on his head, "I'm only a little guy with short stubby arms. The only place I ever drilled an extra bolt was under The Great Roof. I was hanging from one that I had just drilled. I was fifteen hundred feet above the valley floor and looked down at all that air and immediately drilled another one for good measure. Erik, you'll feel that bolt when you're up there. It's probably a little rusty now, but so am I." He laughed a deep belly laugh.

"What about the Stove Legs crack?" I asked. "How did it get its name?"

"Well, back then," he said, "you didn't have all this new-fangled gear. We had pitons that I forged in my basement, but the Stove Legs crack was so wide, it stumped us for a while. One day, I was passing through a junkyard and came across this old potbellied stove. It gave me an idea. I sawed off the legs and drilled holes in the ends. Those legs fit in that crack better than any of us could have hoped."

"What got you interested in climbing?" Jeff asked.

"Isn't it obvious by looking at this devilish face?" he retorted. "Fame, fortune, glory, and women. Didn't get much of the latter, though."

"Why not?" Jeff asked, interested in any subject that concerned a lack of women.

"Too busy climbing," he replied.

On the drive back to his car, Warren said to me, "I've gotta hand it to you, climbing that monster without seeing what you're doing. You know what I'd do, if I went blind?"

"What?" I asked.

"Nothin'!" he chuckled, "Absolutely nothing. I'd finally have the excuse that I've always been looking for, to become the underachiever I was meant to be." Then he erupted into a roaring laugh that began deep inside his belly and spread outward. It lasted for a solid minute and it started Sam and me laughing with him.

On our second day in the valley, we jumped right into our training. "There's nothing better for a hangover than an overhang," Sam said, holding his head tenderly in his hands. We started with a two-pitch climb, a pitch being about 150 feet long, or about the length of a climbing rope. The first consisted of a long, finger-width crack, the rock wall around it, like most climbs in the valley, polished and featureless. The technique is to jam your two hands and one foot into the crack and torque them so they stick fast. Then you stand up on your tortured foot and jam your other foot higher in the crack. Much of your weight is hanging from your fists stuffed inside the crevasse, or the bulgy knobs of your fingers that get wedged between granite lips. In a twisted way, crack climbing is a perfect sport for a blind person; I could feel my way by simply running my hand up the crack until it fell into place. No hidden holds lurked just out of my reach. There were no inch-wide pockets for my desperate toes to miss.

The next pitch involved a layback. I had to lean way back on the rope with my hands locked around a granite flake and flatten my feet against the polished face, using the opposing forces to slowly walk my body up the rock. The pulling force of my arms kept my feet pushing against the rock. Sometimes my arms would bring my upper body too high, and my feet would slide out from under me, slamming my body into the rock. "Bashed elbows and knees mean you're climbing hard," Hans said.

"They're war wounds," Jeff added.

The next route was a three-hundred-foot climb called Bishop's Terrace. We were so excited to be climbing on the most classic rock climbs in the world that I began climbing fast, using my arms and legs to catapult my body up the face in quick bursts of movement. "This speed climbing stuff is easy," I boasted to Hans, who was belaying me from the top, "I'm gonna beat your El Cap record." My cocky statements must have angered the climbing gods, because, seconds later, I sprung up onto a small ledge and, bolting upright, slammed my face into a protruding rock. My nose was shredded and bloody and felt like it had been smashed flat against my face. I prayed that Hans hadn't seen the culmination of my brief attempt at speed climbing. I kept quiet until the top, working to avoid imaginary bulges of rock looming overhead and trying to ignore my squashed nose that was sending jolts of pain through my face. When I reached Hans, he took me off belay as I anchored in. "The next section is a long narrow traverse across a sloped ledge," Hans explained. "If you fall, you'll take a major swing, so you may want to take it slow and protect what's left of your nose, speed climber."

At the end of my first full day of climbing in the valley, my arms and legs felt limp, like an old rubber band that had lost its stretch. The skin on my hands resembled raw hamburger meat, and my feet felt like a hot iron had pressed them. My lips were split, my teeth were smeared with blood, and a quarter-sized scab decorated the middle of my scalp. Not to mention my swollen nose, scraped elbows and knees, and bashed shins. It had been a perfect day of climbing.

The next day Hans took me to a practice area called Cookie Cliff to teach me how to aid climb. Yosemite rock faces were carved by moving glaciers, leaving in their wake perfectly sustained vertical cracks so void of features, even exceptional climbers cannot move up the rock with the sole power of their arms and legs. There are simply no holds to stand on and hang from, so a climber uses a technique called aid climbing in which he wedges a small metal rectangle called a stopper or a spring-loaded camming device with serrated edges into a vertical crack, attaches a three-foot nylon ladder to it, and then stands up on the highest rung in order to place another piece of protection farther up. Once the next piece is in, he clips his second ladder to it and gingerly steps onto the bottom rung, working his way to the top. It's a slow and tedious process, but it would get us over sections that wouldn't "go free."

The approach to Cookie Cliff was over an old forestry road that had been destroyed by a landslide and was never repaired. It was now a jumbled boulder field; I was on my butt more than on my feet. The world's speed climbing champion got a kick out of getting me to the base faster than anyone else had before. He called it a "blind speed approach."

"Efficiency's my thing. You'll learn," he warned. "OK, on your butt and slide. Three-foot drop at the end," he'd say. "Left hand on your trekking pole, right hand against this boulder. OK, down-climb, fat jug—one foot under your left hand, ledge two and a half feet below your right foot." When the trail was smoother Hans would walk in front of me clicking together two carabiners, or two sticks or rocks, whatever was handy. I'd follow the sound. On this day, after making it through the boulder field, he said, "Feel this." He put a smooth metallic rectangle in my hand, and I could feel a tiny row of square holes. "I almost forgot about this. It's way better than clicking 'biners." The rectangle was a harmonica. Hans had found it earlier, hidden away in an old chest full of childhood junk and, for the rest of the way, he stumbled through the classics: "Row, Row, Row Your Boat," "The Farmer in the Dell," and his grand finale, a rendition of "Three Blind Mice." Hans thought this last song was a stroke of comic genius because he kept stopping to sing a few verses and chuckle. I couldn't help chuckling too.

At the base of Cookie Cliff, we stood in front of a perfectly sustained vertical overhanging crack. Just before I started climbing, Hans said, "You'll smoke to the top with me here." Connected to a fixed rope anchored into the top chain, Hans zipped along beside me with his ascenders, examining each of my gear placements. I reached up, feeling the crack's width and measuring the gap with my finger. I needed to match it with a similar-sized piece of gear hanging from my harness. I had learned to organize the many kinds of metal gear that climbers use to protect themselves: stoppers, smallest to biggest, on my right gear loop. Cams, smallest to biggest, on my left loop, and TCUs and aliens in the back loops. I had exhausted myself at first by constantly fumbling through the racks of gear and awkwardly bringing heavy metal pieces up into the crack until I found the right size. "Efficiency is everything," Hans taught. "Especially for you." He meant that as a result of being blind, climbing entailed a little extra work on my part. Although I tried not to harp on my difficulties, I did have to admit he was right. A sighted person, while hanging from a piece, can glance up the crack, moving nothing but his eyeballs, spot the next suitable placement, and after grabbing the right piece, stand up and jam it in. Since I couldn't glance up, I had to stand up on my ladder, scan the crack with my hand, drop back down to find the right piece and then stand up again to place it, hoping it was the right size. Standing up in the top loop of a flimsy nylon ladder, an overhanging rock pressing into my face, with the wind and my trembling leg rocking the ladder from side to side, was considerably more strenuous than mounting a stepladder. Before I'd stand up, I'd clip a piece of webbing from my harness to the piece of gear in the crack so I could straighten my leg and lean back, keeping my hands free for placing the next gear. Standing up one extra time doesn't seem like a big deal, but on a two-hundred-foot pitch, it translates to over sixty extra moves, and on three-thousand-foot El Cap, it translates to more than I would want to count.

As I moved up the crack, Hans coached, "Too big. Try a number two," or "That won't hold. Feel how it's overextended," or my favorite, "Bomber! Don't even bother checking it, couldn't have placed it better myself." At first I nervously checked and rechecked the little piece of metal, sliding it up and down, back and forth in the crack. Then I would tentatively put weight on the ladder, as if I were taking a step into a minefield. "Reach in there," Hans said, his cool voice having a calming effect. "Feel how all six teeth are biting the rock. You could hang a truck off that. Now, stand up. It'll hold." My fingers believed him, but if he were wrong and it didn't hold, I knew the consequences were severe.

Months before, while learning to aid climb on hundred-foot basalt cracks outside of Flagstaff, those consequences were drilled into me forever. Sam led the crack, leaving the "pro" in for me to use. "It'll be good practice," he said. "Just lead on up and clip into them. Practice connecting your ladder and standing up." So, I worked my way up the crack, clipping, standing, and reaching. About fifty feet up, I clipped in my ladder and stood up. Leaning back, I heard a quick, popping noise as the pro broke free from the crack. Then I was weightless, tumbling over backwards, my shocked mind barely registering what was happening.

The next pro ripped free from the face and again the third. Then my feet slapped the ground, but the impact was surprisingly gentle, as if I had fallen back only a few feet. Immediately, I was boomeranging up with the dynamic spring of the rope. The last piece of protection had held. Thank God.

Now, halfway up Cookie Cliff, I heard Hans saying, "Trust it," and although my brain accepted this, my heart still pounded with that memory of a sudden metal pop and the sensation of weightlessness as I lost contact with the rock. Still, I've never lost touch with the sober knowledge that my life depended on my capability; on how well my fingers placed a small piece of metal gear into a crack. I never forgot that my life rests in my own hands. The feeling is both powerful and terrifying.

With one of the world's best climbers looking on, a climber who had survived the valley's most dangerous ascents, I forced myself to trust. "Killer placement. Go for it," he urged me on. When I reached the top and clipped into the anchor chain, Hans glanced at his watch. "Not bad, fifty-seven minutes," he said. "Next time we'll do it in fifty."

The next training was now to do it alone, so Jeff and I headed to the base of the Salathe' Wall, a classic route that rivals The Nose in length and difficulty. The first 150 feet is a classic aid climb in the valley, just a zigzag of various-sized cracks running up the smooth granite face. Unfortunately it was getting dark by the time it was my turn to lead, but Jeff said, "Darkness doesn't bother me, and I know it doesn't bother you." Leading on the Salathe' was tricky, because to get to the base of the aid-climbing portion, we had to scramble up a fifty-degree slope to a small ledge and then traverse far to the right until the ledge narrowed into a toehold. The crack ran up from this point, so if my first piece had popped as I stood up on the ladder, I was looking at a forty-foot fall or, in climbing lingo, a forty-foot crater. I set the first piece of pro and with one foot pressed aggressively into the foothold, tested the ladder with my other. My leg weighting the ladder felt like it was filled with molten lead and that standing up on it would surely snap the fragile metal piece like dry kindling, perhaps even rip through the flimsy fabric ladder. I was convinced I'd hear the swift pop of metal as my heavy leaden body spiraled away. "How will I lead on The Nose when it comes time? Will anything be different?" I asked myself. "I can't back down. I can only go forward," I told myself repeatedly, and after a few minutes, the repetition seemed to calm my mind. Finally I backed up the one piece with two more and connected the ladder to all three. At least one piece would hold. The law of averages was in my favor, but still that first committing step was agonizing. As I stepped up the rungs to get a higher placement, I kept my hands buried in the crack, acting as a fourth, and even a fifth anchor point. I let out a few shallow breaths. On the periphery of my concentration, I heard Jeff's voice imitating me with little mocking cries.

As I got higher, leaving more pieces of gear attached to the rope below me, I gained more confidence. About eighty feet up, the crack petered out and I leaned left and right, scanning for another hold. Then I found it, a paper-clip-wide seam, about three feet up and four feet to the left. I had to acrobatically lean and stretch my body to even reach it. With one foot perched on the top rung, I walked my other foot far out onto the face and jammed a finger into a shallow pocket. With my free hand I reached back, finding the rack of thin metal nuts. My body was leaning almost horizontally as I pushed various sizes against the surface of the seam, but none fit. Then I selected the smallest one. It slid in easily and caught at the bottom of the seam. When I swung over and stood up on it, I tried to block distracting thoughts from my mind, the foremost being that ninety feet up on a rock face, my body weight was being held by a piece of metal no longer than the tip of my pinkie and the width of a credit card. Ten feet higher, the crack widened and I jammed in a number two cam, a piece half the size of my fist. When I reached in, I found that not all the teeth were catching, and I tried to pull it out, but it was stuck. I reasoned, if it didn't budge when I yanked on it, then it wouldn't budge when I stood on it. So, convinced, I stood up. Murphy's Law went into full force, because the piece immediately shot out. A series of quick shallow grunts escaped from my mouth as I swayed precariously to the left, my arms wildly slapping the wall. I didn't even notice at first the heavy piece of metal that had smashed directly into my left eyeball. Luckily my right foot had not yet left the lower ladder, and I recovered my balance. Later I joked to Sam and Jeff that if I hadn't already had a glass left eye, I might now have had to get one.

Resting on a one-inch ledge that at this point seemed as wide as a sidewalk, I stood wiping the blood from my numb eyelid. I ran my finger over the hard glassy surface of my eyeball to see if it had cracked. My skull still vibrated from the jolt. As I regained awareness of my surroundings, I surmised that I had ten or fifteen feet to go. "Reach right." Jeff's faint yell rose up from the ground. I reached right and my hand ran across the rap rings that were drilled into the rocks. I clipped in my daisy chain and the heavy feeling was immediately replaced with relief. I had led 150 feet in just under four hours. The time was painfully slow, pathetically slow, but at least it was a start.

Reaching the ground at eleven P.M., I was met by Jeff's grave words. They burst out as if he had been pondering the thought for a long while. "It's pitch black out. There's no moon, and I forgot my headlamp." The hike out was only twenty-five minutes—that's if you went by the trail, which began a quarter mile down, from a rocky scramble.

"Well, what choice do we have?" I asked. "Bivy here all night, which is out of the question, or fall off a thirty-foot boulder on the scramble out?"

"I vote for the fall," Jeff replied grimly. Jeff shuffled along in front of me, stopping and starting as our way met with repeated dead ends. Each time he tripped and stumbled over rocks or fallen limbs, I couldn't help laughing to myself. I got a secret kick out of his sudden fits and starts, combined with his scared little gasps and under-his-breath curses. Abruptly Jeff stopped in front of me and gasped, "I think there's a very big drop-off in front of us."

"How far down?" I asked.

"Maybe, thirty feet," he guessed. "I can see the tops of trees at our level." I knelt down and investigated the drop-off. It sloped down at a moderate angle and seemed featured with large pockets and grooves. "I think I see a clearing over there. It might be a trail, but there's no way I'm climbing down this thing in the dark." In the day, Jeff's climbing ability outclassed mine, but in the dark, the rules had changed. "I'll climb below you," I said, "and I'll help you place your feet." Jeff agreed with only a hesitant grunt. I down-climbed below Jeff, hanging straight-armed from a hold by one hand while I scrunched up my body and reached far below my feet with my other hand. Finding a hold, one at a time, I gently lowered my feet into it. When I was secure on the rock, I'd grab Jeff's ankle and lower his trembling foot onto a hold. With each step down, Jeff made shallow whimpering noises, and I gleefully mimicked his voice from below. Slowly and carefully, we inched our way down, and, standing on the ground below the boulder, I said, "You'd make a wimpy blind guy."

Jeff took the lead again, and after half an hour of stumbling and shoving ourselves through an impenetrable wall of shrubs and tree branches, I waited for him to be the one to discover that this fortress of vines and branches didn't meet the definition of a trail.

Half joking, I blurted out, "Jeff, why don't you let me take over?"

"Be my guest," he replied, relieved. So, I took the lead and pushed through the next tangle of shrubs. It was a complete stroke of luck that in another twenty feet, I stepped from the thicket onto the flat dirt of a trail, but I never let Jeff forget the slightly inflated tale of the heroic blind man leading his hopelessly lost climbing partner out of the wilderness.

As I walked in front of Jeff, I kept us on the trail by feeling the hard-packed dirt under my feet, versus the spongy earth and small bushes along the border. Sometimes the hard-pack would suddenly become soft, and I'd step into fallen leaves and thin tree branches. Then realizing I was at a dead end, I'd backtrack, stopping frequently to tap the trail with my heel and scan my pole from border to border until I felt the trail open up and turn off in what I supposed to be the right direction. I laughed nervously to think that I guided Jeff, a better climber than me, but in pitch darkness, I knew I was the best person for the job, and to continue to follow would have meant shirking my responsibility as a partner. As I stepped tentatively forward, I tried to feel confident, but the confidence didn't come naturally. I was unsure, questioning each step. I had always presumed that leadership came easily to a chosen few like Jeff, that people like him were born to take command, but now I wondered if this presumption was only a convenient excuse. Jeff might be as uncertain to lead me by day as I was to lead him by night. Perhaps leadership was not so much a matter of raw talent, as raw courage. Leading was the ability to move forward through darkness toward those immense possibilities, unseen yet sensed, while others allowed the darkness to paralyze them.

Soon we began to hear the distant sound of car engines and knew we were nearing the road. I also heard a distant bustle on the trail. "Here come some headlamps," Jeff said, and two climbers emerged, heading toward us. They were probably planning to bivy at the base of the wall for an early start. The first astonished climber saw us moving slowly through a thick blanket of darkness, and as we passed, he remarked excitedly, "You guys must have really great vision."

"Twenty-twenty!" I replied.

The next day our plan was to get some practice pulling a haul bag up the cliff. On El Cap we would bring twelve gallons of water, an arsenal of metal gear, rain suits and fleece, food, and sleeping bags. The whole assortment would be stuffed into a deep rubber tube and would weigh close to 150 pounds. On this day Jeff, Sam, and I planned to climb three pitches up Serenity Crack, getting practice hauling the "pig," bivy on a ledge, and climb and haul the last three pitches the next morning. The air was already stiflingly hot as we hiked up to the base. The route was facing south, and when I touched the rock with my finger, it felt like the top of an oven. As we moved upward, the haul line kept getting entangled in the climbing rope. Our anchors were turning into a jumble of indistinguishable ropes, carabiners, knots, slings, daisy chains, ascenders, and pulleys. Trying to sort it all out under the oppressive sun was proving frustrating.

The first resting point was a hanging belay off some old pitons. With no ledge to perch on, our legs dangled and our harnesses cut into our sides. I had been hanging motionless for an hour while I belayed Sam, and my feet were totally numb with the loss of circulation. My black rubber climbing shoes seemed to be attracting the sun's rays and then channeling the heat into my now scorching feet. Luckily we had brought plenty of water. Jeff unlashed the top of the haul bag and disappeared into it, his body upside-down, his feet kicking in the air. Minutes later he emerged empty-handed. "The water bottles are buried under a huge pile of gear," he said disappointedly. I tried next but was met with the same problem. Our three-foot length of webbing holding us to the rock wouldn't allow us to reach the bottom. Reluctantly we gave up and hung silently from the anchors.

The weather was only growing more oppressive as the sun rose above us. Climbing again, my hands were so sweaty they kept popping out of the crack, almost sending me on a "whipper," a violent, swinging fall. Finally after fighting my way to the top of the next pitch, I began to feel sick. My head was spinning and I was nauseous. I screamed down to Jeff as he climbed beneath me, "Don't let this information throw off your climbing, but there's a possibility I might puke on you." My warning was just the excuse we needed to give it up. We retreated, dehydrated and dejected. Later we heard that this was the hottest day of the year—over a hundred degrees, and Hans told us, "Oh, you should have asked me. Serenity Crack's a winter route. No one tries it in the summer, unless you're into saunas." When we got down, I whipped off my shoes. They were boiled to a pink hue in my own sweat. Blisters were forming on my fingertips. Sam lowered the haul bag and as soon as it touched the ground, Jeff and I attacked it, ripping out all the gear, and finally reaching the water. We poured it all over our faces. Most of mine flowed down my chin onto my shirt. "Hey, save some for me," Sam called from above. When he reached the ground, we dumped our individual bottles over our heads, and silently concurred that water never tasted or felt so good.

On the hike down I kept telling myself that each time we made dumb mistakes, those were mistakes we wouldn't make again. I hoped that was true. To do The Nose, we were going to have to become stronger, smarter, and more efficient.

Throughout the summer, when Hans would pop in after setting another speed record on a valley route, Jeff would persistently suggest that we do a big wall together before attempting The Nose. A big wall is considered any rock face that requires an overnight bivy in order to climb it. Hans recommended The Leaning Tower because it only took two days and would be a good introduction to "jugging" up a rope, hauling weight, and removing gear behind the leader. Jeff said he read somewhere that if you weren't just a little queasy before you did your first big wall, then there was something seriously wrong with you. I was glad to know that I was normal.

After a two-hour scramble over a broken talus field and a roped traverse over a narrow ledge of loose dirt and scree, we organized our gear at the base of The Leaning Tower. When I placed my hand on the wall, I immediately understood how the route got the name, Leaning Tower; it thrusts forward from the ground at a thirty-degree angle. We could hear the far cries of climbers moving up the face, screaming out commands to one another. Then we heard the guttural echo of a climber near the top—fifteen hundred feet above, yelling, "ROCK!" The word pierced the still air like a sharp blade. All of us instantly shrunk down into a ball, trying to squeeze our bodies into the least possible area. The basketball-sized rock sounded like a missile as it spiraled fifteen hundred feet and exploded in the talus field right below us. It sent a plume of dust rising from where it hit. Now I knew how the broken talus field had been formed, and was glad I didn't know that until after I had crossed it. "We're relatively safe in this spot." Hans eased our worry. "The rock's overhang means that the people climbing at the top are at least three hundred feet in back of us."

After Jeff led the first pitch, he tied the rope into a fixed anchor. The rope trailed beneath him and was connected to the overhanging rock by gear he had placed in the crack. At the bottom, I clipped into the rope with two mechanical devices called ascenders. The devices slid up the rope but fortunately wouldn't slide down. Standing on the ground I slid the ascenders as high up the rope as I could reach, clipped my ladders to them, and stood up. The dynamic stretch of the rope dropped me back to the ground. By weighting and unweighting each ladder, I slid the ascenders up the rope with my hands, one at a time, my body following. As I found my rhythm, I found pleasure in jugging the rope, the feeling of my body in motion, moving in perfect rhythm up the rock face. I could hear my breathing, the zip of the ascenders as they moved up the rope, my muscles firing in sequence.

High up on the seventh pitch, the cliff jutted out into a forty-foot roof. As the second climber, I was responsible for "cleaning the pitch." The rope on which I jugged passed continuously through the metal snaplinks connected to pieces of gear wedged in the crack. My job was to remove them. This was easier said than done, because the weight of my body pulling out from the rock kept the pieces wedged in solidly. So each time I'd have to jam a hand into the crack and do a quick pull-up. These few seconds of weightlessness were usually enough for my other hand to jiggle the piece from its grip. Directly beneath the roof, the rope passed through a piece of protection, keeping it pinned in against the rock. Above the piece, it ran out and up the overhanging rock. I hung beneath the piece for a few minutes getting my nerve up to pull it. "What's going on down there?" Hans called from above. I was out of sight under the lip, but he could see that the rope was not bouncing and jiggling in its usual fashion. I took a colossal breath, jammed my fingers in the crack and pulled myself against the rock. My other hand wriggled and worked the piece of protection until it was hanging loose in my hand. My fingers in the crack began to slip, so I let the inevitable happen. I leaned back at first until the rope was taut, then let the rope swing me out and up like a kid on a Tarzan vine, except my rope was only nine millimeters thick and I was twelve hundred feet up and forty feet away from the face. The echo of my yell might have been heard by campers across the valley. Before the swing even came to a stop, I was jugging in fast-motion to get back to the granite. Even though the face was overhanging, I needed to touch something, anything that might loosely meet the definition of solid matter. The rope was also spinning me around in quick circles and, even though I couldn't see the rock, I dreaded the idea of facing the vast open sky. As I jugged up, I repeated in a whisper, "I'm facing the rock. I'm facing the rock." I had always thought I was immune to dizziness, that it was a visual thing; I was one hundred percent wrong.

Near the top I made a big mistake. My tired arm sweeping across the face accidentally brushed a huge rock teetering on the side of a small ledge. "Watch that!" Hans warned, but it was too late. I felt it roll off and brush by my leg as it picked up speed. My hands instinctively shot out, trying to catch it. I touched the corner for just an instant, but its weight ripped it free as it sped away and down. I felt like a football player who had fumbled a pass near the end zone, but the consequences of this screwup could cost more than the game; it could cost lives. "Rock!" I screamed, my voice picking up momentum as I realized what was happening. And above me and below me Hans, Sam, and Jeff were yelling, "Rock! Rock!" All our voices rang out in a deadly chorus across the valley, "Rock! Rock!" Three climbers hiking across the talus field fourteen hundred feet below us scattered. One hiker looked up, ran in one direction, then in another, and then in a third. The giant rock exploded eight feet from his balled-up form.

The rest of the pitch continued through loose rocks. With each move, I felt like my heart had squeezed up into my throat. When I reached Hans, my face must have shown traces of an intense internal guilt, because he said in an amazingly calm voice, "Rockfall is part of the climbing game. It's the risk you take. We've all done it."

On the last pitch Jeff persuaded me to lead. I was still on edge but couldn't turn him down. To say no seemed in conflict with climbers' etiquette and against the crucial teamwork required to make the top. I aided about fifteen feet up to a bulgy overhang over which Hans said I would have to free climb. "There's no crack to place gear, so you have to climb out over the bulge; a couple feet higher, the crack resumes." I moved a few feet above my last gear placement, but the bulge felt blank under my fingertips. I moved out onto the bulge several times, but I felt there was no way to get over it, so I backed down and hung dejectedly in my ladders. It wasn't the fifteen hundred feet of space below that worried me, but the four-foot ledge just fifteen feet below that I'd first bounce off if I fell. "Come on down," Sam urged. "Let me give it a shot." I retreated to the ledge and sat down in a cloud of humiliation.

Jeff said, "Don't worry about it. None of us would ever lead that with our eyes closed."

After that, jugging up the fixed line that Sam had led to the summit, I felt even worse. I didn't want to have an easy excuse for backing down. When I completed a lead, I wanted people to say, "I wouldn't have done that with my eyes open." It's not that I wanted to impress people. I climbed because each time I was able to go one step further, that was one step further than I knew was possible. And when I got to wherever I was heading, I found myself in a place that, at one time, only existed in my imagination.

On The Nose, I wouldn't have the option of backing down. I'll be ready, I thought, perhaps only because I'll have to be ready. That's the way it had always worked in my life, as a child facing the challenges of blindness and as an adult facing a three-thousand-foot wall of granite. I could meet the challenge, but first, I would have to stumble a little farther through the darkness, groping for the right holds that would take me where I wanted to go.

With a few days to go before the big climb, Jeff, Sam, and I decided we needed one last marathon day in the mountains. We needed an honest test to prove that we were really ready. The East Buttress of Middle Cathedral is a classic in the valley, known for its twelve long pitches and its difficult routes. Routes never take a simple straight line up a rock face. Instead they zigzag radically, following the natural path of least resistance. Cracks and flakes will peter out or shoot out over an impossible overhang. When this happens, climbers sometimes have to traverse hundreds of feet to find the continuation of the route. The rock faces of Yosemite have been described as vertical deserts, and to be lost on one is both terrifying and dangerous. When we told Hans we were going to try the East Buttress, he gave us two important pieces of advice, "Bring headlamps and bivy gear."

Hans turned out to be right. As dusk swept over the valley, we were still climbing. We had been counting pitches, and at the end of the twelfth, thought we were reaching the top. We were wrong. Although the steepness of the rock grew a little gentler, the upward rise continued farther than Jeff and Sam could see. Finally it leveled out to a forty-degree scramble through loose dirt and clumps of stunted oaks growing out of shallow ledges. The guidebook stated that, near the top, climbers should begin traversing left, but there were no rock cairns to mark the way. We decided to keep moving up although the way was becoming increasingly blocked by high scrub brush. Farther up, I spent a frantic hour with Jeff and Sam far ahead darting right and then left, looking for the path, and me crab-walking up the granite, doing my best to follow. All of their choices ended in drop-offs. They would crash out of the bushes hoping to see a trail, but instead face the twinkling headlights of Winnebagos rising up from a thousand feet below. With night coming on fast, I caught up to Jeff and Sam, who were sitting down contemplating the situation. "Listen to this," Sam said, reading over the route description in the guidebook one last time. "Do not try this descent at night." For my benefit he added, "It's written in bold letters at the top of the page." It went on to state that many climbing parties had fallen to their deaths while descending the mountain in the dark. With that, Jeff dug into the pack and pulled out the headlamp. He flicked the switch and stated calmly, "Big E, I have good news for you. I didn't forget the headlamp this time."

"Good job," I replied, my heart lifting a little. "But the batteries are dead," he cut in. The guidebook's advice, combined with the dead batteries, was enough to win my vote, and I prepared mentally for a night's bivy on the top. Jeff and Sam weren't yet ready to give up, however. "We've got fifteen more minutes of light," Jeff said. "If we don't find the trail by then, we're screwed." He jumped up and began scouting again, while Sam hung back at my pace. With the last traces of light disappearing, it sounded too good to be true when Jeff yelled down, "I see some cairns. I think it's a trail."

When we reached the supposed trail, I doubted whether it was a trail at all. We were constantly fighting our way through brush, trees, and boulders. My legs were scraped and raw. But all of this was secondary because inches from our left feet, the rock swept away in a continuous drop to the valley floor. "It's steep and narrow," Sam warned. "There's a lot of loose dirt, so watch each step, and if you gotta fall, for God's sake fall to the right." Since I couldn't see the drop-off, it was easier for me to block it out and simply concentrate on making sure each step was a firm one. "We're back on the summit ridge of Denali," Jeff laughed grimly. "In the words of Chris Morris, this ain't no place to be screwing the pooch."

Sam looked over, shuddered, and said, "This is one of the rare times you should be grateful you can't see what you're doing."

"Then, you and I should be grateful too," Jeff added.

Next the trail opened up into a thirty- to forty-degree ramp, smooth in some places and broken up in others. The grade was just shallow enough to walk down by placing my feet flat on the granite and positioning my weight directly over them. A few times it steepened and I had to crab-walk down, and sometimes it steepened so sharply we had to traverse a ways before we could resume. Jeff was walking with me while Sam forged ahead. The moon was beginning to rise, providing just a hint of light for them. "Put your hand on my shoulder," Jeff said. "Maybe we'll be able to move a little faster and get off this thing." As my hand rested on his shoulder, it worried me each time he groaned and confessed how little he could see in front of him. I wondered if I might do better leading him, recalling our last late-night adventure together, but I kept on holding.

Moving fast down a steep section of the ramp, I stepped in a deep groove in the rock, stumbled, and regained my balance by putting a little extra pressure on Jeff's shoulder. "Easy there, home chicken," Jeff said, and then, making his voice sound burly in his best Chris Morris impression, "If you fall, we all fall." If I had really fallen, both Jeff and I knew there were only two scenarios: One, he would hold me up with the strength of his body, or two, I would drag us both off the rock. From time to time, I had traveled this way with Sam too. There had been those who were afraid to connect with me. Perhaps they feared a friendship with a blind person would require too much work, too much adaptability, or even, too much risk. I don't know if Sam or Jeff ever had these same reservations. It seems likely that they once might have, but here they were, climbing mountains with a blind man, a thought that suddenly struck me as so ludicrous, I almost laughed aloud. For the last few years, Sam and Jeff had proudly and readily attached their hopes, their ambitions, and their success as climbers to my success, and beyond that, they had never once hesitated to connect their very lives to mine. I could only imagine my brothers or my father linking their fates to mine in this way, but Jeff and Sam were more than friends; they had become my brothers.

An hour later, I was amazed with Sam's route-finding skills when, in almost pitch darkness, he screamed, "I see the rap anchors." At least now we knew we were on the right path. When we finished five rappels, we stood atop a long, steep talus field. Rocks the size of baseballs to busses lay jumbled on top of each other, and most of them rocked or moved when stepped on. There is no easy way to explain the misery of a talus field, unless you close your eyes and take a three-hour hike over one. For the next three hours, I was either carefully hopping from rock to rock, down-climbing steep boulders, or inching down loose rubble on my butt. Sam and Jeff called out the usual directions. "Loose rocks left." "Butt slide ten feet." "Tree branch, head banger." With each step, I'd plant my upper foot securely on a rock and slowly lower my other leg until my foot touched another rock. Often the distance down was so far, I was sitting on my heel before my toe touched solid ground. Then, leaning heavily forward on a trekking pole jabbed in the ground, I'd delicately put weight onto the lower step. The bones in my knees and ankles ground together like chalk against a blackboard, and I heard myself pledge, more than once, "I'll never do anything else like this again." But a fine line exists between misery and fun, and just before one A.M., eighteen hours after we had begun, when I found myself slumped in the back of Sam's car, the hardships were already drifting away like morning fog. "Hey, let's do that one again tomorrow," I joked.

"Maybe we should have left you there. Then, you'd still be there tomorrow," Sam joked back.

"He can live there permanently as far as I'm concerned," Jeff added.

"Yeah," I jumped in, "Yosemite legends would be told about me. They'd call it 'The Legend of the Blind Stud.' "

"If you listen closely," Jeff said, cocking his head and speaking in a haunting voice, "you can still hear him wailing and whimpering as he stumbles aimlessly through the talus."

# 16
# The Nose

Finally August 6th arrived, and I found myself standing at the base of The Nose in the cool dampness of predawn. Our month of climbing adventures had spanned the gamut, from hauling loads to finding routes up vertical wastelands. Climbing El Capitan would simply be longer and harder than anything we had done. My hands were callused; I had lost fifteen pounds. Although I didn't feel one hundred percent prepared, I was about as ready as I would ever be.

All of us carried loads to the base, but when the gear was piled in a heap, Hans asked sharply, "Where's the small haul bag?"

"I thought you had it in your car," Jeff barked at Sam.

"Why would it be in my car?" Sam retorted sharply. "I had the green pack and the three ropes."

"Where is it?" Hans's friend Shipoopi, who was there to send us off, took charge.

"On the porch, to the right of the door," Hans replied, scowling. So Shipoopi raced back down the trail toward his car to retrieve it.

Hans had spent the previous day carefully making a schedule for the climb. It was a model of efficiency:

leave cabin 4:15
park and begin hiking 5:32
reach base 5:56
finish organizing gear 6:07
last climber off the ground 6:22
reach Sickle Ledge 10:37 . . .

"Look," Hans said, whipping the schedule from his jacket pocket and shoving it in front of Sam's and Jeff's faces. "You've thrown my whole schedule out of whack. Now we're going to have to climb twice as fast to get back on time."

The plan on this day was to set five hundred feet of fixed line up to Sickle Ledge and then rappel down to sleep on the ground. "Sleeping on rock ledges does not make for the best night's sleep. Never give up one more night sleeping on terra firma," Hans said. The next morning we would then jug the ropes quickly and have a big head start on the day.

When the last person left the ground we were already, as Hans pointed out, "Thirty-two minutes and twenty seconds behind schedule." Everyone was feeling strong, however, and we made up for lost time. We each led a pitch. We were moving fast. Jeff's pitch was a difficult face climb, no crack—just tiny nubs to claw at and an occasional tiny pocket, just big enough to fit one finger. He fell on the crux, but his last piece of protection held him, and he only fell about eight feet. It added some excitement to the day. On my lead I aided forty feet up a thin, flared crack to an old piton hammered into a seam. I clipped my rope to it and then lowered down ten feet. Hans called out from below, "OK, now pendulum your body to the right. You'll have to pick up a lot of speed. When you swing as far right as you can, reach your right hand out for an edge in the rock." I did what Hans said, tentatively walking my body to the right, but the rope kept pulling me back. "Commit to it," Hans yelled. "You're not going to reach it by tiptoeing." So, this time, I started by walking in the opposite direction to the left. When I got as far as I could, I leaned back right and began running. My legs didn't really have much of a choice; they just tried to keep up with my upper body, which was already going in that direction, like it, or not. As I swung right, the rope arced me up. "Now!" Hans screamed, and my hand slapped out, my fingertips grazing the sharp edge in the rock. Then I was falling back and dangling once again. I thought about that lone rusty piton and the weird, hollow, wrenching sound it had made when I swung on it. It had sat there for the last ten years taking the full brunt of fierce wind, pouring rain, intense sun. For the last ten minutes, the entire momentum of my body had been torquing it from every possible angle. A hundred climbers pass by this spot every year, I thought, and each of them rely on that piton. What are the chances that fate will choose this moment to end its illustrious career? So with that in mind, and knowing that everyone was watching from below, I committed my body to one more swing. If it popped, it would be a clear message that this climb was not meant to be; instead, though, my hand swept out at the perfect time, and I caught the edge. Beyond it was the beginning of a tiny ledge that ran up and right to the wider Sickle Ledge.

On the ground again we made for the refreshing water of the Merced River. In front of us walked an English couple that had come to climb The Nose on their vacation. They didn't seem to be enjoying themselves, however. They had made it to a few pitches above Sickle Ledge, when they had backed down in a thick mire of frustration. The boyfriend stormed along, thirty feet in front of his girlfriend. Every few minutes the girlfriend would break the silence in her thick cockneyed accent. "It wasn't my fault. How do you expect me to use all those blasted contraptions? You didn't tell me it would be like that. Some vacation. I never want to do anything like that again. It's pure cockamamie, if you ask me." I trailed behind, eavesdropping onto the one-sided conversation. At least for us, I thought, the climb had started with good signs from the mountain gods.

The next morning Hans said, "Just wait, the mountain will show its size." While jugging to Sickle Ledge, Hans attached a pulley called a wall-hauler to the rock. Through it we inserted the rope with the haul bags attached. "It's too much trouble trying to haul up both bags," Hans said, after our twenty-minute crank session with gravity. "This small one couldn't weigh more than fifty pounds," Hans remarked, as I felt a heavy weight being clipped to the back of my harness and heard Hans chuckling below. I realized that I had been chosen for the honor of jugging to Sickle with one haul bag while Hans handled the other with the wall-hauler. As I struggled a few feet up the rope, I must have grumbled, because I heard Hans concede, "OK. OK. Maybe it's too heavy. Let me take some weight out of it for you." When I heard that, though, I felt myself jugging as fast as I could to get out of his reach. The last thing I wanted was for Hans to make allowances for me. As I inched upward, my back and calf muscles screamed under the obscene weight. Then I heard Hans speaking softly, but clearly for my benefit, "Killer! He took the bait."

When I began jugging with the bag, I'd hang from my ascenders exhausted after each step, but soon I got into a rhythm. Stand up and lock off left leg, pull up right jug, stand up and lock off right leg, pull up left jug, rest. It became like a game. When I yelled this back to Hans, he stopped muscling the rope through the wall-hauler long enough to grunt sarcastically, "Oh yeah, fun." I was excited when I reached Sickle, four hundred feet of jugging with a respectable load. I never wanted to be a token blind climber. A mountain was such a huge and awesome force compared to the minuscule life of a human, to have a chance of standing on top, we combined our strengths and talents to become a more powerful force than we ever could have been as individuals. Each of us had to make a real impact, whether we were leading, belaying, managing ropes, or hauling loads.

When we all reached the ledge, Sam led a section with a lot of loose rock, which, if displaced, would have fallen directly on our heads. I put my helmet on, if only to con my mind. I wasn't worried about my helmet surviving a falling boulder; it was the soft stuff underneath it that I worried about. Jeff led a section and, at the top, had to set up a "hanging belay." This meant that there was no ledge at the spot where we would rest, so all four of us, plus the haul bags, almost one thousand pounds of weight, would hang free, suspended over the earth by the six pieces of gear he had placed in the crack. When we reached him, his voice sounded jittery as he told us the reason it had taken him so long. "I kept thinking about all our lives hanging on my gear. Even though my mind knew they were bomber, I kept checking them and rechecking them, and then rechecking them again."

Then it was my turn to lead Hans's favorite section of The Nose, a three-hundred-foot vertical crack called The Stove Legs. "It's the same width all the way up," Hans said, "takes number two cams the whole way. Eats 'em like candy." A dozen of these cams dangled from my harness. Each had a plastic stem attached to a metal head that bit into the rock. "And don't forget what a sacrifice I'm making by not leading this one myself," Hans finished. It was wild hanging by my arms and legs, which were wedged in the smooth sustained crack and then scurrying up fifteen feet higher, until my biceps burned and my hands, dripping with sweat, threatened to pop out of the crack like a soft-boiled egg from your hand. Then I would reach for one of the number-two cams hanging from my gear sling and cram it into the crack, praying it would hold the weight of my body. Halfway up the pitch, I hung from a cam with one arm while my other frantically scanned the back of my harness for my ladder. Clipping the ladder into the cam would enable me to rest, and I needed one quickly. I knew the ladder was there, somewhere, but my hand fished futilely through the jumble of metal and nylon. My grip on the cam began to tingle, then grow numb. I couldn't feel the plastic stem under my palm, and I knew it was slipping. My arms and legs began to tremble with exhaustion, and still, no ladder. The rope that trailed below me passed through a cam fifteen feet down, so losing my hold in the crack would mean a fall of at least thirty-five feet with rope-stretch. If that cam didn't hold, then the fall would be more like seventy-five feet. This grim consequence was beginning to seem probable, when I heard Hans's unalarmed voice calling up from far below, "Look at that gripped look on his face. I love it. Pushing him to his limit," and by his voice, I could tell he was smiling. "Killer! Pushing him right to the edge. Look at him. He's even got the Elvis shake going." The playfulness in his voice and the simple fact that he was joking at a time like this, made me reassess the seriousness of my dilemma. I redoubled my grip on the cam. The one thousand feet of air below me didn't seem like such a big deal anymore. To me, Hans was saying, "No big deal. We've all been there. You're OK. Everything's OK. Just relax and find that damn ladder." The wind gusted against the rock face, lifting me up for just a second, and that gave me an idea. I reached in front of my body, and there it was. The wind had blown it sideways, wrapping it around the front of my body. I carefully unclipped it from my harness, forcing myself to go slow and not panic. No mistakes now. I couldn't afford a mistake. With the last traces of staying power draining from my grip, I clipped the ladder to the cam and finally stood up. Deep breath.

That night we stopped at El Cap Towers, a plush four-foot-wide ledge fifteen hundred feet up. We sat with our legs dangling over the side, eating fruit cocktail, chili, beef stew, and creamed corn, all from cans that we passed around. Hygiene was not an issue after ten hours of climbing. Sam pointed out that my hands were black with grime. We played musical cans, eating from the one in front of us until Hans called out, "Time," which meant we were supposed to pass the can. If it was something I liked, I'd usually try to scoop one more spoonful as Sam was snatching the can away. I was passed a can from somewhere and, dipping my spoon inside, it clinked against the bottom. I even lifted the can upside-down over my mouth and beat the bottom with my hand, but only a few forgotten kernels of corn rolled out. "This one's empty," I complained. "Gimme mine back." I reached out toward Jeff and my finger touched the side of a can, but he leaned back and lifted it out of my range. I lunged toward the can, grabbing Jeff's arm and forcing it toward me. Jeff laughed. "All right, hey, no roughhousing. That's the way people get hurt up here."

"You're the only one who's gonna get hurt," I answered. Then he handed over the can, and I figured I had won my point, until my spoon clinked against the bottom again. "Look, home chicken, you snooze, you lose," he said, exhaling a long belch.

Some fifteen hundred feet below, we could hear traffic and the faint yell of an occasional tourist. In a way, those noises interrupted our sanctuary. We were far above the fray, and I wanted to keep it that way. Horizontally, fifteen hundred feet would be a short walk away, but vertically, it put us in another world.

Later in the night Ellen and my dad, who had arrived in Yosemite Valley a week earlier, drove from their cabin to El Cap Meadows and, with chemical glow sticks, performed a laser light show for us. Sam described the lights dancing in broad sweeping arcs across the spectacular rock faces of the valley. For applause, we flicked our headlamps on and off in quick succession and screamed as hard as we could. Ellen told us later that when she looked up, it was hard to imagine people sitting in the sky, the lights from our helmets blending with a million twinkling stars.

After the show, while Hans and Jeff slept, I lay awake in my bivy sacks listening to Sam talk. His voice sounded restless and a little sad. "It's really cool how your dad's always there for you. I'll bet he's still sitting down there in the dark, looking up. Big Daddy is the epitome of proud." My dad had acquired the nickname, Big Daddy, because of his tireless work behind the scenes, writing letters to sponsors, raising money, helping with logistics, and during the adventure, always finding a way to cheer from the sidelines. And sidelines weren't easy to find on a mountain. "These climbs we're doing are a great thing. They're like George Washington crossing the Potomac. We're making history." Sam's voice grew more animated and went up an octave. "And you know what? I'm a part of it, right here, helping to make it happen," and it seemed as though Sam were just catching on to the validity of his own words. "When I see your dad flying over the summit or cheering us up Heartbreak Hill from base camp or giving us a show from the meadow, don't get me wrong, I'm not jealous, but I just wish, sometimes, that my own father was there, that, maybe, he knew what I was doing."

"Maybe, your dad's been following our climbs on TV," I said.

"I don't think so. My dad and I haven't spoken in almost ten years," Sam replied softly. "When I was eleven, my father gave me a rifle. Shooting at a little square paper target was about the most boring thing I could possibly imagine, but nevertheless I'd go to the target range every day. I practiced until I could shoot the balls off a mosquito from a hundred yards away. I even became a state champion, but it was a rare occasion when my father said 'good job' or 'I'm proud of you.' To my dad, I was always the kid who couldn't concentrate in class, the kid who couldn't tell his left from right, the screwup, and, to him, that's what I'll always be, a screwup. In high school, I placed second in the whole New England conference, and you know what he said? 'You weren't concentrating. You should have hit that one.' So, I realized I'd never really be happy doing something that I didn't love for its own sake. That's when I started climbing."

Sam's daily life was definitely a little unorganized. He was often running behind schedule and juggling a dozen unfinished tasks in his mind, but, ironically, in the mountains, he was by far the most focused person I had ever met. (It was as though Sam's mind were a chariot, hurtling along, pulled by forty horses, all jostling and jockeying for position. No wonder in his daily life he wrecked sometimes when turning a corner. But in the mountains, when the consequences couldn't be greater, he had found a way to make the horses move together. Since those first few days of training, Sam had never again mixed up his lefts and rights when guiding me and was usually the partner I relied on to talk me through a tricky piece of terrain.)

Even when it was not out of a sense of necessity or danger, Sam always made a point to stop in the midst of a long day of climbing to describe to me our surroundings, as though the beauty he witnessed overflowed his spirit and spilled out into words. I had a hard time comprehending the majesty of the mountains beyond my immediate touch, but through Sam's eyes, I came close to grasping it: how a gaping crevasse merged from sky-blue to deep blue to black, how the massive fluted columns of ice near Denali base camp split the sky like serrated knife blades, how the glorious sun rose up over the summit of Mount Rainier, orange and gold and fiery. Sam's words were like paintbrush strokes in my mind, some descriptions delicate and elaborate, others large, sweeping, and colorful. After he finished his descriptions, surprisingly, I never felt like I was missing out on the view, but that I was getting an extra bonus, a picture of the world, spiced up with Sam's wonder, his awe, his hope, and given with friendship and with love. I didn't know how to explain how I felt, so finally I just said, "Sam, you're no screwup. No one standing on the top of Mount McKinley and El Capitan is a screwup. Most people only dream when they're asleep, but you allow yourself to dream when you're awake. All of it, this whole great thing we're doing, started with you dreaming about it."

As we both drifted off to sleep, Sam said drowsily, "Erik, if I can't have my own dad flying over our summits, then, having your dad here is the next best thing."

In the morning Hans said that we were behind schedule. "By last night we should have made it four pitches above to Dolt Ledge." So, he decided to take over the leads. It was amazing how fast we went with Hans at the helm. He would fly up a 150-foot pitch that would have taken the rest of us two hours, in fifteen minutes.

The most excitement of the day was my "cleaning gear" under The Great Roof. The Great Roof pitch consisted of a long traverse under the shadow of a huge thirty-foot overhanging block of granite. Hans's gear protruded from a tiny crack that ran across the ceiling of the roof. Moving across it reminded me of swinging beneath the rungs of monkey bars and trying to get all the way across without touching the ground. When I jugged up to each piece of gear, I found it almost impossible to pull it from the crack while putting my full weight on the rope. I had to unclip one jug, which was psychologically terrifying, and reclip it above the piece I was trying to remove. Then I'd weight the ladder, which now hung from the rope above the piece, and reach back to force the piece out. When it came free I'd swing under the next piece, ready to jug up and repeat the process. Sometimes I had to bounce up from the ladder, totally unweighting the rope for a second while simultaneously cranking on the piece. It was quite a balancing act.

My father had been following our progress for the last three days from El Cap Meadows. Throughout the first day, he sat in the grass, holding his small telescope and craning his neck, but as we climbed higher and higher and his neck grew stiffer and stiffer, he changed angles, and instead, lay all day long, flat on his back, resting the telescope on the bridge of his nose. Noticing my delay under The Great Roof, my dad grabbed Hans's friend, Shipoopi, who was hanging out nearby, and asked for a commentary. Shipoopi grabbed my dad's telescope and peered up at the roof. By this time, Ellie, along with a crowd of tourists, gathered around. "Seconding The Great Roof is way sketchier than leading it. I personally know two climbers who greased in that exact spot he's in right now. Your gear gets all tangled up, you lose concentration and next thing you know you're taking a two-thousand-foot screamer, destination terra firma." Looking around for a reaction, Shipoopi was met with the worried face of my dad and the indignant face of Ellen. "Oh, don't worry, babe," he said. "He'll have no problem. He's bold." But Ellen was already slinking away to sit alone in the grass, refusing to look or listen for the rest of the day. Then my father turned to the crowd. "That's my son up there," he said, pride and worry blending together in his expression.

"Aren't you afraid?" a large woman in a sundress and big floppy hat asked.

"Sure," he responded. "Especially since he's blind."

"Blind?" she repeated, anger and astonishment evident in her voice. "And you let him do that, and you're his father?" She glanced up at the tiny dots hanging under the roof, a shudder passing down her like a wave. "Let's go, honey," she said curtly as she grabbed her husband's arm. "I think we've seen enough." As she charged to their parked car, her husband dragging behind, still squinting up at the rock, my father mumbled, "He also sky dives."

Under The Great Roof I worked on one piece of gear for fifteen minutes, trying everything and growing more frustrated with each unsuccessful attempt. In my near panic, I started forgetting how all my equipment worked. I couldn't remember which ladder was connected to which ascender. I couldn't remember which foot to weight and which to unweight. I think I was beginning to lose it. Hans rapped down so that he was about fifteen feet to my right. "Switch your ascenders around," he said. "The bottom should be on the top." Although he was right and although his advice was helpful, at the time, I still didn't want any help. I wanted to solve the problem on my own. I could tell Hans was being careful not to help too much, because he knew ultimately cleaning the pitch of all the protection he had left in the rock was my responsibility, my problem, and ultimately only I could solve it. Finally, though, I got through it, clumsily, inexpertly, but at least persistently.

When we reached a ledge wide enough for sleeping, the team had been climbing by headlamp for several hours. Even our fearless leader, Hans, seemed worn out. Sitting on the ledge after ten P.M., I listened to Hans and Jeff fixing two more pitches above us in order to save time in the morning. Jeff was the unlucky loser of a stone-paper-scissors challenge to see who would go up with Hans and fix the pitches, but because those two were doing the extra work, they also got the best ledges for sleeping. Sam and I wound up on a grim little ledge, two feet across and sloping off the side. Hans and Jeff's was slightly better, two and a half feet wide and sloping off the side. I tried to sleep by turning on my side and pressing my body against the wall, but I kept slipping down. I'd wake up, the webbing connecting me to the wall pulled taut, my right arm and leg dangling off the edge. So, I gave up on sleeping and entertained myself with a box of Tic Tacs that I had carried with me. Hans and Jeff slept twenty feet below us, and Jeff had made the colossal mistake of falling asleep with his mouth opened. Sam repeatedly directed my throws as I tried to land a Tic Tac in Jeff's gaping mouth. Sam would get a reading on his location with a quick shine of the headlamp. "Hey, what the hell," Jeff would mumble.

"Oh, just looking for my Chap Stick."

"Well, it ain't down here." As soon as it was quiet, I'd start launching again. "No, that one was too long," Sam whispered. "Almost, you just missed his arm." I think I connected, because a few times in the night, Jeff woke up gagging and gasping for air, I'm assuming with a minty fresh taste lodged down the back of his throat.

Sometime in the night, I swallowed my last sip of water. When we had arrived on the ledge, Hans had expected to find a gallon of water, which he had stashed on a previous climb. But the bottle was nowhere to be found. "Our last day's gonna be a dry one," Hans said angrily. I thought about the heat pouring off the sizzling granite and the air that reached close to a hundred degrees in the sun. Hans had found an old crushed bottle lodged deep in a crack, but when he had dug it out, passed it around, all of us taking a sniff, we decided that going thirsty was a far better option. "Climbers are a hard bunch," Hans told us. "They know you're running out of water at this stage of the game, so they leave full bottles waiting for you on ledges. The problem is, they aren't filled with water. The liquid has a slightly more yellowish hue."

In the morning I was very ready to leave my little perch. Only five pitches remained. It was already hot as we started climbing, and I kept having to swallow hard to wet my throat and mouth. My parched body was offset, however, by the knowledge that by noon my dad, Ellen, and the rest of the group would be arriving on top from a nine-mile hike up the back side of the Captain.

Throughout the climb, I had observed Hans in a variety of stressful moments, but no matter how desperate the situation became, Hans's voice only grew gentler. Above the Boot Flake, I remarked to Hans that I had never heard him yell at anyone, even if the person deserved it. "I only let nice people into my life," he responded. "So I don't ever have a reason to yell at anyone." I felt sort of honored that he had given to us so trustingly of his time and of himself. He had let us into his life so openly, I wanted to live up to his faith in us. For the rest of the day I tried to climb harder, move faster, and keep any whining to a bare minimum.

On the third to last pitch I pulled up onto a small ledge and Hans warned, "Be careful about what you grab." When I stood up Hans put my hands on a huge boulder that seemed to be resting completely free from the face. It rose up as tall as me and was twenty times heavier, teetering on the edge. It would have gone over except for a dozen pieces of webbing holding it in. "It's just a matter of time," Hans said. "Let's just hope this isn't the time."

Leading the Harding Roof, a forty-five-degree overhang and the last hard pitch, my hands and neck tingled as I thought of the three thousand feet of air beneath me. When I got to the top of the pitch I fixed the line so Sam could clean it. After he reached me, he led the very last pitch, number twenty-seven, a moderate rolling slab to the top. As I waited for Sam to top out, I hung from the anchor, my feet dangling limply in space, under the lip of the roof. I could feel my weight pressing into my harness and the blood draining down my legs and pooling in my feet. The ground was so far below me, the distance seemed almost unfathomable. I was so high up, I couldn't even hear the sounds of life wafting up from the valley floor. If my anchors snapped, I considered morbidly, I'd fall for a full thirty seconds before hitting the ground. It seemed more fitting that I was hanging from the wing of a plane than from the side of a rock face. Throughout the last four days our progress up the side of El Cap had been so gradual I had enough time to acclimate to each new increment of height; I had eaten, slept, and worked in this environment until it had become my world. Suddenly, however, the veneer of comfort lifted, and I was slammed by the realization of where I was. My heart sunk into my belly and my body tingled and turned liquid, as if all the bone and muscle were mysteriously removed. The webbing connecting me to the rock seemed as delicate as a dry strand of grass, and the metal bolts as soft and flimsy as chewing gum. "They cannot break," I told myself firmly. "The systems are redundant: two pieces of webbing connected from two pieces of my harness to two bolt anchors," and although my rational brain accepted the truth of this principle, one-hundred-trillion twitching chromosomes cried out in defiance. Finally, giving in to impulse, I cried aloud, "Oh, please God, let these bolts hold for just a few more minutes." I kept recalling an old John Wayne movie I once saw. Wayne and a younger character had stormed a hill and taken it from the Japanese. They stood at the top, proudly holding the American flag. "See!" Wayne said to his young friend. "Your fears were all for nothing." That's when one last sniper bullet crackled through the air.

Feeling the rope go taut and hearing Sam's "On belay" seemed like a gift sent down from heaven, and then I was scurrying up over the last pitch and hearing the cheers. I could hear my dad, his voice always the loudest, our friends from AFB, the camera crews and reporters from local TV stations, and even the team who had climbed above us, who had waited around to see "the blind guy." But I couldn't hear the one person I wanted to hear the most. I knew I would have to listen carefully for her voice. Then I heard Ellen softly step forward. "Hey, Erik. Awesome job. You look thirsty. How 'bout a Yoo-Hoo?" I honed in immediately on her voice and wrapped my arms around her, neither of us caring about my five days' worth of accumulated sweat and dirt.

Hiking down the gentle nine-mile descent on the back side of the Captain, I felt more alive than I ever had. Even the heavy pack full of metal gear and ropes didn't bother me. I was on solid ground. I actually found myself leaping and bounding down the rocky trail, even laughing when my feet slid out from under me and I landed on my butt in a pile of rocks. I hardly felt it when later, while charging down an old abandoned forest road, I slammed my shins into a fallen tree, and the bark shredded my legs. With blood oozing in large droplets into my socks, I hopped up onto the log and danced crazily, standing on one foot and then the other, swaying from side to side and waving my arms in the air.

I had lost eight more pounds from my already bony frame, and the vision of rich fatty food pushed me onward. The Iwanni Grill, the only true restaurant in the valley, had always been too expensive for climbing bums, but tonight was a celebration. The problem was that it closed at ten P.M., and we had another three hours plus a forty-minute drive to go, with barely enough time to squeak in. We bolted through the Grill's large oak doors fifteen minutes before closing, and I was surprised to hear a familiar boisterous voice booming through the restaurant. Warren Harding was sitting alone at a table, talking across the room to the passing waitresses and cooks who would periodically pop their heads out of the kitchen. The maître d' would approach his table with reverence and ask, "Can I get you anything else, Mr. Harding?" Black and white pictures of Warren putting up impossible-looking first ascents were plastered all over the walls. Warren was the resident hero in the valley. We asked him to join us and learned that he had driven the three hours from his home on the off chance that we might show up. "How did you know?" I asked.

"It's the nearest restaurant to the Captain. I had a hunch."

I couldn't think of a better ending than sharing a beer with the man who had done the first ascent of The Nose over thirty years before. Sitting over a colossal dinner of prime rib, baked potato heaped with sour cream and butter, salad, cheesecake, and five root beers, I turned to Warren and said, "Thanks for coming. I'm honored." I could feel his intense stare and sat awkwardly waiting for him to speak. Then, unexpectedly, he blurted out, "You son of a bitch," and a jolt of anxiety shot up my spine. Oh no, I thought, he's mad at me. Perhaps angry that a route taking a year out of his life and his very heart and soul to complete, a route that in his day was deemed the hardest ever done, was now climbed by a blind guy. Perhaps he felt that his life's work had been reduced to a laughable scale. "You son of a bitch," he repeated and this time he reached out, grabbed my shoulders, and shook me roughly. I didn't know what to do, so I did nothing, just sat there stupidly, my head bobbing back and forth. "You son of a bitch!" he said for the third time. "You did it!" Then, with relief, I understood. He wasn't angry; he was proud, and I regretted not being able to see his grizzled face. But I could hear his husky voice, barely above a whisper, "You son of a bitch. You did it."

# 17
# The Slag Heap

In the Refugio at Penitentes, near the trailhead of Aconcagua, Chris approached the team over instant coffee and stale hard bricks of bread. "Bad news, boys. The gauchos sent a muleteer through the Vacas to see if the river was passable, but he couldn't even get that far. A huge avalanche has closed off the entire valley. There's a hundred feet of snow blocking the way. There ain't no getting through, unless you brought your chain saw.

Our plan had been to climb Aconcagua's Polish Glacier, an ice climb on the mountain's northeast side. "That'd be pretty cool, to get you up the Polish," Chris Morris said, when I had proposed the idea to him at the end of our Denali climb. Since then, Ellie and I had moved to Denver, Colorado, where she accepted a job teaching sixth grade while my workplace was the great Rocky Mountains, the ideal setting to train. Sam had moved to San Francisco to begin a new teaching job and was out of commission, at least for a while. Jeff, on the other hand, was still living the carefree vagabond life with no serious job to tie him down, so he was raring for another adventure. I had even convinced Hans, the world's fastest climber, to join us.

With the gaucho's news, however, a year of planning, strategizing, organizing, and training was buried under an acre of rubble and snow. I tried not to let the disappointment become personal, as if the mountain were striking out at me. In fact, that's what I like about the mountains; they are oblivious to human ambition, but these natural forces had never hit so close to my own ambition.

"I guess it's the Route Normal," Jeff said, pushing back his chair and laughing sarcastically.

"But the Route Normal's a slag heap," I complained. "The guidebook says it's the world's tallest pile of rocks."

"Yessir! It is," Chris stated emphatically. We were all silent for a minute, contemplating fourteen thousand feet of dirt, rocks, and scree.

"Get ready for some slag climbing." Chris finalized the decision.

"Then, let's climb the damn thing and get this slag heap over with," I thought bitterly, but even as this thought materialized in my brain, I knew it was a mistake to underestimate the mountain, or even worse, disrespect it.

A jeep carried us up a long bumpy dirt road to the trailhead. The sun shone through a stiff breeze. We hiked along a narrow trail cut into the middle of a steep scree slope, to our right the slope rising up hundreds of feet and on the left dropping severely to a raging river. Three hundred feet above it, I could feel a cool damp hint of spray. I stepped forward with one foot directly in front of the other, leaning heavily on my trekking poles and scanning one out in front for rocks or drops in the trail. "Stay right," Jeff said. "Death fall to the left." His voice had a hint of humor in it, but we both knew the message was very serious.

"Would I fall straight into the river?" I asked nervously.

"Oh no," he replied as if to reassure me. "You'd bounce a few times before you hit the water."

"Great."

"Oh, yeah!" he continued, on a roll. "You'd smack a ledge every hundred feet or so. You'd break a lot of bones before you were swallowed up by a thousand gallons of foam." Next we crawled across a dilapidated bridge reduced to just a few planks and began following a trail on the other side of the river. "Now, stay to the left," he said. "Drop on the right. It wouldn't kill you, but you'd be severely pissed off." From then on all drop-offs were divided into three categories, "mildly annoyed," "severely pissed off," and "death."

The next day we worked our way up a long flat valley, our bodies leaning into a constant stream of roaring wind. Jeff described the snow-covered peaks rising up on both sides of us. In the afternoon the trail steepened and culminated in a series of switchbacks. At the top Jeff gasped in stunned disbelief. "There are two things I'm sure of right now. This isn't base camp, and those are our duffels piled in front of us." We were still five hundred feet below base camp; the trail continued up through a jumbled field of *penitentes*—ice pinnacles jutting out of the snow from six inches to six feet high. It's standard procedure on Aconcagua for mules to carry your gear to base camp, but the muleteers must have judged the *penitentes* too dangerous and dropped the loads here.

There were no flat spaces for tents, so we set up camp on the side of the slope in a cold, blasting wind. I had learned from past climbs that this was a very dangerous time of the day. Our bodies, after a long day's effort, were exhausted, dehydrated, and damp. And now with the plummeting temperature and my body no longer in constant motion, I began to shiver. I knew to keep moving, keep working to haul loads, pile rocks for wind walls, organize food bags, anything to keep my blood flowing until I could crawl into the warm cocoon of my tent.

The next day we shuttled loads through *penitente* fields to base camp. Each trip only took an hour, but *penitentes* are a blind person's ultimate punishment for his sins. If I really hated another blind person, I'd drop him from a helicopter into the middle of a *penitente* field and yell down from the open door as we soared off to the nearest Dairy Queen for banana splits, "Have fun. See you in hell!" Even though we were at a higher altitude with cold temperatures, the sun was intense, burning the snowfields into a chaotic array of jagged shapes, deep grooves, and severe angles. Being blind and carrying a sixty-pound pack, navigating around and on top of *penitentes*, is treacherous, slow going. Stepping from one sharp narrow pinnacle to the next, my feet were sliding and my upper body wobbling precariously. A fall would mean a long slide into a deep uneven gash in the ice. I was afraid of breaking an ankle or smashing a knee against the rock-hard points. Chris would hike in front of me picking out the least horrendous path. "Stay in this narrow groove. Keep your feet in it. Now big step onto a *penitente*." My foot hovered over a deep slot. "No! Left . . ." My foot probed for the top of the icy needle. "More left . . ." My foot pressed down, digging in. "Perfect. Only fifteen more feet until scree."

In Yosemite, descending endless scree fields after day climbs, I didn't think there could be anything worse, slipping and sliding over loose rocks, knees cracking, ankles bending and contorting into grotesque angles. But now fifteen feet from the scree, I begged for it. I tottered so slowly across the *penitentes* that I felt like I wasn't really contributing to the team effort. Each of my teammates could have probably made two trips in the time it took me to make one. As we reached base camp, I dropped my load and sat on my pack, waiting for Chris to speak. I expected him to say, "Erik, you hang here. We'll get the rest." Instead he said, "What the hell you sitting around for? Think you're on holiday in the south of France? We've got another load to haul."

Finally at base camp, Chris looked around for a place to camp. "What's it look like?" I asked.

"Oh, it's beautiful," Chris replied, placing a rusty piece of chicken wire in my hand.

"What's this?" I asked.

"Hard saying. There's crap like that everywhere." Splintered wooden beams, rusty sheets of metal, and burlap sacks littered the ground. South American environmentalism is not quite up to that of Denali or Rainier. In two weeks, this empty junkyard would be converted into a tent city, selling everything from Inca Cola and *cervesas* to a full-fledged team of guides, cooks, and porters for the upper mountain. I was glad we had arrived preseason.

For me the worst part of mountaineering is each time nature calls. Curled up in my warm sleeping bag at night, feeling the urge and knowing relief will mean waking up my tent mate and both of us thrashing around to put on a dozen pieces of clothing, I'd lie awake, dreading the moment. On Aconcagua, instead of having to be "grumped," which was an unpleasant part of being my tent mate, Jeff had evolved a system. Jeff would poke his eyes out of the tent and yell out directions. About fifty yards from our tents was a narrow rocky ravine, which Chris had named Growlers Grotto, because from the hundreds of piles of little frozen turds, he had surmised this was the camp's latrine. "Straight, now left, more left, stop, turn around . . . Fire away!" That night, I was feeling bold, and decided to find Growlers Grotto on my own, but I got a little disoriented in the boulders. I climbed over a little ridge and on the other side, feeling the rock wall behind me, decided this was as good a place as any. It even seemed to be out of view from the main camp. Midway through the act, my privacy was interrupted by sharp voices wafting up from below the ridge. "What's he doing?" the female voice called out in a thick English accent. For a fleeting moment, I prayed she was referring to someone else, another blind guy, perhaps, taking a grump on the opposite ridge.

"That's a blooming disgrace," a male voice yelled.

Female voice: "That's an outrage, right out in plain view."

Male voice: "The bloke has no respect!" I imagined the British newlyweds, enjoying the honeymoon of a lifetime, boiling their freeze-dried shepherd's pie under the full, full moon. "Darling," she might have started, "isn't this romantic? Isn't the moon so unusually pale tonight?" Holding hands, they gaze up, their loving expressions quickly changing to disgust when they notice the "moon" moving a bit too much. I desperately wanted to retreat, but I was past the point of no return. By now it was painfully obvious who the bloke with no respect was, but squatting near the top of the ridge, I clung to my philosophy that had managed to keep me safe in the past. "What I can't see, won't hurt 'em."

Above base camp we were back into the familiar. We knew our job. We would shuttle loads to our two higher camps and then make a single carry to our presummit camp at 19,500 feet. From there we'd wait for a clear calm day and go for the summit. On the first shuttle day we made good time, plugging steadily up the intermittent scree and snow. Everyone was excited to finally be getting above the signs of human havoc into a realm more sacred. It was exciting to finally feel the thin crisp air against my body and in my lungs. On the way back to base camp, Jeff and Hans tried their hands at glissading while Chris and I took the more conservative descent down the trail. Descending a mountain is probably the most difficult part for me, and I move slower than a sighted person. I extend my trekking poles to their full length so I can feel the terrain below me. I must make a bizarre sight, waddling along like a giant duck, leaning forward on my poles, butt protruding out, and feet slapping around as they search for flat steps. When we shuffled into base camp, two Argentines met us excitedly.

"Hot tea" one said and thrust a thermos into my hand. I drank some and passed it on to Chris. When Chris handed it back, the other Argentine said urgently, "Now, we get doctor." I was confused. "Doctor?" Chris repeated. "Doctor, for your amigo," he persisted. Later Chris said the man had pointed to me, swaying crazily back and forth and making his eyes very wide. Then Chris let out a sound between a grunt and a laugh. "No! No! Not sick, blind." Chris waved his hand in front of his face. "Blind!" The Argentine waved his hand in front of his own face. "Blind?" he repeated and turned to his friend. "Blind?" he said. They murmured back and forth in Spanish, periodically waving their hands in front of their faces. Chris interjected, "He's not sick. He always looks like that." He slapped my shoulder and this time the sound was more like a laugh. Despite my exhaustion, I laughed too. We proceeded down the trail to our camp, the Argentines trailing behind, watching carefully, not quite convinced of this preposterous story. I forced myself to walk a little straighter and step a little more confidently.

Lying in my tent after arriving at Camp Canada—16,500 feet—I grabbed one of my plastic water bottles sitting in the corner, knowing the importance of staying hydrated. First I dropped some drink mix into the full bottle and shook it up. Then I lifted it up to my lips and took a big swig. Suddenly my whole body shuddered. The drink was noxious, warm, salty, and ammonia-tasting. If I didn't know any better, I would swear I had just drunk a mouthful of drink mix over pee, I thought. Still shuddering, I stepped outside, holding the bottle in my hand. How could a bottle of drink mix and water possibly taste like urine? I wondered if I had a malfunction in my taste buds, and was about to test the theory by taking another sip, when Chris rushed over frantically. "Oh dude! Tell me you didn't just drink out of my pee bottle." Each of us had pee bottles, so we wouldn't have to bother getting dressed and stepping outside in the night, but I had seen to it that they were different sizes than our water bottles. Apparently Chris had lost his pee bottle at base camp, so had begun completing the job in one of his water bottles. "Sorry there, young sportsman. I wrote 'pee' on it in big black letters. What the hell, are you blind or something?" Chris said as I took a few steps and forced myself to puke in the dirt.

By Camp Canada, we had been on the mountain a week, already having completed one cycle of the freeze-dried meal varieties carried with us.

"What's for dinner?" I asked Chris.

"Well," he said, "To make it up to ya for drinking my pee, I'm whipping up something special: filet mignon with béarnaise sauce and a side of asparagus tips, lightly braised in garlic. And for dessert, New York cheesecake."

"Don't forget the after-dinner liqueurs," Jeff added.

"Come on," I said, my mouth watering, despite my lingering sensory memory of pee.

"What do you think's for dinner?" Chris shot back, "The same lumpy nasty gruel we've been eating for the last week."

Digging into a heaping bowl of New Orleans style red beans and rice, I bit something hard that sent jolts through my teeth. "What's this?" I asked in shock, holding up the marble-sized object in my palm.

"Why that'd be a rock," Chris retorted calmly as if reciting the sports scores. "Oh, yeah, the snow around here is kind of old. Lots of rocks and pebbles in there, so bite gingerly boys." He chuckled a secret laugh.

That night, we sat on our packs as the sun went down and the temperature dropped, attempting to stretch the minutes before we were forced into our long night's twelve-hour captivity in the tent. The wind began to blow, first as a whisper and then in short fierce gusts that made me hunker down and squeeze my arms into my body. At times like this, Chris was famous for practicing an attitude he called, "positive pessimism." "It sure is cold," Chris commented, "but at least it's windy."

Then I jumped in, immediately catching on to the rules of the game. "It sure is dusty, but at least there's rocks in our food."

Everyone piped in with their own versions. "This mush sure does taste awful, but at least it's freeze-dried."

Jeff was the first to retreat to the warmth of our tent, but in a few minutes he called out, "The ground sure is hard, but at least there's a hole in my sleeping pad."

That night I lay awake next to Jeff, listening to the erratic wind bursts as it flapped the fabric of the tent and rattled the tent zippers, hoping we would get a stroke of luck and the weather would improve. I reached my hand between the top compartment of my pack and its main body to the silver angel pin, attached unseen to the fabric. My grandmother had given it to me on my last visit. My grandparents' reservations about my climbing trips had never been subtle. On the same visit, I was sitting in front of the TV with my granddad when a segment about my McKinley climb came on the news. During the video clip of me taking my last few steps to the summit, thousands of feet of air below me on all sides, Granddad hauled himself out of his big, stuffed

La-Z-Boy recliner and charged the screen, faster than he had moved in years. His arm waving at the picture, completely forgetting my presence in the room, he yelled, "Don't you know you're blind, boy? Get youself off that confounded mountain 'fore you kill youself." Later, at the kitchen table, after my grandmother dished up my plate, my probing fork continued to come across an endless supply of roast beef. I soon realized that each time my fork raised toward my mouth, my granddad was quietly slipping another piece on my plate. I think his plan was to fatten me up into such a doughboy that I could hardly get out of my chair, let alone get up a mountain. After the meal, my grandmother said, "It's time for you to quit gallivanting around on those mountains. Why don't you settle down like a man of your age should and have yourself some babies?" Knowing that I wasn't swayed, she had fished around in her jewelry box and handed me the angel pin. A friend had given it to her after my mother's funeral. "If I can't talk sense into you," she said, "then, maybe your mama can, and if even she can't, she'll keep you safe."

Curled up in my heavy down sleeping bag, I touched the tiny pin, felt the thin wings like those of a butterfly, and the intricate garland around the head. It would be kind of sick to try to use my mother's spirit to change Aconcagua's weather patterns so we could stand on top, but I hoped it would give me the strength to make safe rational decisions, to surround myself with a strong team, and not allow my aspirations to defy the crushing power of this mountain.

The next morning, we awoke to a foot of fresh snow blanketing our tent, so we stayed cozy inside, figuring we'd be sitting through a bad-weather day. Around one P.M., a strange little pigeonhole of sun brought us out of our tents. Chris, already pacing outside, said, "Guess what, boys?" and not waiting for a response, continued, "Yessir, we're moving. Maybe, we'll even have time to get to the next camp before it craps out again."

Inside the tent, as I packed up, Jeff, beside me, moved unusually slowly. His upper body swooned back and forth reaching for his possessions and his clumsy hands stuffed gear haphazardly into his pack, sometimes missing the opening altogether. When I asked him if he was OK, he mumbled back, "Don't worry about me. Everything's just fine," but halfway up a steep scree field to camp, it was obvious that everything wasn't fine. He had been stopping every five minutes as he hiked beside me. "You OK, buddy?" I said, grabbing his arms. Jeff was leaning heavily over his ice ax, head hanging down. "Everything's dizzy," he slurred. "I feel like I'm gonna pass out."

"Tell me what's going on," I said, a little scared.

"I took an antihistamine," he whispered. "Four of 'em." All of us had suffered from a dry high-altitude cough and stuffed-up nose, caused by breathing in so much dust. Through the night I could always hear someone hacking away in their tent. "I could understand the need for an antihistamine," I told Jeff. "But four of 'em?" I asked.

"I thought it was a rest day," he grumbled, "and then home chicken had to go and change the plan."

As the clouds rolled in and the wind picked up again, we were nowhere near camp and clearly in trouble. Chris got right in Jeff's face and yelled, "Come on, Jeff, get it together. Weather's comin' in, and this ain't no place to be screwing the pooch." All of us took a portion of weight from Jeff's pack and as I stuffed what seemed like a giant load into my already overstuffed pack and slipped and staggered up the slope, I completely regretted that decision, but also knew we had no choice. For the next three hours, as the fury of the storm came down on top of us, we stuck by Jeff, who seemed to improve a little with no weight to carry. Chris hiked along right behind him, slapping his ski poles together and yelling out, "Ya, ya, mule. Keep it movin'. When you're back to normal, you and I are gonna have a word."

When we came into our 17,500-foot camp, named The Nest of the Condors, we were being pelted by hard nuggets of hail. Jeff plopped limply down on his pack, head between his knees, as the rest of us gathered rocks for wind walls. I kept busy, walking in straight lines out from the campsite, swinging my feet and trekking poles, until I kicked a rock with my hard plastic boots. Then I'd haul the rock back and place it on the wall. The temperature was plummeting, and I would have been getting cold if I hadn't been so preoccupied lurching around under the weight of large rocks and between carries, tending to Jeff. I pulled my down jacket from my pack and wrapped it around him and then worked fast to set up our tent. When it was up, I grabbed his sleeping pads, sleeping bag, and various stuff sacks, which others had dropped at the head of the tent, and laid them out. Then I helped Jeff inside and he collapsed facedown. Rolling him over and taking off his boots, I got him inside his sleeping bag and every few minutes would check his breaths by putting my ear to his lips. His breaths were so faint, I could barely hear them against the rattle of the wind. So I put my hand to his lips and felt a trace of warm humidity. I knew if he fell asleep in this state and at this altitude, he could easily stop breathing, so whenever I felt he was drifting off, I'd yell in his face, "Hey Jeff, how you doing? What's going on? What are you thinking? Tell me about all those Argentine babes you're gonna hit on when we get down," and when that got no response, "Hey Jeff, just think, this's the second time I'm saving your life," and Jeff murmured back, "Super Blind."

Around midnight, Jeff's breathing seemed to be coming easier and more audibly, and I could tell the antihistamine was wearing off. In the morning, with Jeff still a little groggy but basically back to normal, Chris lived up to his word and lectured Jeff, reminiscent of a loving father disappointed in his son. "You sorry #!%$#@. If you ever pull that one again, I'll skin your hide."

The wind howled through the next day. From The Nest of the Condors, the team could finally see the summit. Jeff looked up and described the high cirrus clouds, like paintbrush strokes streaking across the sky. "They call 'em mare's tails," Chris added. "When you see those it means high wind at the summit." As if to affirm his statement, vast plumes of snow shot hundreds of feet vertically into the air, obscuring the summit for an entire minute. "To make snow do that," he said, "the wind has to be blowing at least a hundred miles per hour. This ain't a travel day, boys."

"You're absolutely positive this time?" Jeff asked caustically. "You're not gonna suddenly get a wild hair to go for the summit?"

On bad-weather days, time would creep by and then explode in quick bursts of excitement. Our tents were set up only a few feet from each other, so we could pass books, food, Walkmans, et cetera, back and forth. Hearing a tent door being zippered open, I rolled over quietly and reached for my arsenal of ready-made snowballs piled in the vestibule.

"You always launch 'em too early," Jeff whispered. "Be patient, until his door's fully open." I lay still as Chris whistled and rattled a stove.

"Now," Jeff roared, as he yanked down our door's zipper. Chris was ready for it with his own attack. A snowball thudded against the tent above me. Ice chunks spilled onto my shoulder. Then I whipped mine directly toward the former sound of whistling. It rocketed through his open vestibule and exploded right on his sleeping bag. When you have just experienced a small victory, I've found it's best to quit. I zipped up our fly and went back to my Walkman.

The wind hadn't stopped in the last week. It had pretended to stop, teasing us as we lay trapped in our tents. The mountain would grow still and calm like a vacuum, and then it would abruptly send a blast shaking the flimsy poles of the tent, lifting it up and slamming it down again. The guide wires would pull taught and grow slack, twanging like rubber bands. I had felt wind on McKinley, but not like this. There it would blow strongly for a day or two and then subside. This wind seemed different in the way it would begin as a whisper and grow into a shrieking roar, enclosing us in its sound, so that I would have to scream at my tent mate to make myself heard. It would blow at the tent from different angles, from one side and then the other and then straight down. Then it would seem to be swirling around the tent, coming from everywhere at once. Yes, this wind was different from Denali. It had personality. It was alive.

Trudging up to our presummit camp, backpacks bulging with gear, Chris asked "So, Big E, how long you wanna do this kind of stuff for?"

"Until I'm forty or so. Then I think I'll get it out of my system."

"Not me," he quickly replied. "I want to do this forever." Then he hesitated, as if he had spoken too much. "But I'm just an old climbing bum," he laughed. "Strong back, weak IQ."

"You're sort of slow-witted," I added, "but at least you're stupid."

Until now our free moments had been filled up by Chris's jokes about the misery of mountain climbing, but now I realized that his jokes were not complaints. I think there are times when you really love something, but you're embarrassed to admit it because you know the thing you love is only a slag heap. You make fun of the mountain and yourself for your decision to be here when, underneath, the jokes are really praises. Secretly I had learned to love it too, every moment of it—the way the rock and scree felt under my boot as I probed for a secure step, finally finding it, my leg driving my body up another foot; the way the wind felt as it roared against my face and past my ears, cutting me off from the world, so that it was only me and the staggering force of the mountain.

At Piedras Blancas at 19,500 feet, we all tried to fall asleep early, but for some mysterious reason my right eye felt like an active volcano, ready to explode out of my head. At high altitude on Denali, it hadn't ever felt like this. I wondered if it was just a one-time fluke, but the cynical part of me feared that my one remaining eye was changing, perhaps, beginning to build in pressure, like my left eye had done in college. Now my eyeball felt like internal fingers were pushing outward, trying to poke holes in my eye's surface. Throughout the long night, I squeezed my eye shut and kept my palm pressed against it, trying to combat the cruel little fingers. By the next morning I was exhausted, and found it hard to think about anything other than the pain. I knew I had to stay focused, because, as a team, we had even bigger problems. Despite our prayers to the mountain gods and our requests for forgiveness for once writing off this fierce mountain as a slag heap, sometime about midnight I woke to hear the wind returning. I was beginning to understand how someone could go insane. Jeff called it "Argentinean wind torture." I had begun giving the wind different names at each subsequent camp, imagining they were all part of an extended family. Lying awake in a tired delirium, I greeted the wind, "Hello Uncle. I met your nephew down at sixteen. He was very blustery but not nearly as cold as you. I met your wife down at seventeen. She was a fierce one. She roared in my face and turned my nose white. One of these days, I'll have the honor of meeting the head of the family. He's bound to be a tough old bastard." The wind responded in a colossal blast that lasted several minutes, and my tired brain wasn't sure whether the wind was giving me all it had or whether this was just a tiny taste of its fury.

By the fourth day at Piedras Blancas, the wind had not abated. We were out of food and fuel. "The latest we can leave for the summit is noon. We'll wait until then."

But when the weather had not changed and Chris made the decision to try, we all knew the attempt would only serve to satisfy our need to learn firsthand the mountain's limitless power. Three hours later, we stumbled into Independencia at twenty-one thousand feet, acclaimed as the highest man-made structure in the world. In reality it was the remnants of a rock wall protruding from a deep pile of snow. We hunkered behind it. One hundred feet above me it sounded like a thousand freight trains or a fleet of jets taking off. Protected by four layers of fleece and a GORE-TEX shell, I was still cold. My fingers were losing sensation through my mittens. "It's over," Chris yelled. He was only a few feet away but I could barely hear him. His words seemed to be swept away as soon as they left his mouth. "Above us is an exposed ridge. It's the windiest part of the mountain. There's no way. It would be suicide." We all reluctantly agreed. I respected Chris's ability to know when we were outmatched. I was intensely sad, but also relieved because I wouldn't have to face the head of the family. I stood facing the deafening sound one last time, still feeling a remnant of my desire to go on, and as if to answer my urge, the wind gusted hard against me, almost knocking me off my feet. "Next year," I said, and my heart felt heavy and cold as I forced my body to turn around toward camp. Later in the tent, the disappointment of the climb swept over me like a river of scree. I escaped outside, pretending to organize my pack, so Jeff and Hans wouldn't see the tears that were spilling out in scorching waves. Jeff followed me out into the whipping wind. "When you try big things," he said, "you gotta expect to fail sometimes." The thought was so simple, yet, at the same time, profound, and I knew he was right. His words took the edge off my sadness and gave my brain something to hang on to throughout the long hike down.

On the twenty-two-mile hike out from base camp, Hans and I teamed up. He hiked in front shaking a box of Tic Tacs and using his own special lingo to guide me. "Iceberg" meant an immovable rock in the trail. "Ankle burners" meant a series of icebergs. "Rollers" meant loose rocks that could turn underfoot. Clearly bored, Hans went a little overboard. "Iceberg protruding six inches at a thirty-degree angle to the right, left edge of trail. Rollers, scattered at eight inch intervals, moving from left to right, varying sizes from three to seven inches. A combination of ankle burners and rollers, an average of two to three ankle burners to every roller, culminating in one large iceberg, flat top, rising at a twenty-degree angle." The information was more than I needed to function, but I think Hans was trying to give me a taste of sight. For three hours Hans had been happily spouting information. I wondered when he had time to breathe. Nearing the trailhead, Hans became bored with this game. "Let's switch," he said. "I'll take the hiking sticks and you take the Tic Tacs." At the trailhead, the rangers were gathered in a large tent. They had heard about the blind hiker who would be arriving any minute. As we arrived, I was walking in front of Hans, my feet braced for any random terrain. I shook the Tic Tacs in large sweeping movements, stopping periodically to scream dramatically, "Over here, this way. Big step over a little gully." I only knew about the gully because a few moments earlier I had stepped in it myself. I hoped the rangers didn't notice. Hans stumbled along behind me, butt out, head bobbed forward, swinging the hiking poles wildly in front of him. Sometimes he would stop as if he had lost track of my voice and begin rotating his head and probing one pole tentatively in front of him. "This way, come on, you can do it. Only a few more feet." I'd shake the Tic Tacs loudly. When we neared the rangers' tent, Hans whispered, "It's going to be a delicate maneuver between two parked jeeps. Don't blow it." Tic Tacs held high over my head, shaking in a salsa beat, my knee banged against the jeep door. "Left a little," Hans barked, trying not to move his lips. We were both laughing as we thought of the rangers watching in awkward silence the two gringos, the guide almost as clumsy as the blind man he was supposed to be leading.

Passing the rangers, I picked up a rock off the side of the trail and squeezed it tightly in my hand. "Maybe I'll do this forever."

# 18
# I Did Not Die

After returning from Aconcagua, I flew to my grandmother's house in Florida. One of the sad rituals I always performed while there was to visit my mother's grave site. Back in high school, the pastor had told me that in times of struggle, I would need my mother's love and strength even more than in times of happiness, and, I had to admit, he was right. After our crushing failure on Aconcagua, I had felt a powerful longing to be near her. So, I wanted the visit to her grave to be something special, but it was more of an obligation because I never knew quite what to do while standing there. I thought that her grave would be where I could commune with her, an earthly pathway to the heavens, but when I talked to her, I was never sure if anyone was actually listening. Not that it wasn't beautiful, the hot sulfur air of the Panhandle, hot all through your body, just the way she liked it, and the peaceful country cemetery set back from the main road, almost lonely. When I stood beside her grave, I mostly thought about her death, the last moments of her life, which she spent alone in the emergency room, slowly bleeding to death through a crushed artery, waiting for help that didn't come in time.

I thought about her open casket, which would have made her seethe with embarrassment. In the funeral parlor it was as if she were giving her opinion for the last time, because despite the mortician's best efforts to ply her face into a peaceful expression, my grandfather said that she looked like she was "just about to cry." Mostly I thought about what she had told me in the midst of her depression. "If I die, I want to be cremated and have my ashes scattered over the South China Sea."

I got uncomfortable when she talked of her own death. My rock-stubborn brain, which had only accepted blindness after I walked off a dock and almost broke my neck, refused to take her seriously. My older brother Mark rebutted her with his usual smart-ass responses. "Quit trying to get attention. You'll outlive us all, sitting in a rocking chair like Nana, grouching and carrying on just like always."

She had defied all our predictions, though, and was killed that very year, and no one in the family, except me, had taken her request seriously. "If she were cremated, there'd be nothing left," my grandmother had explained. "I don't want to sound morbid, but this way, I can always know that she's still there, with her beautiful blonde hair and beautiful face. If there were nothing left, I couldn't bare it." So instead of cremation, my father decided to lay her to rest at the Mount Carmel Cemetery, close to her mother's home and right beside a small country church with her grandmother and grandfather buried beside her.

My mother had traveled the world. She had stood before the Taj Mahal, had walked along the Great Wall of China, and had ridden on the backs of camels in Egypt. The end of her life brought her right back where she began—to a small farm town growing peanuts in the winter and cotton in the summer. When they placed her in the ground, I thought how far away Jay, Florida was from the South China Sea.

The Florida air was steamy in contrast with the cool dry air inside my grandmother's little white Toyota as she pulled onto the dirt strip of the cemetery and I opened the door. "I get to visit whenever I want. You go visit a while and I'll sit right here under the air conditioner," my grandmother said. Seigo and I got out and walked across the grass until my foot touched the brick border that I knew would lead me to my mother. I slid my right foot along the bricks until I reached the end, and then I sat down on the hot ground and placed my palm flat on the bed of little cut rocks.

The air buzzed with life; birds chattered, mosquitoes and gnats swarmed around my face, darting in and out of my ears. I tried to ignore them and reached out to touch my grandmother's pots of flowers placed carefully on the site. She kept my mother's grave decorated with fresh flowers—lilies, azaleas, and birds of paradise, my mother's favorite—arranged in clay pots baked in her own kiln. I had let go of Seigo's leash and he immediately began rooting around in the flowerpots. I tugged him back. Something about Seigo trampling around happily and indiscriminately in the carefully arranged flowers and on top of my mother seemed sacrilegious. Seigo plopped down and gloomily laid his head on the grass, panting hard in the stifling humidity.

Whenever I came to this place, I expected something to happen. I know it sounds silly, but I wanted this place to pulse like the beating of my heart as if it were alive with the soul of my mother, like the feeling some get when entering a giant Gothic cathedral, the feeling I get when I'm in the mountains—the vastness, the ancientness, the immense power opening my heart to the presence of God. But here, God was strangely silent.

This time I was determined to get a sign, something small but real. I wanted to feel her. I wanted to know she was close to me here. Of all the places in the world, this should be our cathedral, our mountaintop. Instead I always went away feeling lonely, unfulfilled, with unanswered questions. My brother would take pebbles from her grave around in his pocket. Once, he had placed them in my hand. I squeezed them until they cut into my palm, but I only felt the heat of my own hand. I scooted around and touched my finger to the engraving on her gravestone, ELLEN BAKER WEIHENMAYER, 1939–1985. GOOD MEMORIES ARE EVERLASTING.

No charge pulsed up from below. The stone was still. I tried to conjure up her image, but it was distant. Her face could have been anyone's and her voice was a blend of others I had known more recently. Despite my effort to channel my thoughts and energy on her, all I could feel was the stifling midday sun like a blanket, the annoying gnats swarming around my face and ears, and my sweaty T-shirt plastered to my body.

I redoubled my efforts, but my stubborn mind refused to focus. Everything kept getting in the way. Seigo continued to pant in rapid fire. My grandmother's little Toyota idled too loudly. A soft wind kept puffing in my face, like an Aconcagua wind but gentler. It still shocked me how my mother, a laughing, living, sometimes angry force could be lying lifeless in the ground, and on top of it all, my memory of her was dying too.

Seigo, fed up by the relentless gnats, stood up abruptly and shoved his snout into my ear, pleading with me to leave. I laughed in shock, feeling the cold wet nose against my skin. Then he rolled over and waved his helpless paws in the air, and I couldn't help but chuckle, despite the somber setting. I give up, I thought. The life around me was conspiring against me, demanding my attention: Seigo, the puffing wind, the idling engine. And suddenly, I was aware of it all, an explosion of birds chattering and singing above, a tractor roaring and rumbling in the distance, the grass whistling below me and the sky buffeting above. All these sounds exploded into focus like they had never before. And it forced me to wonder whether these were distractions or the very clues that I had been seeking.

Later my grandmother and I sat in her warm kitchen surrounded by the delicious smells of pot roast and brown gravy, canned pickles, and fig preserves. This was a place that hadn't changed since my mother's death, and that is when the memories came alive. I especially loved hearing my grandparents' stories of my mother as a little girl, so lively, strange and magical. The story I had been hearing over and over, ever since I was a little boy, was my mother rooting around like a pig under the kitchen table, coaxing her three-year-old brother, Kenny, to give up his precious candy. "Oink oink!" she'd snort. "Feed the piggy." And he'd drop another piece into her snout.

My favorite story, though, happened when she was only a tiny little girl. The family had gone to the Jay Diner, which offered the town's first jukebox. Country music was pouring out and my mother found it hard to sit still in that soft booth. She stood up, leaning restlessly at the edge of the booth, and began to sway, tapping her little feet, and dancing to the country music. Her eyes were closed, as she laughed and hummed and danced. Most of the patrons watched her, moving so joyously, oblivious to anything else. When she opened her eyes, she saw that they were staring. As if waking from a dream, she looked down at her feet, then up at all the smiling people, and lunged desperately behind my grandmother. She hid behind her for the rest of the meal.

The image of my mother, only a tiny girl, so full of innocence, so full of beginning, got stuck in my head, my brain continuously pushing it to the surface. That laughing, dancing little girl did not fit in the cemetery. It seemed impossible, like trying to fit a puzzle piece into the wrong slot. The two images could not be reconciled, the little girl and a lifeless corpse, a coffin, a heavy headstone. How could the two be the same?

Finally in my grandmother's kitchen, I summoned up the courage to share my frustrations at the cemetery, how I couldn't feel my mom's presence through the distractions. As I told her this I felt more stupid. Instead of laughing, my grandmother rushed into her closet and drew out a newspaper clipping as if she had been waiting to share it. "I've been saving this," she confessed. "I clipped it out soon after Ellen died." Then she began to read.

*Do not stand by my grave and weep.*
*I am not there.*
*I do not sleep.*
*I am a thousand winds that blow.*
*I am a diamond glint on snow.*
*I am the sunlight on ripened grain.*

*I am the gentle autumn rain.*
*When you awake in the morning, hush.*
*I am the swift uplifting rush*
*Of quiet birds in circling flight.*
*I am the soft star shining at night.*
*Do not stand by my grave and cry.*
*I am not there.*
*I did not die.*

And then I knew that my mistake was that I had looked for her in only one place, as if her whole essence were crammed into an angel pin or into a box, buried in the ground, when nothing so small could contain her. Suddenly, in my grandmother's kitchen, it was so obvious I laughed aloud. The signs I had been looking for were the wrong signs. I hadn't felt especially connected to her grave because she wasn't there any more than she was anywhere else. She was all around me in all the glorious distractions. She was the puffs of wind and the explosive chattering birds. She was the living breath in Seigo, the innocence and the playfulness. She was the idling engine and the little white Toyota and all that was inside it. She was my grandmother and the palpable love that passed between us. She lived in me and in every fiber of every tiny dancing child; and she was other things too, the warm touch of the sun on granite, the stark crunch of the snow under my feet. She was the vast echo of the mountain above me and the solid earth below me and everything in between. She was the great force of the world and all that comprised it. She was everywhere and everything, and I knew instantly that I would never be alone, that even on a cold night in my tent high up on a mountain peak, all I would have to do is to reach out and touch the cold still air, and I would find her.

# 19
# The Song of the Sirens

In late December, 1998, for the second time in my life, I found myself back on the slag heap. I can't wholeheartedly say that I was thrilled to be back, but I had had a year to pine over last year's failure, and the story desperately needed an ending. Aconcagua is a harsh land. Some critics called it, "the world's tallest rubble heap," and the less creative, simply "an ugly brown heap of rocks." Below base camp the water collected from streams is flecked with brown swirlies and vague tastes of mule dung and higher up, the ancient ice is layered with rocks and grime. Despite all of this, I found myself boarding an Aero Argentina jet with my climbing partner, Chris Morris, heading for Mendosa.

When I decided I would return to Aconcagua, I began racking my brain for sponsorship, and ironically it was intense eye pain from glaucoma that had given me the idea where to look. At high altitude on last year's Aconcagua expedition, my right eye felt like it was going to pop, and now it was beginning to affect me at lower and lower altitudes. Recently, while camping out at eight thousand feet, I had writhed in agony through the night and gone through almost a full bottle of Advil and now, in Denver, only five thousand feet, I had been waking up at night with a dull throbbing ache in my eyeball that often extended to my whole head. Ellie had first noticed a gray fleck growing in my pupil, which soon expanded to cover the whole pupil, making it look cloudy. Eventually there was no visible separation between the white part of my eye and my once-black pupil. When I finally went to the doctor, he tested the pressure in the eye, and just like when my left eye had been tested almost ten years ago, my right eye pressure also registered off the charts.

My current doctor had suggested several treatments: first, a benign series of eye drops and secondly, a radical laser procedure called cyclophotocoagulation. The doctor explained the grim procedure. Using a laser sixty times more powerful than the ones used in a doctor's office, he would blast away at the front membrane of my eyeball, which would hopefully damage the membrane enough to allow fluid, currently trapped in my eyeball, to pass through it. He had put a pencil eraser in my hand. "If I focused the laser on that eraser, it would be reduced to a charred black nub. Honestly, I don't know if this will work, but if it does, it sure beats the alternative." I respected his frankness and willingness to be proactive, when others might have too readily accepted the inevitability that I would lose my eye. The procedure began less than pleasantly. I lay on my back on a skinny metal table with my doctor standing over me, jamming a blunt needle through my lower eyelid. He listened for the three distinct pops as the needle broke through three layers of cartilage. "Try to keep your eye open," he warned. The only sign that the needle hadn't gone too far or ruptured my eyeball was the three popping sounds and the fact that my eye socket hadn't filled with blood.

"One surgeon pushed the needle in too far and froze the patient's brain stem," my doctor remarked as he stood over me.

"What happened to him?" I asked, as I forced my eye open and tried to calm the uncontrollable twitch in my legs.

"Oh, he died in a fit of convulsions." And this was only the anesthetizing part.

* * *

After my third cyclophotocoagulation, my eye membrane was too fragile to do another, but my eye pressure had only been brought down to fifty, a marked improvement but not enough to totally eradicate the pain. After discovering the procedure hadn't worked as well as we had hoped, my doctor did his best to console me, his hand on my shoulder. "Well, at least I didn't freeze your brain stem."

After sixteen years of blindness, one thing I've learned is that life is never meant to be easy; exciting, challenging maybe, rewarding from time to time, but never easy. Ironically when I finally accepted this reality, that's when life got easy. So, after reconciling myself to glaucoma, I decided to go to the experts. I called the Glaucoma Research Foundation, an organization concerned with both glaucoma research and prevention. Almost immediately they signed on to sponsor the climb. Despite impressive advances in medical technology, when it came to acute glaucoma like mine, doctors were still reduced to blasting away at the eye or ripping it out. Glaucoma had ravaged my eyes, but maybe, in a tiny way, I could prevent it from happening to others. On last year's Aconcagua expedition, the pain was crippling, but this year, I was prepared with an arsenal of glaucoma drugs, which would hopefully keep the pressure at bay. The climb would show glaucoma sufferers that they could live healthy, active lives, persuade people to seek out regular eye checkups, and most importantly, the resulting media attention might just bring a slightly faster cure to glaucoma.

During our failure of the previous year, the mountain had worn us down, beaten us into submission and, in doing so, had earned our begrudging respect. The wind was the worst part, scouring the dry rocky soil and turning sky to dust, which cakes your face and coats your lungs. It was a relentless wind, puffing, whipping, swirling, and howling, a wind that had become my personal nemesis and had taken on living proportions. I laugh at the phrase often quoted in climbing literature, "conquering the mountain." In a head to head fight, the mountain will far outmatch the strongest climbers. Chris Morris had said, "The best you can hope for is to sneak to the summit when the mountain blinks."

That is what I like about mountains. It is a realm where humans haven't reached godlike status, a realm that demands humility. Human frailty is amplified, human ambition nullified. Chris didn't think much of ambition. The mountains had taught him to accept the world for what it was. If I said, "This weather sure sucks," he'd shrug and reply with a hint of a grin in his voice, "Yessir! It does at that," and immediately go back to whatever he was doing. Sometimes I would make the mistake of saying, "I wish it wasn't snowing so hard," or "If only the wind would stop for a while."

"You know what I think about wishing!" he'd shoot back. "You can wish in one hand and crap in the other and see which one fills up first." Or when he was in a more poetic mood, "If *if*s, *and*s, or *but*s were candy and nuts, we'd all have a merry f------ Christmas."

"If you ever decide to stop climbing," I said, "you should become a philosopher . . . for simple people, of course. Imagine yourself standing over your minions—mostly old crotchety climbing bums, general freaks and dirt bags—proclaiming important revelations about not crapping in your hand."

On our last Aconcagua expedition, we had been on the mountain for eighteen days, on the upper mountain for a week. Every day, plumes of snow rose hundreds of feet straight up from the summit while a gauntlet of wind hammered our faces. Long strings of clouds called mare's tails raced across the sky, an ominous sign of bad weather to come, and by noon each day, the mare's tails had expanded into dark lenticular clouds which dumped heavy snow and dropped the temperature fifty degrees. As usual, we had reached our high camp in raging wind and snow. We lay shivering in the tents listening to the insane flapping of tent walls until Jeff checked his Walkman and called out, "Hey, I'm getting some tunes." It was a faint, fuzzy disco station, originating from Mendosa hundreds of miles away, playing cheesy, B-rated throwbacks from the seventies. The first song was more appropriate than any one of us wanted to admit. It was titled, "She's a Bad Mama-Jama," and the song was right: she was about the baddest mama-jama any of us had ever confronted. The song gave me a sunken feeling, and I couldn't help but believe it was a mocking taunt from the mountain gods. We had all tuned in with our own Walkmans and sung along defiantly from our three separate tents, our straining voices practically drowned out by the screaming wind. "She's a bad mama-jama. Just as fine as she can be! Her body measurements are perfect in every dimension. She's got a figure that sure enough gets attention. She's poetry in motion. A beautiful sight to see. I get so excited viewing her anatomy."

This year, Chris and I left for Aconcagua later in the season, a day after Christmas. Last year's failure had made me bolder. My plan was to be aggressive, to move up the mountain every day, even during marginal weather. In a year it was easy to forget the bad weather driving us back, the thin oxygen sapping our strength. So, I began to doubt whether we had been aggressive enough. Maybe we had let our chances slip away. This year, I decided, we'd push the route aggressively to high camp and then wait for a perfect summit day. As much as I loved to climb, I was not coming back to this place a third time.

I had the whole climb planned out. After summitting, I would use the radio phone at base camp to call a flower shop in Denver and order flowers for Ellie. I even had the note planned out. It would read, "I miss you. We summitted. I love you." And it all would be delivered to her in her classroom in front of all her sixth graders, a big bouquet of red roses. "What do we have here?" she'd ask amusedly, and when she spoke in this voice I could actually picture her blue eyes sparkling. All her students would press around her, craning forward to see the card.

Among Chris, Hans, and Jeff, Chris was the only sadist who I could persuade to accompany me on a second attempt. A new climbing partner, Mark Howe, also joined us. Mark was an amazing athlete. On the day of our first meeting, he had just returned from a bike ride. I learned that he had ridden his bike sixty miles from Boulder to the Long's Peak trailhead, run to the top of Long's Peak—elevation 14,255 feet—and back to the trailhead again, then ridden his bike home.

Mark's and my climbing experiences could have been entitled "The Turtle and the Hare." On our forty-mile trek to base camp, we crossed desert terrain, dotted with scraggly shrubs and crisscrossed by rivers which we had to ford. While I plodded along, placing one foot carefully in front of the other, Mark raced ahead, usually having tents set up and water boiling by the time I arrived. But mountains are an ironic testing ground, because athleticism isn't an assurance of performance. At base camp, Mark woke up with a pronounced gurgle in his lungs, a sure sign of high-altitude pulmonary edema. If Mark didn't go down immediately, he would drown in his own lungs. So, in only three days, just as our tiny trio had begun to bond, we sadly said good-bye to Mark. With him gone, Chris and I were completely thrown. I had planned this second attempt with minute detail, and just like last year, when an avalanche had poured into the Vacas Valley and cut off our route, everything had changed. Chris was quiet throughout the morning as we pared down gear. Neither of us wanted to confront our severely narrowed options. If Chris or I were to become injured or sick, we would have absolutely no safety net. In the afternoon, Chris said abruptly, "Everything will need to go perfectly now or we'll have to go down."

The next day and all that week, we inched our way up the mountain. By each afternoon, the clouds would roll in, the wind would pick up, but mornings were generally clear, giving us enough time to make it to the next higher camp, set up the tent, and be securely inside before the weather turned ugly. With long fifteen-hour stretches in the tent to kill, it was unfair to a climbing partner to become a slug. Making an effort to converse was an obligation. As tent mates, however, I was a bit introspective and Chris seemed quietly content with the long gaps of inactivity, so words didn't always come easily. At camp one, at sixteen thousand feet while I was listening to a book on tape, Chris's voice crowed out, breaking the solitude with a question, as if he had been pondering the issue a long time. "You've got a pretty good woman, don't ya?"

"I'm pretty lucky," I replied.

"She's gotta be pretty special to tolerate a dirtbag like you. How's Ellie feel about you leaving for such a long spell?"

"You and I have a goal to focus on, but it's a lot harder for the ones we leave at home, just waiting for news of a summit. It's hard on Ellie, but once she told me she didn't want our life together to be ordinary."

"Then she got what was coming to her," Chris laughed sarcastically.

"My climbing team knows me as Super Blind Guy, but Ellie's seen my soft underbelly."

"God help her," Chris interjected.

"Ellen flew over the summit of McKinley and watched me take my last steps. She met me at the top of El Cap, but she's also witnessed a few blunders. When we first got married, I tried to impress her by doing up the breakfast dishes. I was in my own little world when Ellen came in and started laughing. She asked me if I always washed dishes like that, like she had some much better way that she wasn't going to share with me. Naturally I was annoyed, so I asked her what her secret was. Then she really confused me because she answered that her secret was to use 'liquid soap.' So now I was really steaming and asked her what the heck she thought *I* was using. She said, 'Why don't you taste it and find out.' So, I did, and that's when Ellie lost it. She was practically rolling on the floor. I still don't think it was my fault. Why does a bottle of maple syrup feel so much like a bottle of dish-washing soap?"

"I think it's a conspiracy, Big E," Chris chuckled. "Maple syrup companies everywhere trying to screw with the soft underbellies of blind people." And, as usual, when Chris was overtaken by his own cleverness but was also a bit worried he had taken the joke too far, he gave me a hard slap on the leg.

"Being blind has its advantages too," I stressed. "When Ellie and I had been dating a while, I got curious about how much she weighed. I didn't want to ask her directly; I didn't want her to think I was a pig. It wasn't as if knowing Ellen's weight really mattered that much. I just thought it was a boyfriend's prerogative to know. When she was stopping off at my apartment after a workout, I asked her if she wanted to weigh herself on my bathroom scale. Ellen got quiet and I could feel her eyeing me suspiciously, but I think she figured she was safe; it wasn't like I could look over her shoulder, but when she stepped on the scale, she got a little surprise. She didn't count on my talking scale blurting out in its computer voice, 'one . . . hundred . . . and . . . twenty . . . seven . . . pounds.' That's when Ellie rushed out of the bathroom and saw me smirking around the corner. She called me a cheesy little schemer."

"She should have just taken a few swings at ya," Chris remarked. "That's what I'd have done."

As Chris and I slept, the humidity of our breath froze against the tent ceiling, so that the next morning when the warmth of the sun touched the tent, we were awakened by large cold droplets of water splashing onto our faces. This Aconcagua version of Chinese water torture was enough to get us packing and moving up the mountain. This year, Chris and I had worked to perfect our hiking system. Since on Aconcagua we weren't roped together like we had been on McKinley, finding a way to follow Chris was an added challenge. Chris hiked in front of me at a fast clip, saving his voice by tapping the tip of his trekking pole on rocks to be avoided; but the biggest additions were the large bear bells I had ordered from Alaska. Last year, when we had turned back at the bottom of the exposed ridge at twenty-one thousand feet, we had all felt the staggering wind blasting down from the summit, and I knew if we had continued, hearing my partners in front of me would have been impossible. So this year I attached the bear bells to Chris's pack and the wrist loop of his pole, so his movements would be easier to follow, hopefully even in high wind. If Chris wanted me to move left or right, he'd simply extend a pole in that direction and jingle the bell.

Often Chris would slow down to look around, and daydreaming, I'd bump into his back, stabbing him in the calf with the sharp point of a pole. "Ooh! That was a good one," Chris would shout in mock enthusiasm. "If I'm not mistaken, I think you drew a little blood." Occasionally I'd even manage to drive a pole down the back of his boot and I'd have to yank the thing out while waiting for the wiseass response from Chris. The silence was almost worse, as I pulled and twisted the pole, the groove at its end stubbornly caught in socks and flesh. When he heard me bearing down on him, understandably he'd get a little nervous. "Gear down there, big shifter," he'd say. "I'd like to keep a little skin back there."

Chris always got me back though. Below camp two, he remarked, "This trail is pretty smooth."

"Never comment on how good something is," I warned. "It upsets the mountain gods." And I was right, or so I thought. In the next moment, the trail became very rough. Chris zigzagged us across piles of jumbled boulders and through deep uneven ruts, all the time jingling the bear bells energetically. "You see!" I said exasperatedly. "Talk about how great it is and look what happens." That was when Chris began chuckling, and I suddenly understood his little game. He had left the trail and was leading me over the worst terrain he could find. An instant later, my pole shot out and was swatting hard at the sound of the bells, but Chris was already leaping across the boulders, just out of range.

A few hours above camp one, we traversed along the side of a steep loose-scree slope. Every step sent piles of various-sized rocks skittering down the slope and dropping into a fierce glacier-fed river. With each step I couldn't help morbidly imagining my own body tumbling down the bank like the loose rocks. Eventually we worked our way down to the river where we had to cross. The river was only fifteen feet wide but cut a powerful path through a deep gorge. Chris stepped out onto a slippery boulder and yelled out, "OK! Step to me. Whatever you do, don't slip." We scrambled out over the river on a succession of increasingly smaller rocks until we stood on the edge of an overhanging hump of ice. The river spewed forth ten feet below me, and cold, stinging spray splattered my face. Chris stopped on the edge, surveying the best way across. "We're going to have to jump it, Big E," he shouted above the noise. "There's no other way. Now I want you to listen to me carefully. This ain't no place to be screwing the pooch." And now I was nervous; for Chris, this gem of a phrase was like heavy artillery, only unleashed when things were really serious. "You're going to stand on the edge of the ice. Get a solid stance, and don't slip." To hammer home the point he picked up a rock and said, "You hear this?" He launched it into the fuming torrent, and I thought I heard a vague grinding sound beneath the roar. "If you didn't drown immediately, in about a hundred feet, the river would suck you back under the glacier . . . You'd definitely die." I stood on the edge, contemplating the jump. "It's about nine feet across, and there's not much to land on, just a sixty-degree slope of ice and scree. You're gonna just have to trust it. When you land, your front points will stick and you'll fall forward with your palms." Then his monkey-like frame leaped across. On the other side he yelled, "Alright, go for it, Big E," but my legs felt like they were fused to the ice. I leaned forward, and holding the end of a pole, reached out as far as I could. "You can't reach the other side. You just have to trust it. You have to jump." I was still frozen. "Don't think about it anymore," he yelled. "You'll psych yourself out. Make it a good one, though, because if you fall, you'll definitely die." Why did he have to keep repeating that? I thought. I imagined him glancing nervously downriver to where the water poured darkly under the glacier. "I'm just getting ready," I yelled back, and thirty seconds later, "I don't think I can do this."

"It's the only way across," he shot back.

There are moments in our lives when we can move forward in small increments, increasing the challenge bit by bit, but there are other times when security is merely an illusion, when we must summon our courage, gather up our past skill, and proceed by the power of sheer faith. To this day, I cannot explain how I triggered the circuits that enabled my legs to crouch, my body to lean forward out over the abyss, and then my legs to spring, so that I launched across, through the roar of the river and the mist that rose up like cold frost. On the other side the front points of my crampons bit the ice and my momentum drove my palms forward flat against the slope. When I knew I was safe, I lay against the slope, my cheek pressed against the ice, my chest heaving. My body felt like it was melting into the frozen ground. "Good job," Chris said. "You didn't die."

Maintaining our aggressive schedule, Chris and I bypassed camp two, sitting at the top of an exposed col at seventeen thousand feet, and humped our heavy loads up an endless mixed-snow-and-scree slope to camp three at nineteen thousand feet. "How far do you think we have until camp?" I asked Chris as we rested on the slope, my head hanging and my chest leaning heavily on a trekking pole.

"Well . . ." Chris replied, "It's hard saying, not knowin'."

Higher up the slope Chris climbed far ahead to scout out the route, and I was left alone to pick my way through the rocks and snow. I concentrated hard and found I could stay on route by stepping in the frozen boot holes of previous climbers, an exciting game of connect the holes. When I caught up to Chris, I panted, "Morris, you better not be getting any ideas to leave me here on this godforsaken mountain."

"What could you do about it if I did?"

"Ellen tried to leave me once. You know what I told her? We were walking through a remote village in Africa, and somehow or another, I began to annoy her. She started walking really fast and told me she was going to leave me there. I tapped along behind her with my cane and shouted out, 'You may leave me here, but eventually I'll track you down. You'll be happily remarried, probably have forgotten all about me, but I'll find you. I'll swim across the ocean through a school of sharks, crawl a thousand miles on my knees, and drag my bloody carcass across your manicured lawn and into your house. You'll be drifting off to a pleasant night's sleep when you'll feel a gnarled bloody hand around your throat.'

"If you leave me here, Morris, you might get away with it, but one day when you least expect it, you'll hear a little knock at your door."

"Well, that confirms it," Chris said, laughing. "You're officially an asshole."

When we arrived at camp three, both of us were hurting. "How do you feel?" Chris asked as we set up the tent.

My head pounded. My stomach was queasy. I doubled up with coughing when I breathed too deeply. "If I felt like this at sea level," I said, "I'd be calling nine one one."

The next day we traversed across *penitente* fields to Piedras Blancas, our high camp at 19,500 feet. When the snow steepened, we stopped in the wind to put on crampons. We only had a few hours to go, so I wasn't hurrying. Chris, on the other hand, always in high gear, was impatient. I was sitting with a crampon half on my boot when Chris, hovering above me, said abruptly, "If you move this slow on summit day, we won't have a chance." I hurried to finish the job, but nervous from the lecture, caught the tip of my pointer finger in my crampon bail and ripped off the pad. With blood pulsing down my hand, I shoved it angrily into my glove and hoped it would cut off the bleeding.

By camp, I was fuming. I was sick of Aconcagua, the tormenting wind, and the impenetrable maze of rocks that never gave me a break. I was tired of Chris too, from the sour smell of his feet when he took off his socks, to his impatient crusty lectures, to his blunt Alaskan witticisms. One day blurred into the next as we sat in our cramped tent waiting for the wind to abate. My Walkman had broken, so I couldn't even escape into my book on tape. At least the radio worked, so I found myself listening to endless disco over the one Mendosa station. I had no diversion to occupy my brain. I couldn't stare out the tent at the fast moving gray clouds; I couldn't even stare at the tent walls. I was reduced to my own thoughts. I could keep my mind busy for a few hours, thinking about home life, the food I would eat, my future goals, but slowly those thoughts began to be replaced with ones of doubt. I thought about Ellie and how unfair it was for me to be away so long, devoting myself to such a selfish, dangerous goal. I thought about that living wind, and decided it would never quit. I thought about Chris's harsh words: "If you move this slow, we won't have a chance," and I feared he was right. On top of it all, the glaucoma eye pain that the drugs had been keeping in check were no match for this extreme altitude. The pain broke loose with savage fury, making my eyeball feel like it would burst. It was the worst at night when I'd lie awake, writhing in pain, a fork stabbing my eyeball. It was then when the pain and fear and panic seemed to conspire against me, burrowing their way into my belly and filling it up so tight, I felt I would surely suffocate. To combat it, I'd force myself to repeat reassuring mantras and to breathe deeply in rhythm. "Breathe . . . relax . . . breathe . . . relax . . . calm . . . down . . . you're . . . OK."

By our third night, feeling the panic rising up inside me, I woke up Chris. "Let's play a game," I suggested. "Maybe twenty questions or I Spy."

"I don't play games, and I especially ain't playing I Spy with a blind guy," Chris replied groggily and then rolled over and fell back asleep.

In high school, I read the Greek novel, the *Odyssey*. In the long voyage home, Odysseus and his crew pass the Island of the Sirens, where beautiful maidens sing out to passing sailors with voices so melodious and haunting that they are drawn to the island, the original goal forgotten. As it turns out, though, the maidens are really monsters and the sailors are gobbled up, never to be seen again. To fight their allure, Odysseus ties himself to the boat mast and the music nearly drives him insane. Stuck on a mountain at almost twenty thousand feet is no different. The Sirens were calling out to me, the music so strong that I wanted to tear open the tent fly and run headlong into the frigid night, tripping and sliding down the rocks until I reached the comforts of the world, until I reached my wife, my friends, my family. "Come down! Come down! Come down!" they chanted. "Hamburgers and French fries and milk shakes await you." The Sirens even took on the voice of Ellen. "Come down," she urged softly. "I'll still love you if you fail."

Finally I couldn't take it anymore. I had no one to turn to but Chris, so once again, I woke him up.

"I don't know what's happening to me. I think I might be going insane."

"Talk to me, Big E. Tell me what you're feeling," he said alertly.

"I feel like I can't wait anymore. If we don't summit soon, I think I'll have to go down."

"It's the thin oxygen talking," he warned. "You'll get down and be disappointed in yourself because you'll know you didn't give it your best shot."

"Maybe I don't want this," I said, unable to control the tears that began to slide down my face. "Maybe, everything I thought I wanted . . . Well, maybe, I was wrong."

"Hang in there, Big E. You've got to remember why you're here. We'll be down soon enough, and then you'll be missing your old salty buddy."

"Oh! When I get home," I said. "Maybe I'll do something completely different. I'd like to do something simple, to work with my hands, maybe a carpenter, or even better, a pie chef. How wonderful it will be to make pies day after day: blueberry, apple, cherry, and chocolate cream. And every evening, when Ellie comes home from work, I'll meet her at the door with a new kind of pie, steaming hot and fresh from the oven. I'll make pies from dawn to dusk and be happy, and I'll never dream of mountains ever again."

Chris, suppressing a laugh, cut me off. "I'm telling you. It's the altitude. I'll bet you a million bucks, when you get down, you'll never bake one pie."

Even if he was wrong, I could see myself escaping from this mountain to the warmth and comfort of my own kitchen, and surrounded by stacks of voluptuous, fresh-baked pies, a vague yearning would seep over me and I would begin to hunger for a mountaintop, an unquenchable appetite that just couldn't be satisfied with pie. I'd be kneading the dough and pouring the fruit and scheming about ways I might get back to the slag heap, in all its austerity and beauty. I'd pray to return again and again, despite the rocks in my food, the *penitente* fields, the wind and perhaps for the sake of these things. Then, lying in the tent next to Chris, I knew the awful irony of the Sirens. The powerfully hypnotic pull of their music also worked in reverse.

At two A.M. the next evening, Chris looked outside. "It looks clear," he said. We boiled water for oatmeal and drinking water and began the long process of getting dressed in a space little bigger than a car trunk. Knees, elbows, and shoulders collided and my body strained and contorted as I pulled on long underwear, layers of fleece, and a GORE-TEX shell. Next came two layers of socks, vapor barrier socks, inner boots, and then stiff frozen plastic boots; finally, three-layer gloves, hat, balaclava, and goggles. We checked our summit packs for snacks, water, shovel, stove, bottle of gas, lighter, sleeping bag, down jackets, extra gloves, first aid. And then I was struggling out the tent door, zipping the tent fly behind me, dizzy in the thin air. Leaving so early, we hoped we would beat the huge winds that began howling near the summit by noon. We made good time until twenty-one thousand feet. But approaching the ridge traverse, we heard a noise above us, like jet planes taking off. The wind patterns had shifted. On previous days, while observing from below, we had noticed the strongest winds built up in the afternoon. Now, in a cruel statement of superiority, the winds had decided to rage earlier. As we crested the ridge, they met us at full gale force, screaming off the summit and hammering us in our faces at sixty miles an hour. We hid behind a pile of rocks, putting on our down jackets. We were both beginning to shiver, and our fingers and toes were going numb. "This is the same place it turned us back last year," I said angrily and laughed to myself; this year, I thought, the wind was even worse, much worse.

"Yessir, it sure as hell is." Even Chris's normally accepting voice showed a trace of bitter disappointment.

As we shoved forward into the wind and I pulled the collar of my down jacket around my face, I quickly realized I had an even bigger problem than the cold; I couldn't hear the bells anymore. Maybe they had frozen, or maybe the wind was just too loud to hear them. The system I had thought was so brilliant was useless. Chris kept stopping in front of me and trying to get the bells to jingle, and when that failed, clicking his poles together, but I still couldn't hear him.

"Feel my boot holes," Chris yelled. "Try to stay right in them." But there were long sections where the wind had scoured the slopes bare and I couldn't connect the holes. Chris must have seen me wandering off the mark, so his quick mind acted instinctively. He put his pinky fingers in his mouth and whistled at the top of his lungs. My head shot up, as the shrill piercing sound cut through the wind. I moved toward it. Every few minutes for the next three hours, Chris stopped and whistled. It was a bizarre game of mountain Marco Polo. Chris would watch in horror as I wandered off toward a cliff. He'd whistle with every last bit of breath, and I'd begin following him again.

It was the coldest weather that I haven't turned back in. Often we had to stop and windmill our arms and chorus kick our legs to keep our extremities from going numb. "By God!" Chris yelled out in one of our many chorus sessions. "I think my left toe is frost nipped. We gotta keep moving."

We knew, if we could only make it to the Canelleto, the protected snow gully that led to the summit, it might be sheltered from the wind. So many times I thought we were going to have to turn back, so many times I decided that we had no chance of making it. I waited for Chris to say the words that would turn us back: "I think this is as far as we should go," or "Big E, this just isn't our day." A part of me actually hoped he would say them. But he just kept moving and whistling, and I kept on following. About eight o'clock in the morning, we rounded a corner, and the wind simply stopped. Chris shook a trekking pole and the bell, dangling from the wrist loop, jingled; we both laughed. We were in the Canelleto, only two thousand feet to go.

Even though, thankfully, the wind had stopped, the Canelleto was a spooky place. Some of those who had tried to stand atop Aconcagua had taken their last breath in the Canelleto. The day before, we had heard about a climber who had disappeared and was spotted near the top of the Canelleto, leaning frozen against a rock. The gully, long and steep and protected from the wind, would seem a perfect place to stop and rest. Climbers sit down amongst the boulders for a moment's rest and promptly freeze to death. Dying of exposure is supposedly a very peaceful way to go. Before death, climbers are overtaken by a strange feeling of intense warmth, so that they are often found sitting in the snow, with most of their clothes lying next to them. I knew that somewhere along our path, we would pass right by the missing climber. I was glad I would not be able to see his half-naked corpse, the fragile warmth of his life stamped out so easily, resting now like so many boulders strewn across the mountain. I shuddered and willed my brain to clear itself of the lackadaisical fog that crept over me, with such little oxygen to breathe. The steep walls of rock rising up on both sides of the gully created the sound of closed-in space around us, like an echo passing through a mausoleum.

As the terrain changed from snow to a hodgepodge of boulders, I couldn't seem to get my breathing into a rhythm. "You're starting to move mighty slow," Chris said.

I lifted my tired head. "You better not leave me here, Morris."

"Yeah, I know. You'll hunt me down and kill me," he grunted out in his best Dirty Harry impression. "Not far now. I could throw a rock to it."

Forty minutes later when we were still moving, I grumbled, "Either you have one heck of an arm, or you're a bold face liar."

"I swear it looked a lot closer from below."

Fifteen minutes later, at 10:37 A.M., Chris said, breathing heavily, "Big E, guess what? You probably won't even believe me."

"What?" I replied in an altitude daze.

"We're here."

With those words, I sank down exhaustedly as my hands touched a series of cold, rough rocks. The rocks were no different from the ones I had felt farther down, but in my investigation, I noticed a few formed a pile. From this rose a smooth metal structure forming the shape of something familiar. It was a cross. I had heard about the little metal cross that signified the very top, perched at a point on the mountain where climbers say there is simply no place else to go. I touched it for a long time, maybe too long, but the cold touch of metal under my fingers was the only sensation that convinced me we were truly here, after two long years of trying. Chris gave me a hug and said, "Good job, Big E, but for the last hour, you've been moving slower than my old dead grandmother." I gave Chris a tired smile, because I had learned long ago that, for mountaineers, insults were the highest form of praise and affection.

"You're an impatient old sod," I said. "Can't a guy just relax and enjoy the scenery?"

"And I suppose you're not even tired," Chris said sarcastically.

"Not at all," I lied, forcing my voice to sound upbeat.

"I have a feeling," Chris said, "when we get down off this pig, you're going to rewrite history."

"Why not?" I responded. "It's my history."

From my perspective, the summit of Aconcagua offered no stunning view, no dizzying panorama with the world dropping away before me. For me it was only a chaotic pile of boulders with a cold metal cross protruding from the center. But a summit is so much more than the view. I may be biased, but when people say they summit mountains for the view, I don't believe them. No one suffers the way one does on a mountain simply for a beautiful view. A summit isn't just a place on a mountain. A summit exists in our hearts and minds. It is a tiny scrap of a dream made real, indisputable proof that our lives have meaning. A summit is a symbol that with the force of our will and the power of our legs, our backs, and our two hands, we can transform our lives into whatever we choose them to be, whatever our hands are strong enough to create.

The way down from the summit was long and grueling. I slid down the icy scree behind Chris, having a hard time believing that only a few hours earlier, we were trudging up the same slopes. When we finally reached our tent, the sun had actually peeked out, and I lay on the warm rocks, deep exhaustion penetrating through my every muscle.

"Want some jerky?" Chris asked, slapping a bag of greasy dried meat in my hand. I sat up, suddenly realizing I was famished and, with barely a breath, gobbled down a half dozen strips. "Uh oh!" I said, feeling the jerky in my belly gather into a tight hard ball and fight its way back up my throat. I leaned forward on my palms and heaved into the rocks.

"Alright!" Chris said jubilantly. "Isn't this three for three?"

He was right, I thought. I had hurled on all three of my continental summits: on McKinley, in the igloo, after the summit; Kilimanjaro, on the caldera, before the summit; and now, on Aconcagua, I had just earned myself a perfect record. That gave me an idea. "Well," I said, "if for some reason, I can't be the first blind person to climb the seven summits, then, at least, I can be the first blind person to puke near the top of all seven. In a way, that might even be a harder goal to beat."

The next morning in our tent Chris woke up early in a fit of coughing. "Big E? You awake?" His deep hoarse voice was only a whisper. "You got any water?" I gave him my last half quart and he downed it in one swig. "Now, young sportsman, that's how you drink water!" He smacked his dry lips, starting to come awake.

"Sorry about your voice," I said. "It was a long day."

"Ah, it's OK," he rasped.

"Were you scared up there? I mean with just the two of us?"

He chuckled and said, "It isn't every day that I climb to the top of a seven-thousand-meter peak with a blind guy. You might say I was a little stressed."

"You gonna climb with me again?" I asked sincerely.

Chris paused for a long moment, so long that I thought he had drifted back to sleep. Then he said, "If you don't think I get pleasure out of getting you up there, out of being a part of this whole thing, well then . . . you're just crazy."

There was something about his words, spoken in his typical Alaskan gruffness, and his rough ruined voice, destroyed by a long day of whistling in the wind, that made my heart swell with pride for what we had done, and for the fact that we were here, on this mountain, together.

That day we packed up and scurried down the scree slopes to base camp. As we dropped altitude, I could feel the energy and vitality returning to my oxygen-starved body. As soon as we arrived, I ordered flowers for Ellie over the radio. Below base camp, along the rocky trail, despite the countless trips, slides, and stumbles, my feet felt light. The mountain could beat me up as much as it wanted now. I could walk a thousand miles. All I could think about were the flowers. They'd be delivered any moment now, bursting through her classroom door, in front of all her students, with her sparkling blue eyes full of surprise and, then, relief as she read the note. "I miss you. We summitted. I love you."

# Epilogue

In January 2000, I lost my right eye to glaucoma. Ever since Aconcagua, the eye had become worn-out and was beginning to shrink and grow gray. The severe altitude of Aconcagua hadn't done much to preserve the eye's longevity either. After the surgery, lying in the recovery room, I asked Ellie groggily, "It won't gross you out, your husband having no eyes?"

She laid her face on my chest. "I'll always love you," she said firmly. "Every night before we go to bed, you can take out your glass eyes and I'll kiss them goodnight."

"If you do that," I laughed sleepily, "you'll always be the apple of my glass eyes." And then I regretted laughing as hot pain seared my bandaged socket.

For a few weeks afterwards, I was bogged down in depression over the loss, but with so much to be done, so many possibilities, there was no room left for sadness, and two months later, with my eye socket scarcely healed, I climbed the three-thousand-foot vertical wall of ice, Polar Circus, the crown jewel of the Canadian Rockies. I had learned to climb frozen waterfalls in Ouray, Colorado, in spite of a few experts who thought the idea was crazy. "You have large, sharp, metal ice-tools in your hands, and you can't swing them indiscriminately at the face," one climber stated. "If you do, you'll knock off giant, refrigerator-sized chunks of ice which will fall down and crush you." Ice climbers use their eyes to know where to swing; they look for deep-blue healthy ice versus rotten white ice. They look for the divots, made by earlier swings, for concave dishes, for the slope above a bulge, but I learned that I could use my ice tools as extensions of my hands and scan them across the face. When I found the spot I thought would make a good swing, I'd tap the point lightly against the face, listening for the right pitch. A shallow tinny sound, like the tap of a fork against a dinner plate, meant shattering ice; a hollow reverberation, like the *dong* of a heavy bell, meant large chunks of potentially fracturing ice, but a deep *thunk,* like the sound of striking old stale peanut butter, meant a good stick. There were those who thought you had to be able to see to ice climb, but I had learned well through the years that when I strove to look beyond convention, I came away understanding that there are infinite ways to climb a mountain, not just one.

On the final pitch of Polar Circus, I hung by my leash from two metal ice-screw anchors buried in the fat ice wall, waiting for Mike O'Donnell, our climbing leader, to finish the next pitch. Before I went blind, I remember seeing a picture of a climber far up on an ice face in Chamonix, France. He was a speck of color on an endless river of ice that rolled and dropped away beneath him. As I hung, I took my glove off and ran my bare palm across the surface of the ice. It was as cold and polished as the surface of my bedroom window on a winter's day, and I had to draw in a breath for the sheer beauty felt through my fingertips, and for the fact that I had become the speck of color in the picture, the massive rounded columns of ice rolling and dropping away beneath the reach of my hand.

When I returned home in the spring, Ellie and I moved to a new house in Golden, located in the foothills of the Rocky Mountains. Ellie and I had taken a break from unpacking boxes to explore some titles for this book. "Why don't you call it *Climbing Blind: Are We There Yet?*" Ellie suggested, and from there, we thought up other titles that would never make it to the book cover. "How's this?" I offered. *"Get the Hell off that Mountain, Blind Boy!"* and even better, Ellie's next suggestion of, "*Dragged to the Top Kicking and Screaming: a Blind Man's Journey*."

We were laughing hysterically when Ellie became silent, and I could sense she was smiling. "I know how you could end the book," she said softly.

"How?" I asked, very interested.

"With a very special event," she said.

"What do you mean?" I asked. Ellie sidled up next to me and whispered, "We're having a baby."

Emma Louise Weihenmayer was born on June 21, year 2000, at 3:57 A.M. There is so much to learn about parenthood. Sometimes being a father is about as intense as climbing Denali, Kilimanjaro, and Aconcagua, all in a day. Because I'm blind, I tried to convince Ellie that I couldn't change diapers, but for some reason, she didn't buy it. Ellen and I also discovered that I needed to develop some kind of system for dressing Emma. Apparently, pink socks don't match well with her orange plaid dress. The reward, however, is greater than any summit—feeling her tiny delicate fingers wrap around my forefinger, hearing her babble with happiness when I sing to her, feeling her round perfect cheeks, quite often dimpled by a smile.

It was a perfect Colorado morning when I strapped on Emma's front pack, which enabled her to rest against my chest. I fumbled with all the confusing straps, first connecting a shoulder strap to the waist clip and the waist strap to a shoulder clip, realizing my error and unclipping and reclipping it all over again. I lowered Emma into the pack, guiding her wiggling feet through the leg holes. With Emma hanging from my chest, harnessing up Seigo was a challenge. I crouched down and stretched my arms, wrestling with the buckles and loops as Seigo twisted his head around, trying to give Emma a kiss. Lastly, I searched for her bonnet, crawling around the carpet under the table where I thought it had been dropped, with one hand cupping Emma's head and the other scanning for the little hat. Finally all the elements were in place and I took a stroll to the coffee shop down the street to bring Ellie a slice of banana bread. The sun's warmth shone through the crisp still air, as Seigo, Emma, and I navigated down the narrow sidewalk. A branch brushing the top of my head gave me the sign to turn right, a sharp decline and a veer to the left told me we were approaching the intersection. The end of a gravely patch of ground and the chatter of a sprinkler let me know when to jog right into the parking lot. On the way home, controlling Seigo with my left hand, holding Emma's head with my right, and with two slices of banana bread resting in the crook of my arm, I passed the elementary school, hearing the high laughing shouts of children at play. A little boy yelled over to his friend, "Hey, look over there." I waited for him to finish with "at that blind man with his dog." But instead he shouted, "Look at the little baby."

"Seigo," I said, "we've been replaced," and laughed with full acceptance.

Breathing in the pungent high desert smell of wild grass and sage and feeling the warm weight of Emma against me, I had everything I could possibly need. Some have said, "If you could only see, your life would be so much easier." Easier, definitely, but more exciting, more satisfying, I'm not sure.

"It's all enough," I said to Emma, running my finger softly across her cheek. Then I stopped on the sidewalk and held her up to the west, toward the Rocky Mountains. Emma's chubby arms waved and batted in the air. "Somewhere along the way, you may lose something you thought was important," I said, "but everything you need to fulfill you is inside you or right in front of your eyes. You just have to reach. It won't often be easy, little angel, but it will always be a great adventure."

# EVEREST

*The best and most beautiful things in the world cannot be seen or touched. They must be felt with the heart.*

—HELEN KELLER

In April 2000, Erie Alexander and I spent our eighth long day in a cramped tent above twenty thousand feet on Ama Dablam, a steep technical Himalayan peak, only four miles as the crow flies from its larger neighbor, Mt. Everest. Our snow platform was so small that our tent's back right corner hung over a five-thousand-foot cliff; of course, I made Erie sleep on that side. Ama Dablam has been called the Himalayan Matterhorn and the most stunningly beautiful peak in the world. Translated literally as "Mother's Jewel Box," the sacred peak looms forbiddingly over the Khumbu Valley, with two perfect ridges extending like shoulders from its summit and a huge overhanging glacier glittering like a diamond at the neckline. The peak made a perfect pre-Everest training ground for our team to learn to work as one unit, to assess our strengths and weaknesses, and to familiarize ourselves with local customs and the plethora of water- and airborne diseases that incapacitated most first-time Himalayan climbers.

Through our vestibule, Erie and I could hear our team's four strongest climbers a thousand feet above in a loose rocky gully. Our last-ditch struggle to push the route higher after a month of trying was beginning to fizzle; the monsoons had blown in from India a month earlier than predicted, giving us only an hour of sunlight to climb before the winds howled and the rock would be covered with a slippery layer of snow and ice. Bowling ball–size chunks of ice zipped down the icy gully and exploded in the talus near our tent. Beginning to run out of food and fuel, and finding our progress stalled once again by another storm, PV, our team leader, finally made the inevitable call over the radio from high up in the gully. "Guys, you don't know how much it hurts to say this, but the risk's too high. I'm turning us back." We all reluctantly concurred, knowing well the tricky balance between pushing yourself to your limit and remaining in control of the situation. As it turned out, no one would reach the summit of Ama Dablam for an entire month, when late in the season one Russian struggled to the top in horrendous weather and lost his fingers in the process. So an hour after PV's announcement, we had packed up our personal gear, broken down tents, and rappelled down the fixed lines, stiff with rime ice, with our forty-pound packs pulling us over backward.

On the descent, Erie, far below me, slipped on a loose icy rock and took a 150-foot fall down a sixty-degree slab, landing miraculously on a small ledge. Although he was banged up, his helmet saved his skull, and his heavy padded pack saved his spine. Erie used a rope lowered by two teammates and climbed back to safety, but that night in the tent his body went into shock; his lungs began filling with fluid—the deadly high-altitude disease called pulmonary edema—and his blood oxygen saturation dropped into the 40 percent range, nearly lethal. Our team doctor, Steve Gipe, quickly put Erie on bottled oxygen and led him down the face and across the long boulder fields to Base Camp while the rest of the team worked higher on the mountain to shuttle loads back and forth across the treacherous face. At about 10:00 P.M., after a twelve-hour push through the storm, we came into Base Camp together and met Dr. Gipe, who already had Erie in a gammoff bag—a portable hyperbaric chamber—and was arranging Erie's helicopter evacuation.

After Erie's fall and our failure to reach the summit, there were plenty of detractors who viewed our practice climb as a disastrous beginning, but I didn't see success as simply standing on top. In fact, if we had summited in perfect weather, I don't think we would have accomplished as much as we did. We had stuck together, made good decisions, and taken care of each other to the end. The mountain had erected a powerful barricade, forcing us to cross through it, and on the other side we found our strength.

A year and a half before Ama Dablam, PV had introduced himself to me at an outdoor retailers show, having heard about my climbing history. "Dude, you ever climb Mt. Everest?" he asked eagerly five minutes into our conversation.

"No," I replied longingly.

"Dude, you wanna?" he asked. Later, he told me that Ellie, standing beside me, had shot him a warning look that practically melted the lenses on his sunglasses. PV could have made a living as a rafting and climbing guide, having made unprecedented African river descents of the Omo and the Tekeze, and climbed dozens of high peaks around the world, including Everest in 1998, but he took defiant pride in the fact that he never mixed his passion for climbing with financial gain. Instead he had made his living as a geophysicist, discovering oil deposits through Asia and Africa; in the process he befriended Uzbek chieftains and got himself chased through the desert by Somali warlords. Right from the start, I got the impression that Pasquale Vincent Scaturro, called PV by his friends, took a perverse pleasure in bucking the system.

I had an idea for sponsorship: the National Federation of the Blind, a consumer group of blind people fifty thousand strong and with chapters in every state. Their mission was simple and revolutionary, at first angering the bureaucratic establishment of blindness professionals: blind people working on behalf of themselves, taking their destiny into their own hands. When I visited their headquarters, the president, Dr. Maurer, was immediately elated. "Our goal has been to associate blindness with a sense of adventure, to wipe the dust off the image of blindness. If you are successful, the sighted world won't envision a blind person pining away in a dark room anymore, but standing on top of the world."

With sponsorship set, PV and I set to work organizing the team. PV wanted good team players with plenty of Himalayan experience, no egos, no superstars. I wanted climbers with whom I had a history, who knew my climbing style. Picking the team was like dividing up sides in a game of dodgeball.

PV invited Luis Benitez and Didrik Johnck, two eager young climbers who would make strong work horses, and our team doctor, Steve Gipe. He also asked his closest climbing partner, Brad Bull. On his first Everest expedition, Brad was blown out the back door of his tent and into a crevasse by a faulty gas stove that exploded in his face. In 1995, he returned only to be turned back three hundred feet below the summit by dangerous avalanche conditions. Descending to Base Camp with less than a week left in his climbing permit, he rested for a mere two days before struggling up again and making the summit. Brad's father, Sherm Bull, also joined the team. At age sixty-four—if successful—Sherm would become the oldest man in history to stand on top. When I met Sherm during a practice climb of Mt. Evans in Colorado, he told me, laughing, "It's not like I'm trying to be the oldest man to climb Everest. I'm just getting old trying." This trip would be Sherm's fifth. Twice he had made it to the 28,700-foot South Summit and stared longingly across a twelve-thousand-foot abyss to the true summit protruding from the sky like a solitary island. On his third try, he had slipped on a steep section of bullet-hard ice above the South Col and taken a two-hundred-foot ride, breaking three ribs and compressing his vertebrae, so now he was able to brag that he was an inch shorter. Sherm was as driven and focused as anyone I had ever met, living a tightly scheduled, type-A surgeon's life in Connecticut, yet his four attempts on Everest had beaten into him a profound humility and an extraordinary repertoire of do's and don'ts. Sherm patiently answered my endless questions about different parts of the route, which type of oxygen mask to use, and how many liters' flow to set my oxygen bottle, and his voice was always soothing and rational, like my own father's.

I invited Chris Morris and Jeff Evans, my closest climbing partners, and Mike O'Donnell, who had taught me to ice climb and whose technical skills would be invaluable. I also brought on two high-altitude filmmakers, Michael Brown and Charley Mace, both Colorado residents. Even Eric/Erie Alexander (who got his nickname when his name was butchered on our climbing permit) had made the decision to return. His pulmonary edema had developed into full-blown pneumonia, lingering in his lungs for six months, and he was well aware, as we all were, that once you've had pulmonary edema, the chance of getting it again dramatically increases. Erie had labored over the decision through his long recovery and finally asked me tentatively, "Are you guys gonna kick me off the team?"

"No," I replied. "That's gotta be your decision."

"Then I'll go," he said quickly. "Whether I'm strong enough to make the summit I've got my doubts, but I know I'm strong enough to help get you there."

With only a few months to go before we left for Mt. Everest, Kami, our climbing sirdar who was also with us on Ama Dablam, was still having immense trouble recruiting Sherpas for our expedition. Kami's first obstacle was combating a rumor floating through the Khumbu that it wasn't just one blind person tackling Everest, but a whole team of blind people. Kami had been vigilant in convincing them that, first of all, there was only one of me and, second, I wasn't going to need any extra help from them. One brave Sherpa, Ang Pasang, two-time summiter of Everest, was persuaded aboard, and the rest followed. A second rumor (almost a backhanded compliment) circulated through the Khumbu villages only a few days after I arrived. Because I wasn't flopping on my face every few minutes, the Sherpas thought I was lying about my blindness. Women constantly approached me in the alleys of Namche Bazaar and waved their hands in front of my face. Of course, I'd feel the wind from their hands and flinch, which only confirmed their suspicions. "I can't win," I said to PV. "First, they won't climb with me because I'm blind, then they think I perform too well, so I must be cheating."

Finally, at Dingboche, I was so annoyed by their suspicion that I resorted to drastic measures. I asked Kami into the kitchen tent. "Kami," I said, "I want to give you a message to take back to the Sherpas." I then pulled down my left lower eyelid, leaned my head forward, and my prosthetic plastic eye plopped into my open palm. I heard Kami let out a long breath. "I can take the other out if you want," I said, worrying slightly that I might have offended his traditional Sherpa sensibilities. "No!" he said firmly. "Not necessary," and his words were accompanied by loud swallowing and quick breathing.

While still in Katmandu, we stopped by Bohdanat Temple for a blessing by the local remposhe. My team lined up, and the head monk laid katas, beautiful silk scarves, around our necks. When it was my turn, he remained quiet for an uncomfortably long moment. I pictured him looking inquisitively at my long white cane. Finally he spoke, his voice was high and singsongy, like the voice of Yoda from *Star Wars.* "Are you climbing the mountain too?"

"Yes," I replied quietly. All I wanted was to receive the blessing and move on as anonymously as possible. My neck tingled, crying out for the absent scarf.

"You are climbing Mount Everest?"

"Yes!"

"And you are blind?"

"Yes!"

"You cannot see?"

"No, I can't!"

Finally my bent form felt the kata placed around my neck and I scurried past, but could clearly hear him asking the climber next in line, "He is climbing the mountain? He is blind?"

Surprisingly, the greatest doubt didn't emanate from the Sherpa community but from Himalayan veterans in the United States. Climber and author Jon Krakauer wrote me a sincere letter attempting to talk me out of my plans. "I am not at all enthusiastic about your trip to Everest next spring," he wrote. "It's not that I doubt you have what it takes to reach the summit. You've already shown that you have plenty of what it takes. It's just that I don't think you can get to the top of that particular hill without subjecting yourself to horrendous risk; the same horrendous risk all Everest climbers face, and then some. It's a totally different world above 8000m. All kinds of things go haywire up there and the consequences are so much more serious when they do." I didn't believe I would have to subject myself to more risk than other climbers. In fact, I believed the opposite. I wasn't going up there as a guided client with people I didn't know. PV and I knew that the definition of a team wasn't simply a group of individuals in the same place doing the same thing, but instead a group of friends, not only committed to reaching the top, but to taking care of each other and being a self-contained unit, responsible for and to each other.

Krakauer's letter gave me pause, but I respected his honest attempt to dissuade me, and knew his attitude toward Everest had been badly tainted by the '96 disaster. However, it was a quote from Ed Viesturs, one of America's premier Himalayan climbers, read to me from *Men's Journal*, that floored me. "More power to him, and I support his going," Viesturs said, "but I wouldn't want to take him up there myself. Because he can't see, he can't assess the weather or the icefall or the ladders you have to crawl across. There are areas where he will have to move quickly. Trying to dance through them will be very difficult. When I guide, I like people to become self-sufficient. With Erik, they'll have to be helping him, watching out for him every step of the way. For me, the risks are too great. It will be the hardest ever guided ascent of Everest, if they pull it off."

It was tough going forward in the face of experts who thought I would be a liability up there, risking my own life and that of my team. What did they know that I didn't? I had always prided myself on being one of the reasons for the success of my past expeditions. I had never been short-roped and hauled to the summit, to be spiked in the snow like a football.

In most people's minds, the notion of a blind climber is equivalent to that of a Jamaican bobsledder. At first, it's hard to connect the two. So I don't blame Ed for his assumption that my "helplessness" surpassed that of even the most inexperienced guided client. I tried to put myself into Viesturs's mind and conjured up the comic image of me lying in the tent, an assembly line of teammates latching my harness, locking my crampons, and battening down my helmet. I had only shaken Ed's hand once, so I couldn't figure out how he presumed to know about my talents, strengths, and my ability to contribute to a team. He hadn't seen the sixteen years I had been climbing, the years learning rope management, crevasse rescue, and avalanche safety; he surely didn't see the days spent on big-walls when my teammates had hung from the anchors placed by the blind guy; he hadn't seen the years taken to become independent, learning to build snow walls, cook meals on gas stoves, setting up tents in whiteouts; he hadn't seen the times I had taken weight from teammates' packs to carry on my own back, or the times I had nursed sick friends in the tent. In fact, he hadn't seen any part of my life except for the fact that I was blind.

I shouldn't really have been so shocked by their reactions, having heard it all before. When I had started rock climbing on top rope, people had been supportive. "Good for you," I heard—when there was a fat rope to dangle from—but when I had talked about learning to lead climb, most argued that you needed to see to place the gear in the crack. So I had learned to lead climb anyway with the help of a few supportive friends. When I wanted to climb ice, most had warned, "It isn't stable like rock. You need eyes to know where to swing your tools and know whether it's a good stick." So I learned to ice climb anyway by feeling the face through the metal tips of my tools and assessing my placement by the sound of my tool striking the ice.

Before I had climbed Mt. Rainier as a practice climb for Mt. McKinley, an alarmed guide had said to me, "There's no way you can climb it safely, and as far as McKinley goes," he laughed, "well, that's ten times harder than Rainier." After I climbed McKinley, experts said, "I can understand how you got up McKinley. It's all snow; you don't really have to see where you're stepping, but Aconcagua, that's a different story. It's way too rocky and inconsistent. You'd have a lot of trouble finding your footing." The next winter, I summited Aconcagua.

The pattern continued, with expert after expert telling me I would never be able to surmount each new challenge. But I had pushed on, even though I often staggered beneath their pessimism, feeling like I was being buried under a mountain of "you can't."

But this time, maybe they were right. Perhaps I had finally gone too far. . . . Yet there was still a chance that as before, they were wrong. Those experts could probably demonstrate a dozen different climbing knots and a dozen more pulley systems to drag an injured climber from a slot. If you asked them to describe the South Col, they could map out the route inch by inch, through the Khumbu Icefall past the Geneva Spur to the Hillary Step. There is no arguing the point that they know a lot about climbing and a lot about Mt. Everest, but they didn't know a thing about me. People's expectations had a way of turning into boundaries. So I decided to throw the world's expectations in the garbage and go to Everest to see for myself.

After crossing through the Khumbu Icefall for the first time, I understood why the experts believed I had no chance. Only a half an hour above Base Camp loomed the crux of the whole mountain, two thousand feet of jumbled-up ice boulders piled atop each other, from the size of baseballs to skyscrapers. Looking up at the icefall from Base Camp, Chris explained, "Imagine a massive two-mile chunk of ice and then imagine an atom bomb exploding smack in the middle."

The icefall is essentially a slow moving river of ice, complete with gentle eddies and violent class-five rapids. The glacier proper inches down the broad valley of the Western Cwm and, reaching a steep flank, pushes out over the abyss until it collapses under its own weight. Unseen by the human eye flows a second layer of ice, made soft and pliable by the massive pressure from above. The soft bottom layer flows downward like liquid plastic, while the heavy brittle surface layer tumbles, collapses, splits, and splinters, like old decaying skin. Ice reacts to shifts in temperature, so in the predawn morning when the temperatures were coldest and in late afternoon in the hottest time of day, the icefall came alive, popping and groaning, and exploding with avalanches. At any moment falling ice could crush a climber, but during these two times of day, it was a good idea to be nowhere near the icefall. The trick was to time your movement through the icefall so that you approached the bottom by first light and arrived into Camp One by early afternoon. On my first carry through, I took a dreadful thirteen hours.

I began the day with PV in front of me, jingling the bear bell from the loop of his ski pole, and with Brad behind. We slid and stumbled up the loose rocky moraine, layered unpredictably by a thin veneer of ice. At the edge of the icefall, we strapped on crampons and, for the next hour, climbed a series of steep, almost vertical ice steps, which emptied onto a subsequently higher stretch of frozen lake. Brad looked around at the huge walls of blue-mirrored ice surrounding us and said it looked like Superman's winter palace in the blockbuster movie. Above the lakes, the terrain turned to uneven humps of ice with deep zigzagging grooves. Between each precarious step, I'd bend my legs at bizarre angles, trying to drive all eight crampon points beneath my boots into the ice. Soon the grooves had deepened into full-fledged crevasses, and crossing them was rarely straightforward. The first major crevasse lay just beyond the last lake. It offered a jagged, boot-wide snow bridge six steps long. I stood on the edge for a long time feeling the snow bridge with the tip of my pole and then put one shaking step in front of the last, like a tightrope walker, until I could stretch my poles forward and get a purchase on the other side.

Fifteen minutes higher we came to the first ladder crossing, three sections of ladders lashed together and anchored on both sides by screws imbedded in the ice. Two Sherpas, nicknamed the Ice Doctors, were responsible for preparing and maintaining the ever-changing route through the icefall by anchoring seven-millimeter lines through the labyrinth and carrying ladders on their backs, which they laid across the crevasses too wide to jump. Kami believed my total success on the mountain would hinge on my ability to make it over the icefall's thirty ladder crossings safely and quickly. I stood on the edge listening to Luis's crampon points clanking loudly on the aluminum ladder and echoing off the solid ice walls. Halfway across, the clanking went silent as he stared into the deep abyss and murmured, "I think I see Texas down there." Each of us had been given a small plastic container of holy rice by a Sherpa monk to be sprinkled sparingly over the snow in times of fear. Before crossing, Jeff opened his container and dumped the entire contents into the hungry mouth of the crevasse. Chris was next, practicing a little positive pessimism as he moved slowly across. "This ladder's rickety but at least it's swinging in the breeze." Then, it was my turn. I had practiced a lot in PV's yard on a ladder resting a few feet off the ground on cinder blocks, but there, it had only been one ladder, not three, and if I stepped off, my foot would touch the earth and we'd all laugh nervously. Here, however, as I probed a foot over the crevasse trying to feel the ladder rungs while throwing generous curses to the wind, I knew that if I fell, my weight would shock-load the suspect ice-screw anchors and I'd hang suspended from a deeply sagging seven-mil line in the middle of a forty-foot-wide crevasse. Plenty of climbers crawled across the ladders, but I wanted to walk; I knew my whole team was watching, predicting my entire chance of success by this performance. I moved across in slow motion, sliding my ascender gently forward on the line and lowering each foot as the team yelled out, "Front foot more left. More left! . . . Too far. Too far! . . . You've got it now." With three ladders lashed together, the whole precarious system wriggled and swung in the wind beneath me, and my own legs, twitching with exhaustion and fear, made the ladder vibrate out of control. When

I finally stepped onto the snow I had to slump against my poles, furiously inhaling and exhaling for a good five minutes; I'd forgotten to breathe.

For the rest of the day, different team members took over guiding me: first Mike O. and Sherm, Jeff and Erie, and then Luis and Didrik. We followed a thin trail of kicked-out boot marks weaving and undulating through the labyrinth. A typical section required me to jump over a crevasse, landing precisely in the chipped-out boot holes on the other side, step across a series of broken-up ice boulders with a thousand-foot cliff to my right, climb fifty feet vertically to the top of a serac and immediately down the other side, then traverse along a boot-wide trail passing inches away from the edge of a gaping crevasse.

Part of the beauty of the mountains for me was the consistent rhythm of internal movement as I kicked steps up a steep snow face, breathed, and swung my axe. This type of climbing had little to do with seeing but was much more dependent on good balance, endurance, and mental stamina. Most of McKinley had been this kind of climbing, but in the icefall not once could I let my guard down and take a consistent step; not once during the day was I able to establish any semblance of rhythm. I constantly leaned hard on one pole while scanning the other pole for the next placement, and each of my thousands of steps had to be dead-on. One mistake would mean a broken ankle, shattered kneecap, or much worse. I wasn't sure which was more exhausted, my body or my mind. Never in my life had I faced terrain so totally patternless.

Jeff, tired himself and gasping for oxygen, cut the communication down to its fundamental elements. "Big serac, move fast," and I'd plainly hear its heavy echo overhead. "Clear traveling for the next ten steps . . . well, at least for the next five steps. Rope left, clip in. Slot coming up . . . two steps." Then he'd pause. "At the edge . . . jumping . . . now across. Your turn, Big E." Getting through that day was a staggeringly difficult exercise in focus and communication. More than once, I found myself making bargains with God. "Just let me make it through, and I'll never leave home again. I'll settle down, donate more to charity, go to church every Sunday."

One hundred feet away from Camp One, moments after Luis said optimistically, "We're home free. I can see the tents," I measured the distance over a crevasse with my pole and leaped. The crevasse, however, turned almost at a right angle, so my right foot touched the edge and went in. I pitched forward in the snow, grasping out for solid ground. Luis turned around and reached for me, but holding his own poles in his hand, only managed to blast me squarely in the nose with his ski pole handle. I quickly pulled my leg from the hole and writhed in the snow. Blood gushed from my squashed nose and I thought there was a good chance it was broken. So when I stumbled into camp, thirteen hours from when I had begun, my brain in a delirium of exhaustion, my face green with high-altitude nausea, my nose swelling like a golf ball and dripping fat droplets of blood, I wasn't the image of a sturdy Himalayan veteran. I sat down in front of my tent. Mike O. knelt in front of me and popped off my crampons. Later he said I looked like I had just gone ten rounds with George Foreman. I lay back in the tent, PV handed me some mac and cheese, and as I drifted off, a doomed feeling came over me. I didn't want to quit, but I couldn't imagine crossing through the icefall another ten times, the number needed to acclimatize and to shuttle provisions to the higher camps. I was severely disappointed. This was exactly what I didn't want, to be coddled up the mountain. That night in my dreams, I could hear the murmuring voices of the experts, "You're out of your league. You have no business here. What were you thinking?"

But I also thought back to a week before, when Pete Athans had appeared at Base Camp and shared a meal with our team. Pete, who had been atop Everest seven times, more than any other Western climber, had stood up after dinner and read to us his favorite Tibetan saying, "The nature of mind is like water. If you do not disturb it, it will become clear." Chris Morris, in his simple philosopher's way, had practically given the same advice earlier that very day. Sitting in the intense sun, I had felt his eyes look me up and down. Then he had said, "You're scared, aren't ya, Big E? Well if you want my advice, just don't think about it. I know it sounds stupid, but I swear it works."

You're right, I thought, it does sound stupid. I pictured Chris Morris's head stuck in the dirt like an ostrich, trying desperately to ignore great shards of ice looming right over him. But when I had heard Pete speak the Tibetan words, I wondered if I had dismissed old Chris Morris too quickly. My mind was always working overtime, strategizing all the options, planning for every contingency, but there was a point when I needed to let go of all that. On the trek into Base Camp, standing above Namche Bazaar, Jeff described his first view of Everest, the upper mountain surprisingly void of snow; just windswept and jagged black rock. The harsh image melted a part of my solid will. Suddenly I told myself, You could turn around right now. Nobody would stop you. Standing next to Jeff, my mind churned with fear, self-doubt, and endless self-questioning. Perhaps the way to approach such a monster of a mountain was to break it down into more manageable chunks, to clear my mind, so heavy with expectation, and try to experience the climb moment by moment, step by step. I would try not to worry about everything that lay ahead but focus on the beauty and friendship that was all around me, and no matter how high I got up the mountain, I would celebrate that as my summit.

When I got down to Base Camp, I immediately went into our communications tent, affectionately called the Love Dome, where our computers were set up, powered by a series of solar panels and linked to the world through a satellite that passed over the Himalayas once a day. A voice synthesizer had made one computer accessible to me. I wrote Ellen a letter and, though I didn't want to worry her, couldn't help pouring out my fears and how homesick I was. "To be honest," I said, "the icefall is by far the most terrible terrain I've ever crossed. Thirteen hours is a god-awful time, and the icefall's just the start."

Ellie's letter came the next morning. "I know the comforts of home are calling you loud and clear, but nothing this challenging comes without a cost. To be honest, I want you home more than you will ever know. I want to go to a concert or watch a movie with you. I want you home so that you can play with Emma. But mostly I just want to hold your hand and hear your voice. If you find yourself wishing yourself to be home because it's too hard, or scary, or cold, think about where you are and say to yourself, my feet will touch this rock or this ice just this once.

"Erik, you are on one terrific journey. Know that when you do come home, regardless of the outcome, Emma and I will love you endlessly and wholeheartedly."

During our rest at Base Camp, we'd all awake to PV, standing outside our tents singing off-key, "Da-da-da-dee-da, Heeeere comes the sun." At Base Camp, no one left their cozy sleeping bag before the sun warmed their tent except PV, who routinely stood alone in the predawn, calling the play-by-play of the sun's slow crawl over the mountains and across the moraine. "Only forty feet away . . . now twenty feet . . . just five feet. Reach out of your tents, dudes! You can touch it." Then still lying in my bag, I would feel the distinct line of the sun moving like a wave up my legs and body until it touched my face and instantly bathed the frigid tent in friendly warmth.

While at Base Camp, I tried to soak up as much comfort and rest as possible, saving every scrap of energy I had for the upper mountain. PV, on the other hand, as our leader, could never rest. There was too much to be done. Organizing before the climb had been more than a full-time job for PV. His garage had been converted into an expedition supply room where he had supervised the packing of 120 oxygen bottles, 100 fuel canisters, 45 six-gallon buckets of miscellaneous food, 35 tents, all organized into 70 expedition duffels, prodded through customs, and carried to Base Camp on the backs of 110 yaks. At Base Camp, he was constantly busy fortifying collapsing tent platforms with rock walls, sifting through endless barrels of gear, and tweaking the solar panels that powered our satellite phones and computers.

As I shuffled into the dining tent, PV was excitedly preparing camp for the arrival of his son, Adam. As a junior in high school, Adam had been severely injured in a wrestling accident and was now a partial quadriplegic. With the support of PV and the Scaturro family, he had forged on. At Adam's brutally competitive wheelchair rugby games, PV was his loudest fan. It had always been Adam's dream to make the nine-day trek to Base Camp and see the mountain his father had once climbed; so with a special wicker chair carried by six amazingly sturdy Sherpas, his dream was about to be realized. The Base Camp moraine was a shifting hodgepodge of rocks of various sizes over ice—only slightly less chaotic than the icefall. It had taken me almost a week to memorize a path to the toilet tent, navigating down and across loose icy gullies, weaving through piles of boulders, dead-ending, backtracking, and zigzagging. So it struck me as a colossal and futile effort as I listened to PV shovel and lift aside rubble, attempting to carve a flat, wheelchair-accessible trail through the disorder. "Life goes on," PV had said as we relaxed one day in a teahouse, "but it's hard to watch your son get hurt." I got the impression that for PV, this climb meant something personal. It was about a reaffirmation of life after tragedy, about stubborn faith and irascible love and the defiant will to bulldoze a flat trail through the impossible.

On Good Friday, we woke to six inches of fresh snow. After breakfast, Jeff subtly stationed himself behind a rock and began pelting PV and Brad with snowballs as they busily duct-taped the sagging tent poles of the Love Dome. They made such easy targets, loudly peeling off tape strips, even I began chucking a few in their direction until Jeff pegged me in the back of my head. One by one, everyone was infuriated enough by Jeff to be drawn into the battle. Chris and our Base Camp manager, Kevin, teamed up with Jeff while Erie, Sherm, and I joined forces and huddled behind our own pile of rocks. Since my aim was least accurate, I was assigned to packing and readying snowballs for Erie and Sherm, but soon I got bored and made a last stand in the small valley between the fortresses, firing away at the slightest movement in the rocks. Only one throw paid off with the satisfying whap of hard ice against human flesh, but in return, I took a beating. Pemba Sherpa, innocently carrying a pot of water toward the kitchen tent, took a hard shot to the head from Jeff, so by late morning, Jeff had single-handedly drawn the Sherpas into the battle, converting the mild-mannered pacifists of the Khumbu into bloodthirsty outlaws. For the rest of the day, I listened from my tent to the distant shrieks of resting teams, ambushed commando-style and pummeled with snowballs by marauding bands of Sherpas.

On Easter Sunday, we all met in the dining tent for an early morning service. Sherm began by remarking that no church on earth could rival the grandeur of this place: the glacier moraine of Base Camp at almost 18,000 feet, surrounded by the steep 23,500-foot pyramid of Pumori on the west; the Khumbu Icefall on the east, grumbling and exploding like a cannon shot; the jagged 26,000-foot ridge of Nupse on the southeast; and to the southwest, the near-vertical Lola Pass constantly sending avalanches roaring toward Base Camp.

"Easter is about a resurrection," Mike O. said. "Climbing for me is a renewal, a rebirth. It doesn't matter what mistakes or shortcomings I've had in the past. The mountains give me a chance to cleanse my soul with hard work and sacrifice, with humility and devotion to this team. And when I return home, I feel like I've been given a new chance to live better, to commit to being a better friend and a better father to my daughter, Katie."

Erie closed the service with a prayer, and we all bowed our heads and folded our hands on the little tin table. "Dear God," he said, "give us the will and the patience to climb this awesome mountain and come home safely to our loved ones. Help us to make good decisions, to take care of one another, and to leave this mountain with our friendships strengthened. And we know, God, that a prayer is not just a wish-list, so if standing on top is not to be, give us the wisdom to understand your great plan for us and the courage to carry it through."

For Easter dinner, we all settled again in the dining tent. Adam had arrived, and as he called out directions, I pushed his wheelchair along one of PV's trails and into the tent. Tenzing, our cook, was serving up the usual local fare: cabbage, cauliflower, Nepali flat bread, boiled potatoes, a Chinese version of canned Spam emblazoned with Chinese characters and a picture of a smiling pig, and finally, dahl bat, a Sherpa specialty of rice and lentils, which sounds quite harmless but ranked as our undisputed least favorite. Our meals were a deluxe treat for our invincible Sherpa teammates, accustomed to the variety of local parasites and a bacteria count running in the billions, but reaped serious havoc on the Western palate. There wasn't a refrigerator to be found in the Khumbu, so the perishables, carried up to Base Camp on the backs of yaks, repeatedly freezing solid at night and thawing in the noonday sun, went a little past their prime. Giant slabs of greasy yak meat hung from the roof of our cooking tent and was whittled away with each passing meal. Raw eggs had made the trip to Base Camp miraculously intact. With our already skinny bodies wasting away at the intense altitude, we welcomed the protein, but the eggs were also questionable. Each morning, Chris would call down the table, "Who's up for a little E. coli and toast?" Jeff was the most intestinally challenged of the team, dashing for the toilet tent a half dozen times a day and having already lost twenty-five pounds from his lean frame. About every third meal, I'd turn silent, my face green with nausea, and my breathing quick and deliberate. Someone across the table would shout, "Clear the deck. Big E's gonna blow." Then the team members sitting between me and the tent door would jump back, clearing a narrow path for me to barrel past.

The only one blissfully unaffected was Chris. "You could slurp yak dung up with a straw and be just fine," I told him.

"Some people get sick . . . some people don't," he said, greedily adding bacon bits, mustard, and taco sauce to his dahl bat.

A month into the climb, our dread of dahl bat had become so fierce, that Maurice, our NFB liaison, was inspired to write a song and, after dinner, strum it on his guitar.

Tenzing, oh Tenzing!
I don't mean to make a fuss.
You're boiling up that dahl bat,
And taking good care of us.

But I've got that feeling down deep inside me,
Like a great volcanic ooze.
It must be what they've been tellin' me,
'bout those old dahl bat blues.

After trekking and climbing so long,
I'm hungry, tired, and hot.
Now what's that you're layin' before me?
A steaming plate of dahl bat?

Just one more hill to climb,
And one more hour to go.
I've just gotta pull off the trail here.
Look out down below.

I'm finally getting stronger.
I might just have a snack.
You say you'll get me something,
And promise to be right back.

Oh don't say it, Tenzing!
Please tell me that it's not—
Not what I've been dreadin',
Another plate of dahl bat.

On my second trip through the icefall, the landscape had totally changed. Above the first long vertical section, the fixed line snaking through the boulders had been buried in five feet of ice rubble by a twenty-ton chunk of ice that decided to calve off in the night; farther along, the normal floor of ice had simply dropped away, leaving a wide, forty-foot-deep chasm; and near the top, a steep traversing snow slope had sloughed away, replaced by a seventy-foot vertical wall.

Despite the inconsistencies, I felt much stronger than the first time and was determined to cut my time down. I was already seeing a difference in my ability to embrace chaos. When standing at the edge of a crevasse, I paused only for a moment, scanning my poles across to the landing spot, before leaping. With the ladders, I'd clip into the rope, find the location of the first few rungs and confidently place my foot. I found that the distance between each rung was perfect for locking my back crampon points over one rung and my front points over the next, and I could feel when my boots were securely locked. The ladders were actually becoming easy—the only part of the icefall through which I could rely on my own balance and the consistency of the rungs.

Finally above the icefall, the route crossed through the Western Cwm, a U-shaped, gently sloping valley surrounded by huge ice walls. When the sun came up, the cwm went from brutally cold to brutally hot, the sun's rays reflecting off the walls and valley floor like an oven. Reaching Camp Two at the head of the cwm, I had stripped down to long underwear, but still felt like I was going to pass out; Brad's thermometer registered 109 degrees.

The second crux of the climb began a few hours above Camp Two. The Lhotse Face ran about two thousand feet, consisting of an ice slope of forty-five to seventy degrees. When we approached the face in the early morning, Brad pointed out to me all the sleeping-bag-size rocks imbedded in the snow. Dr. Gipe peered up the face and, seeing the falling rock, said quietly, "Not today—my wife and son would not approve," and returned to Camp Two. In the early season, wind scoured the face free of snow, transforming it into hard blue ice. Loose rocks a thousand feet up the face, dislodged by the wind, would rocket down the slick ice and land with a *whoomph* in the snow below. We hadn't anticipated such dry conditions, and stupidly, we had forgotten our helmets. The rocks whistled past my head like small fierce missiles, as I flattened my shuddering body against the face.

Jeff, afflicted with another bout of the Khumbu crud, had headed down to Base Camp. Erie's resting heart rate wouldn't go below 120, a sign that he was not acclimatizing well, so he chose to go only partway up the face and descend before nightfall. The rest of the team inched their way up to Camp Three in eight hours; the last two hours, I pushed forward on sheer will.

That night, the NFB posted a headline on our Web site, "Blind Climber Sets High-Altitude Record." I laughed. The record broken was my own, set on Aconcagua three years before. We had made it to almost twenty-four thousand feet. Physically, we were pushing the limits of what our bodies and brains could endure, and we all spent a cold, sleepless night on small tent platforms cut halfway up the Lhotse Face. Severe altitude headaches, nausea, vomiting, and panic attacks wracked the team. My headache was so bad that I passed the night on my stomach with my forehead pressed against the cold ground. Others tried to cut down on the misery by yelling jokes back and forth among the tents, but there was so little oxygen in the air, people kept forgetting the punch lines. The team had been participating in a high-altitude NASA study designed for astronauts experiencing oxygen deprivation, and had been performing memory games over our handheld radios to a researcher at Base Camp. The researcher had let slip that we were all experiencing signs of bilateral brain lesions, a phrase I didn't understand technically but which definitely sounded bad. PV was convinced that spending a night at Camp Three was a crucial part of the acclimatization process. "If a climber can make it here," he said, "he has a fighting chance to make it all the way." So even though my body was exhausted and my brain had retreated into a stupor, my spirits were as high as our altitude.

To warm us up, Kevin read racy e-mails from girlfriends and wives over the handheld radios. "Oh baby. When you get down, I'm gonna hang on you like a monkey. We'll take all our clothes off and smear our bodies with suntan oil and bask in the sunshine. Then we'll go swimming and you'll playfully try to catch me, but I'll slip away, and we'll laugh and giggle. Then I'll . . ."

One was from Ellie, written to Kevin.

Hello Kev,

Oh my! Can you believe what they've done? I am so proud of Erik and the way he's handled the hardest part of the climb. I'm praying for a restful trip to Dingboche and then good weather for the summit push.

I could tell from Erik's letter after the first time through the icefall that he dreaded going back. He's never sounded so down before, so I know it's hell for him.

Can't believe he made it through so fast this time. Thank God he's got such a wonderful team to help him see just how brave and talented he is. I wish they could just go all the way up the mountain, but I understand the importance of coming all the way down again.

The team was on Tom Brokaw last night. Erik's been getting mail from all over the world. As you sit in your tent, realize this whole thing is larger than it seems. You all are helping a blind man reach the summit of Mt. Everest. Imagine what parents of newly blinded kids are thinking. Imagine what the whole world is thinking!

Love, Ellie

P.S. Tell those supposedly world-class climbers that the next time they climb in an area where sleeping-bag-size boulders are falling around them to please wear their helmets.

By early May, oxygen bottles, fuel, food, and tents were in place up to Camp Three. So we made the long trek down to Dingboche at 14,500 feet with the idea that a three-day rest in thicker oxygen would return some strength to our sore muscles and heal our cuts and ailments. The descent was a rocky and bouldery nine-hour day in which I kicked many rocks with my toes. Around 6:00 P.M., we came down across a long rutted meadow below the small village of Toogla. A cloud had risen up the valley and I could feel it engulfing my fingers and face like rain. It was then that I heard the cheers filtering through the dense moisture in the air. By then I should have expected it. Just above the icefall on my first trip through, still an hour and a half from Camp One, Charley and Brad were waiting patiently with hot Tang and candy bars; on every descent after the long forays above Base Camp, Kevin and the Base Camp crew would station themselves on folding chairs in Superman's Palace and welcome us in one by one with whistles and applause. Now, above the last five-hundred-foot hill leading into Dingboche, Mike O. and Erie were there to greet us with sodas. The two had reached the teahouse and, before eating dinner, had hiked back up the hill to wait. By the time I sank down at a table in the warm teahouse, the kitchen had already closed, but Chris, sitting across from me, shoved a piled plate of vegetable fried noodles at me and with his mouth crammed with food sputtered, "Chow down, little buddy!"

For the next few days, I made a point to move as little as possible—except for the thousands of times I needed to bend my elbow and open my mouth. The upper mountain had shaved twenty pounds off me, so the schedule revolved around eating: double orders of omelets and French toast, massive platters of mixed fried rice, deep fried mo-mos filled with veggies and yak meat, pizzas loaded with garlic and mushrooms we called "PV Specials" in honor of our leader, who had taught the recipe to the teahouse cook, apple pies, chocolate pudding, and lots of Sprites. At night we played hearts with my Braille cards. Of course, Jeff cheated. PV or Brad across the table would ask me, "Do you have a spade?" and before I could scan my fingers across my cards, Jeff would answer, "Nope. He doesn't."

On our third day in Dingboche, we heard the terrible news over the radio that Babu Chiri Sherpa, the most famous living Sherpa climber, nine-time summiter of Everest, had been killed. He had been walking without crampons outside his tent at Camp Two and had slipped into a tiny hole in the snow, which turned out to be a hundred-foot hidden crevasse. His body had finally been located after the claw marks he had made as he desperately tried to hang on had been spotted at the edge of the crevasse. We all sat in the teahouse in silence. I had met Babu on my first icefall trip when he was coming down. As he leaned in I felt his powerful barrel chest against mine and his gloved hand on my back, warm and confident. It didn't matter how much experience you'd had or how strong a climber you were; if you let your guard down for just a moment, the mountain would be waiting. I fought to keep my mind in a positive space, but my goals seemed meaningless. Suddenly, the cost of this climb was much too high. I could feel my own body tumbling into a crevasse, could hear the massive avalanche rumbling toward me, but something still pulled at me to see the climb through. And one thing in which I had never lost faith was this team that I was a part of. Our commitment to stick together and to take care of each other wasn't just a bunch of empty words. We had already proven it. Individually, we all exhibited weaknesses, but when we came together and contributed our skills, talents, and insights, we became an entity strong enough to rival the mountain itself, and it was the knowledge of this that gave me just enough courage to head back up there for the final push.

On May 9, despite bad weather predictions, we headed up again, our seventh time through the icefall and on to Camp Two. Waiting through a long week, our bodies grew slack and listless in the extreme altitude. At night, I'd sit in my tent listening to the wind roaring near the summit as if the mountain gods were running a very loud vacuum cleaner. The summit of Everest sits directly in the path of the jet stream, so in the winter, wind hammers the summit at speeds approaching two hundred miles per hour. In the summer, the monsoons move in from the south and bury the upper mountain with snow, dangerously loading the slopes. Between the winds and the monsoons there often appears a brief weather window, typically a few days in May. Climbing teams all over the mountain positioned themselves for this one fleeting respite.

On our sixth day, we got set to head up, at least to Camp Three, where the wind wasn't quite as lethal as at the South Col, but we woke in the predawn to a powerful snow and lightning storm. I was severely disappointed but, sitting at the edge of my tent, I soon became absorbed by the powerful stabs of lightning exploding around us. With each crash, I could hear the echo reverberating through the cwm and bouncing off the surrounding peaks and ridges, giving me a quick but dramatic view of our massive surroundings. I felt so puny and fragile in comparison, like a tiny blade of grass blowing in the wind. So later that afternoon, when PV made the decision to head down and wait at Base Camp, my expectations were crushed, but another part understood that there was absolutely nothing to do but plaster a weary smile across my face, make a few shrugging jokes about "here we go again," and start down.

When I arrived six hours later, an e-mail from home was there to console me.

To My Studly Mountain Man,

As I was reading your last awesome e-mail, I didn't pay any attention to Emma who was sitting in her high chair. By mistake I left her whole bowl of food on her tray. When I looked at her again, oh my God, it's going to take a while to clean up apples, apricots, and oatmeal cereal.

Emma and I toasted you at dinner. I had wine and she had grape juice and we drank at the same time. Then we went for a stroll, and Destinee, next door, made silly faces at Emma, and she got into a giggle fit. She's a happy little clam. Then we wrestled a bit and she tried pulling my sock off. She scowled cause she couldn't get it over my heel. "Don't quit," I told her. "You're a Weihenmayer."

After Emma was in bed, the phone rang and I thought the call was you. So, when I heard this lady mispronounce our name trying to sell me a mortgage, I said, "F*** you." I think I'm really missing you. I'm praying all good things for you and filled with the anticipation of running into your open arms.

Excited, anxious, neurotic, impatient, and in love with her mountain man,

Ellie

I had dreamed about Everest since I had begun climbing, and it was almost beyond my imagination just being here, experiencing this legendary mountain for myself. For half my life, I had been acquiring thousands of skills and special techniques that would keep me safe in the mountains. Our Everest planning had taken two years, the physical training, a year. I had run the foothills of the Rockies a hundred times, had sprained my ankles a dozen. I had shivered through endless blizzards near the tops of mountains around the world. For two months, we had been shuttling loads up and down the mountain, while pushing through tremendous doubt and fear. So by mid May, as time dwindled away, I found myself at Base Camp, awestruck and disappointed as I thought about all we had been through to get to this point. Mike O. and I sat in our tent engaged in long conversations about what constitutes success. You could do everything right, make few blatant mistakes, and still fall short. I worked hard not to buy into the idea that standing on top meant tremendous success while falling a few feet short meant utter failure. This savage unpredictability was the very element I loved and hated about mountains, and made this pursuit an adventure, not just a sport. But even though I could rationalize falling short, it was no less painful.

As summer approached, temperatures rose fast. The frozen lakes surrounding Base Camp were now flowing rivers. The black ice supporting the rocky moraine had melted out around our tents, leaving them perched atop narrow, three-foot-tall plateaus of ice with the tent corners sagging over the edges. With the warmth, the icefall would become an impenetrable impasse as crevasses opened wide, avalanches raked the slopes, and ice walls crumbled. Because of the increasing danger, climbing permits required climbers to be off the mountain by the last day in May. As yet, no one had even attempted a summit bid. A few smaller teams had been driven off the South Col by high winds and loaded snow slopes. Many teams, discouraged and homesick, had already given up and broken down their camps.

On May 20, our long wait paid off; four days of high pressure were predicted. We headed up, again fighting a gusty wind blowing spindrift in our faces. It was my ninth time through the icefall, and we knew it would be our last attempt. This time I made it through in just over five hours, feeling so good that Jeff and Sherm convinced me to continue on to Camp Two that same afternoon.

At Camp Two, we sat in our small dining tent, piled with oxygen bottles, freeze-dried food packets, and candy bars, debating whether to head up or delay another day. The argument for going was obvious. A week now remained in the climbing season, and the weather had been predicted to deteriorate in a few days. In the afternoon, however, Brad had counted around fifty barely moving dots on the Lhotse Face. For weeks, the rumor had circulated that other teams wanted to avoid going to the summit on the same day as me, afraid that I'd get in their way, slow them down, or pull them into a disaster. But now as my team watched the throngs creeping up the fixed lines, some considered waiting, believing just the reverse. Two significant rescues had already taken place on the upper mountain. That afternoon, we had gotten a radio call from Camp Three that a sick climber needed help descending the Lhotse Face. His team was scattered across the mountain, and despite repeated efforts, not one of them was reachable on their designated radio frequency, so two Sherpas volunteered to climb the face and bring him down. Our team doctor, Steve Gipe, met them at the base of the Lhotse Face with bottled oxygen collected from Camp Two, and diagnosed him with the onset of cerebral edema. His only chance was to keep descending. Steve returned to camp, shaken and disgusted. "He was a wreck. He hadn't drunk any liquid for two days. He shit himself." I was amazed and thankful our team had stuck together.

The second epic of the day had occurred when a young Englishman had fallen one hundred feet while coming down from Lhotse summit. He got sucked too far to the right and attempted to descend a steeper slope than the normal route. Since Everest and Lhotse share the same route for most of the Lhotse Face, as nightfall set in, PV, peering up the face with our telescope, managed to spot him, sitting motionless, almost indistinguishable from the isolated rocks. Now bleeding, missing a crampon, and disoriented, the Englishman radioed for help. Simoni, an Italian climber resting at Lhotse Camp Four and ready to head for the summit the next morning, traversed over the large steep rock band called the Turtle, put the Englishman on his back, and dragged him to camp while the injured climber pleaded for Simoni to just let him die. Finally safe in his tent, Simoni radioed down to us in a slow soft voice, "I am very tired. No summit for me this year. I guess I'll be back next year." He summoned a weak laugh.

After that, our team debated long into the night. "If we head up tomorrow," Chris said, "there's a good chance we'll get sucked into a rescue. Then we'll have to divert our strength and our numbers to drag a zoid down."

Another said, "This may sound terrible, but I've made a commitment to this team. If anyone gets in trouble, I'm there for you, but I don't feel obligated to anyone else on the mountain."

Chris replied, "I'm not saying I'm right or wrong, but I'd have to go. I just couldn't pass someone dying in the snow." Finally, the argument for going won out. A rescue was a good possibility, but the closing weather window was an eventual sure thing.

In the morning, before we left, Kevin radioed up from Base Camp to wish us off. "I wrote a little poem last night to get you guys pumped up. Here it goes:

"May your vision be laser-focused on the rest of Everest,
For it's been over two years in the making.
And now it's right in front of you.
May you be strong,
Both mentally and physically,
To get you through the trying moments.
May you be brave and swallow some pride,
When the times get tough,
And when someone is in need.
May you be swift in areas,
And proceed with caution in others,
But always be sure-footed.
May you keep on laughing,
To ease the tension,
And keep your spirits up,
For we have had too many successes to stop now.
May you climb as a unit,
Bound together by a cohesiveness
Of friendship and knowledge.
May you all reach the summit,
Or your personal best,
One step at a time.
May I meet you guys in a couple of days,
At Superman's Palace,
For a handshake and a hug.
. . . Climb high, my friends."

Above Camp Three on the Lhotse Face, I was setting my own high-altitude record with every step. I had gone on a one-liter flow of bottled oxygen, and the mask felt like it would suffocate me. All morning, as we neared the long traverse to the Yellow Band, I ripped my mask off several times, convinced it wasn't providing any oxygen, and tried furiously to breathe energy into my depleted muscles. At sea level, three or four hard breaths would bring me back, but at twenty-five thousand feet, I still hadn't recovered after a dozen. For an hour I even hung the mask around my neck, thinking I could do better without it, but the crunch of Jeff's footsteps in front of me kept getting farther away. Finally, Sherm caught up to me. "This thing isn't working," I said breathlessly.

"Don't worry," he said. "It's supposed to be miserable," and he explained how I could test the oxygen flow by pressing my tongue against the cold stream of oxygen escaping from the small valves inside my mask. After that, I constantly reassured myself with the tongue test. Even though I still didn't think I was feeling the effects, it gave me confidence to know it was working.

We moved slowly up the steep Yellow Band, traversed along a snow slope for many hours, and finally staggered up the Geneva Spur, the last forty feet almost a vertical scramble through a loose snow-crusted rock band. As soon as I popped my head above the spur, I felt like a soldier emerging from his foxhole into the war zone. I breathed hard for a long time while the jet stream, funneling through the South Col, blasted me full in the face. My sweaty body beneath my down suit went instantly cold as I hauled myself above the spur onto a small icy platform. To my left I could hear the ground dropping away, but somewhere to my right stood the South Col, the flat, windswept notch below the last two thousand feet of Lhotse on the right and the last three thousand feet of Everest on the left. From guidebooks, I knew I had just topped eight thousand meters and had entered what has affectionately come to be known as the Death Zone, a point at which muscle tissue breaks down and the body begins to eat itself. I celebrated the milestone with a sudden bout of nausea, dropping to one knee, lunging my upper body forward, and dry heaving in the snow for a good five minutes. Jeff had been to altitude with me before and knew better than to worry. Instead, he turned his face up and whooped a rebel yell at the blustery sky, as

I made loud retching noises. "How could I ask for anything more," he yelled to no one in particular. "I'm at eight thousand meters with Super Blind and he's puking his guts out. It sure is a fine day in the mountains!"

After our rest, we followed a narrow traversing trail leading into the South Col, our last camp. The distance was miniscule but, at this altitude, seemed agonizingly slow. The jet stream wind, funneling through the col and rocketing out the other side, obstructed my hearing, so I kept losing track of Luis in front of me. I tried to scan my pole and stay in the frozen boot marks, but the frozen snow slope seemed to terrace down to the left, with possible trails at each level. Apparently, I kept picking the wrong shelf, because Luis kept turning his head, shouting urgently, "Don't go left. Right. More right." And then for emphasis, "Don't go left, whatever you do." Finally I relented and trailed right behind him, grabbing a loop on his backpack.

At 2:00 P.M., Luis, Jeff, and I straggled onto the flat floor of the col, scoured of snow and scattered with rocks, abandoned oxygen bottles, and even the mummified remains of a body. As I walked, the collapsed remnants of tent fabric, frozen in the snow, caught on my crampons. All of the team had already arrived and were laboring furiously in the wind to erect the few remaining tents and chip out a pile of oxygen bottles that had frozen into the snow.

When we all finally piled into our four tents, we had a big decision to make. In order not to waste precious oxygen bottles, and because our bodies would deteriorate quickly at this altitude, our plan had been to rest only seven hours, tank up on liquid, and leave that night at about 9:00 P.M. A few felt good enough to travel, but many were exhausted and dehydrated. We discussed the matter over the radios from our tents, and although we were fully aware the weather might change at any time and jeopardize a later attempt, we made a controversial decision to wait one more day. In this high-altitude malaise, with the summit so close and with so much time invested, it would have been easy for the strongest among us to lose sight of our original plan, to pile out of the tents and salvage their own attempt, but not one team member even voiced this option. We were taking a substantial risk with the changing weather, but there was strength in numbers. The mountain's 170 fatalities and the dozens of frozen corpses on the way to the summit proved that individual skill and stamina wasn't always enough. In the Death Zone each climber's margin of safety rested, in part, on the shoulders of the whole team. We passed the next twenty-four hours resting on oxygen, hydrating on hot soup, and playing cards in Braille. As usual, Jeff cheated by looking over my shoulder. But high altitude had lulled his thinking. With an oxygen mask on, each of his breaths over my shoulder was as loud as Darth Vader's.

An hour before we left, as we organized our gear one more time, a Scottish climber, who had summited just that day, crawled into our tent. He obviously didn't recognize me with my down hood pulled low and oxygen mask covering my face, because he said, "A long brutal day that one is. Not a thing easy about it. I surely don't envy you. You're gonna have a helluva time getting the blind guy up there." Before I had heard the Scotsman's assessment, I was already more than nervous. Besides the normal pre–summit day worries of a long ascent and descent, the cold, and the wind, I felt another, more personal fear rising to the surface. I had heard plenty of times that above eight thousand meters, one's mind was reduced to that of a reptile. Since I couldn't see, I relied heavily on my brain to check each step, to clip into ropes safely, to constantly assess how I was performing. I worried that a lack of sight along with severely impaired reasoning could be an overwhelmingly fatal combination.

Thankfully, my thoughts were interrupted by Kevin's fuzzy voice over my radio from Base Camp. An e-mail from Ellie had arrived.

Hey Erik,

I guess you'll get this at one of the higher camps. As I write, I'm thinking of you up at Camp Four—so high up. I'm hoping you are feeling okay and not too nervous about the summit.

Today, I went to this old church built in the 1800's to say a prayer for you and the team. The door was locked and I found the minister who let me in. He rubbed Emma's back and she leaned toward him to get a little more rubbing. Then, without asking any questions, he left us alone. Emma crawled around on the red carpet and smelled the old wood and candle wax. I tried to sit in one of the hard pews with my hands folded, but Emma was scootin' all around; she was playing with the song books and bibles and pencils and then she crawled back and looked at me for a long time. I looked back at her, not sure what to do. So I picked her up and walked to the pulpit. I kneeled down on this pillow thing with a brass railing in front of me while Emma stood up, leaning on the railing and looking up at the ceiling.

Above our heads was a painted, blue blue sky with gold stars—no clouds, just clear sky and stars. I figured that was my sign. You'd have your chance to summit.

Now I don't know the outcome yet. I'm writing this on the evening when you are all at Camp Four, extending your stay for better weather. I'm going to include a disclaimer here so that if you don't get the good weather, let's not blame this special church. But I kind of think it'll happen, that you'll be able to go for the summit. I'll keep praying for you.

Love,
Ellie and Emma

We left our tents a little before 9:00 P.M. on May 24. Because of our twenty-four-hour delay and the apprehension of other expeditions to share a summit day with me, we moved across the South Col with only one other team behind us. We had no worries of the typical hoards clogging the fixed lines but could direct our full focus toward the mountain. The wind was blowing so loudly through the col that I couldn't hear the bells jingling from Chris's ice axe. Chris and I expected this, so for the first two hours he clanked his metal axe against rocks he passed. Finally, we worked our way around to the mountain's leeward side, where Everest itself protected us from the wind. Chris had lost his voice, so his verbal directions were sparse. At each anchor, he'd hold the new line with his hand, so I could locate it and clip in. Chris was moving in front of me at his usual rock-solid pace, and I was right on his heels. We were making unbelievable time.

As we got higher up the mountain, four distinct changes had begun to work in my favor. Earlier, in the icefall, each step was very specific, but the terrain above the South Col consisted of steep forty-five-degree snow faces a hundred yards wide, intermingled with ten-to-fifty-foot crumbly rock steps. I could stay in the kicked boot holes of Chris or kick my own steps. Where I stepped had become less important than maintaining internal balance. I could breathe, scan my ice axe, and count on the next step. The slope was often so steep that I could lean forward and feel the rock or snow steps with my gloved hands, and I had trained myself long ago to save energy by landing my feet in the same holds my hands had just left. Finally, when I needed it most, the mountain had given me a pattern.

The thin oxygen of extreme altitude reduced us to a crawl. It was like moving through a bizarre atmosphere of syrup mixed with a narcotic. My team, struggling just to put one foot in front of the other, moved so slowly, it gave me more time to scan my axe across the snow and feel my way forward. The third equalizer was the darkness. With just a trickle of light produced by headlamps, my sighted team could only see a few feet in front of them. Bulky goggles blocked their side vision, and oxygen masks covered much of their visual field. Also, the pure oxygen trickling through their masks would flow up and freeze the lenses of their goggles so that they constantly had to remove them to wipe the lenses clean. Those brief moments when eyes are exposed to the elements, corneas will freeze, and the intense rays of the sun reflecting off the snow cause instant snow blindness. Not once did I ever have to worry about these complications.

In addition, my teammates had chosen smaller masks that rode low and tight across their cheeks and hung mostly below their chins. This allowed climbers to see better and prevented pure oxygen from seeping into their lenses, but also allowed plenty of pure oxygen to escape into the wind. I, on the other hand, had the luxury of choosing the largest mask I could find and wore it high on my face, getting the most benefit from the oxygen flow and the ambient air around the mask. I'm sure I made a freakish sight with my gigantic mask covering my goggles, like a day long ago in wrestling practice when I had put my sweatshirt on backward, with the hood covering my face, and chased the terrified freshmen around the mat. The consistent terrain, the altitude, the mask, and the darkness were great equalizers. I wouldn't go so far as to claim these gave me an advantage, but it was a matter of perspective.

The mountain had gotten desperately harder for everyone else, while it had gotten slightly easier for me.

For two and a half months, all the decisions, the logistics, the backup safety plans had been implemented and executed by PV, and now, somewhere below the Balcony, the exhausting burden of leadership finally took its toll. Suddenly feeling listless and unable to catch his breath even with his oxygen bottle at full flow, PV had arduously turned back. He managed to convince Brad and Sherm, next to him, that he was strong enough to descend alone, in retrospect, a ploy that might have turned deadly, but PV's weary brain had never stopped calculating the big picture. He had refused to divert any energy from the team's summit effort. Through periodic radio checks as PV dropped altitude, I could hear his characteristically hyper voice growing flat, and just below a steep ice bulge, only an hour from Camp Four, PV sat down in the snow. "I'm very tired," he said. "I don't know if I can make it. I might need some assistance." PV's one warning before we left the tent was "If you sit down, you'll stay there." So, beginning to panic, I ripped my radio out of my pocket. "Is anyone near PV who can help him down?" I asked. "Is anyone reading me?" I repeated myself several times to empty static.

A few weeks earlier, Dr. Gipe had received the sad news that a close family friend had been killed in a skiing accident; a three-thousand-foot day in the Death Zone just didn't seem fair to his family, so that night, he had never left his tent. His decision was a tough one to make, but extremely fortunate for PV's sake. "This is Gipe at the South Col," finally came over the radio. "I'm strapping on my crampons right now. I'm going out to get PV." Dr. Gipe met PV about a half an hour from camp, up again and staggering slowly toward the tents.

With the first crisis of the night averted, Chris and I plodded up a steep gully, which led us to the Balcony, a flat snow platform, ten feet wide. Michael Brown arrived first at about 2:00 A.M., with Chris and me right behind. All night, the weather had remained clear, with high clouds to the southeast and distant lightning flashes illuminating the sky, but at the Balcony, our luck suddenly ran out. We walked into a blasting storm. Wind and horizontal snow raked our down suits and covered us with a layer of ice. The lightning strikes were now on top of us, exploding like a pyrotechnic show. Chris later said he couldn't see his feet through the blowing snow, which stopped us short, since the southeast ridge above narrowed to fifteen feet wide. Mike O.'s and Didrik's headlamps had simultaneously flickered out, and one of Didrik's crampons had popped off. "Someone come and help us," Mike yelled over the radio. Charley headed back and found them sitting in the snow only twenty feet away.

Chris and I huddled together in the wind, waiting for the others to arrive. "What do you think, Big E?" he asked. "It's lookin' pretty grim." When the others trickled in, Sherm wanted to go on; Charley wanted to turn back, and Erie thought we should wait. For forty-five minutes, we waited, periodic arguments breaking out whether to go on or descend. I was beginning to shiver and forced myself to bounce up and down, and to windmill my arms. We were so close, and I was feeling strong. Turning back was a crushing proposition, but I also wasn't willing to go bullheadedly forward and throw my life away. My mind was starting to settle on the possibility of turning back, when Kevin's voice from Base Camp crackled over my radio. Throughout the expedition, Kevin had been learning to read the satellite weather reports we received every few days over the Internet. From the weather map, it appeared the storm was moving rapidly to the northeast toward Bhutan, and where we stood on the Balcony, we were directly northeast of Base Camp. "Hey you guys, don't quit yet," his voice sounded urgent. "The storm's cleared down here. It just might pass over you."

"Weather is also clearing here," Kami said from Camp Two below.

Chris glanced over at me. Beyond my right hip, shining through the storm clouds, he could see a star. "Let's see if this thing breaks up," he said. Sherm must have felt good tidings too, because he pushed on. Chris and I followed.

Following the narrow exposed southeast shoulder, I felt the first warmth of the sun about 4:00 A.M.; so high up, no other mountain blocked the sunrise. The weather had thankfully turned spectacular.

Still hours below the South Summit, we were stalled out again. The fixed lines, running up the steepest slope yet, had been frozen over by a hard windswept crust of snow. Jeff and Brad moved ahead, pulling the lines free, an exhausting job at twenty-eight thousand feet. The job was quickly wearing Jeff down, but he said later that with each gasping breath as he heaved the rope free, he envisioned the two of us standing on top together. Soon he was beginning to feel faint and dizzy. As he knelt in the snow, Brad, behind him, examined his oxygen equipment and assessed that his regulator, connecting the long tube of his mask to his bottle, had malfunctioned. The internal valves responsible for regulating flow were notoriously prone to freezing shut. "Who's got an extra regulator?" Brad called out over the radio, but tired bodies and brains could not recall who had thrown in the extras in the pre-summit shuffle. "My day's finished if I can't find the extra," Jeff yelled testily.

It may not have been PV's time to summit, but he wasn't through benefiting the team. "Calm down," he advised, lying weakly on his back in his tent. "Everyone take a deep breath. Ang Pasang and Sherm are carrying the extra regulators." Luckily, Ang Pasang was only a hundred feet behind. Together, Brad and Ang Pasang screwed on Jeff's new regulator.

By 8:00 A.M., we had struggled on to the South Summit, 28,700 feet. After a short rest, Chris took off for the summit, cranking it into "Morris gear," and Luis took over in front of me. From the South Summit, the true summit is still at least two hours away across the three hundred-foot-long knife-edge ridge, up the fifty-foot vertical Hillary Step, and finally traversing up a long slightly broader ridge to the summit.

Jeff, exhausted from his two-hour struggle pulling lines, stopped short in front of me. "I'm wasted. I've gotta go down," he said reluctantly. "This'll have to be my summit."

For a moment I wanted to goad him on the way we had done each other on winter training climbs of Colorado fourteeners. "If you wanna turn back, just say the word," we'd jab. "Of course, I'll have to tell everyone you were a whiney little crybaby." But 28,700 feet above sea level wasn't the place to motivate with bravado or ego, so assessing that he was strong enough to get down, I rested a hand on Jeff's shoulder and wished him a safe descent. Jeff had been with me from the beginning, practically introducing me to the mountains. He had shown extraordinary patience as I stumbled along experimenting with brand-new trekking poles. We had even stood together on the summit of Denali and El Capitan, so I knew that reaching the summit of Mt. Everest without him wouldn't feel complete. Suddenly, a wave of heavy exhaustion passed over me, and I felt weary and crumpled. "Maybe I'll go down too," I readied my lips to say, but then Luis was crunching through the snow in front of me, and I forced myself to revive.

Down-climbing the twenty-foot vertical snow face on the backside of the South Summit leading onto the knife-edge ridge went against my survival instinct. The ridge is the width of a picnic table and always heavily corniced with snow. To the left is an eight-thousand-foot drop into Nepal, and on the right, a twelve-thousand-foot drop into Tibet. PV had told me that while crossing the ridge on his 1998 attempt, he had driven his ice axe into the snow and, after withdrawing it, had stared through the small hole into the early morning light of Tibet. In 1995, on Brad's second attempt, a climber in front of him had taken his first step onto the ridge just before the entire right half of it dropped away. The climber jumped back to safety, but a second later he would have ridden the cornice into Tibet. This year, the ridge was drier and more stable. Frozen boot steps traversed along the lefthand side. I'd scan my pole until it dropped into a boot mark, then cautiously lower my foot. I knew I couldn't make a mistake here: six hard steady breaths, another solid step, and a relaxed, focused mind like clear water.

Climbing the Hillary Step, I felt I was in my element, feeling the rock under my gloves. I stuck the crampon points of my right foot tenuously into a tiny crack and the left points into a cornice of snow, slid my ascender as high as it would go on the rope, and stood up and quickly reached for the next knob of rock. At the top, I awkwardly belly-flopped onto a flat ledge, slowly pulled myself to my feet, and began traversing the last slope to the summit. For forty minutes I trudged upward. My heavy sluggish muscles felt as if they were pushing through wet cement. With each step closer, the real possibility of standing on top began to trickle through my focused brain. I had speculated success in a conceptual way and as a way to motivate myself when I was down, but it was dangerous to believe it as a fact. A team could be turned back for so many reasons at any time. Just keep moving, I thought. You're not there yet.

Then a body moved down the slope toward me and I felt thin wiry arms beneath a puffy down suit wrapping around me. "Big E!" The voice rasped, so hollow and wispy, I had trouble recognizing it as Chris. His voice tried to say more, but his quaking words dissipated in the wind. Then he leaned in against my ear. "Big E"—his voice gave way to tears, then struggled out in an immense effort—"you're about to stand on top of the world." Then he quickly let go and hurriedly moved down the slope.

Luis and I linked our arms, and in a few steps, the earth flattened and the massive sky closed around me on all sides. "This is Erik, Luis, and Ang Pasang," I said over the radio. "We're on the top. I can't believe it; we're on the top."

"You're the best, Big E!" Kevin yelled from Base Camp. "I love you guys." I could hear the entire Base Camp crew cheering behind him.

"You're the strongest man in the world," PV said.

I turned around, surprised to hear more crampons moving up behind me. "I wasn't gonna let you stand on top and hear about it the rest of my life," Jeff said, with a little pep left in his voice. One of the greatest joys of my summit was that Jeff hadn't turned back at all. From the South Summit, he had watched us down-climb onto the knife edge ridge and move toward the Hillary Step. Later he told me, "I simply had to follow." Behind Jeff came Erie, Michael B., Didrik, Charley, and Mike O. Sherm had been the first on the team to summit, becoming the oldest man in history to stand on the top of the world, but better than his record was the fact that his son, Brad, had stepped on to the summit right behind him. Nineteen team members made it to the summit: eleven Westerners and eight Sherpas, the most from one team to reach the top in a single day. So it was a crowded summit as we all stood together, hugging and crying on a snow platform the size of a single-car garage.

Another storm was rolling in from the north. "Weather's changing fast," PV called up on the radio. "You guys need to go down immediately." I turned to head down with Erie, when Jeff said, "Wait a second, Big E. You'll only be here once in your life. Look around. Think about where you are and what you've done." So I suspended my nerves for a moment, reached down and touched the snow through my gloved hand, listened to the Sherpa prayer flags flapping in the wind, and heard the infinite sound of space around me, as on my first rock climb. After I had gone blind almost twenty years ago, I would have been proud to find the bathroom, so I said a quick prayer and thanked God for giving me so much. Then it was time to go down.

We descended through heavy snowfall but, thankfully, little wind. Erie took over guiding me, down the Hillary Step, across the knife edge, and contrary to his fears that he wouldn't be strong enough to make the top, he was stronger and more lucid on the way down from Everest's summit than most were on the top of a peak in Colorado. Reaching our tents at about 3:00 P.M., I hugged Erie. "Today," I said, "you were my guardian angel. I'm glad you're here."

That night, Kevin radioed up to report that he had called Ellie on the sat phone with the news. "She screamed loud enough to break the neighbors' windows." He laughed. The next days were exhausting as we fought our way through the screaming wind of the South Col, down the Lhotse Face—where my rubbery legs refused to obey my brain—and finally one last trip through the icefall. At the bottom, in Superman's Palace, of course, the whole team was waiting, and the party lasted long after the sun had sunk below Pumori.

Despite our success, plenty of detractors voiced their opinions on Internet chat rooms and in letters to the editor. I've heard all the ridiculous assumptions.

"Now that a blind guy's climbed it, everyone's going to want to climb it. They're going to think it's easy. People will probably get hurt."

"Why are people thinking this is such a big deal? Anyone can be short-roped to the top by nineteen seeing-eye guides."

My teammates constantly come to my rescue with carefully crafted comebacks like "Before you start spouting a bunch of lies over a public forum, get your facts straight, dude!"

"Don't let 'em get to you," Chris Morris said after I shared with him their comments. "You climbed every inch of that mountain, and then some."

I knew he was right. There were some who would never be convinced, others who still had no idea what to think, but many others for whom the climb forced a higher expectation of their own possibilities. I don't climb mountains to prove to anyone that blind people can do this or that. I climb for the same reason an artist paints a picture: because it brings me great joy. But I'd be lying if I didn't admit my secret satisfaction in facing those cynics and blowing through their doubts, destroying their negative stereotypes, taking their very narrow parameters of what's possible and what's not, and shattering them into a million pieces.

When those parameters are rebuilt, thousands and thousands of people will live with fewer barriers placed before them, and if my climbs can play a small role in opening doors of opportunity and hope for those who will come after us, then I am very proud of what we were able to achieve.

Although making the summit of Mt. Everest was a great honor, far and away the greatest honor of my life was the decision made by so many trusted friends who said "buzz off" to the doomsday predictions of the experts and linked their lives inextricably to mine.

Thank you to Pasquale Scaturro, team leader; Brad, Sherm, and Reba Bull; Chris Morris, Kami Tenzing Sherpa, Jeff Evans, Ang Pasang Sherpa, Luis Benitez, Chuldim Nuru Sherpa, Eric Alexander, Pemba Choti Sherpa, Didrik Johnck, Pemba Gyaljen Sherpa, Dr. Steve Gipe, Ang Chumbi Sherpa, Mike O'Donnell, Lhakpa Tsering Sherpa, Michael Brown, Ang Kami Sherpa, Charley Mace, Phurbu Rita Bhote, Kevin Cherilla, Pasang Nuru Sherpa, Maurice Peret, Ang Chuldim Sherpa, Kim Johnson, Ang Sona Sherpa, Temba Sherpa, Tenzing Sherpa, Chirring Sona Sherpa, and Mingma Tsering Sherpa.

Special thanks to the National Federation of the Blind, sponsor of the 2001 NFB Everest Expedition, and to Dr. Marc Maurer, Barbara Pierce, Dr. Betsy Zaborowski, my wife, Ellie, and my dad, Ed Weihenmayer, who all proved that you don't have to be on the mountain to be an invaluable part of the team. Thank you to Sam Bridgeham for dreaming big and setting me on course. And to Hans Florine for his extraordinary leadership on El Capitan.